EDUCATION
POLICY

WITHDRAWAL

Education at SAGE

SAGE is a leading international publisher of journals, books, and electronic media for academic, educational, and professional markets.

Our education publishing includes:

- accessible and comprehensive texts for aspiring education professionals and practitioners looking to further their careers through continuing professional development

- inspirational advice and guidance for the classroom

- authoritative state of the art reference from the leading authors in the field

Find out more at: **www.sagepub.co.uk/education**

EDUCATION
POLICY

IAN ABBOTT | MICHAEL RATHBONE | PHIL WHITEHEAD

Los Angeles | London | New Delhi
Singapore | Washington DC

Los Angeles | London | New Delhi
Singapore | Washington DC

SAGE Publications Ltd
1 Oliver's Yard
55 City Road
London EC1Y 1SP

SAGE Publications Inc.
2455 Teller Road
Thousand Oaks, California 91320

SAGE Publications India Pvt Ltd
B 1/I 1 Mohan Cooperative Industrial Area
Mathura Road
New Delhi 110 044

SAGE Publications Asia-Pacific Pte Ltd
3 Church Street
#10-04 Samsung Hub
Singapore 049483

© Ian Abbott, Michael Rathbone and
Phil Whitehead 2013

First published 2013

Library of Congress Control Number: 2011934111

British Library Cataloguing in Publication data

A catalogue record for this book is available from
the British Library

Commissioning editor: Marianne Lagrange
Editorial assistant: Kathryn Bromwich
Project manager: Bill Antrobus
Assistant production editor: Thea Watson
Copyeditor: Peter Williams
Proofreader: Caroline Stock
Marketing manager: Catherine Slinn
Cover design: Lisa Harper
Typeset by Kestrel Data, Exeter, Devon
Printed in India at Replika Press Pvt Ltd

ISBN 978-0-85702-576-0
ISBN 978-0-85702-577-7 (pbk)

CONTENTS

ABOUT THE AUTHORS

Ian Abbott is Director of the Institute of Education at the University of Warwick.

Mike Rathbone was Director of Continuing Professional Development in the Institute of Education at the University of Warwick.

Phil Whitehead is the course leader for the secondary PGCE (Teach First) at the University of Warwick.

The authors have worked in schools and in higher education for almost fifty years, teaching all age groups from pre-school children to postgraduates, including the training of head teachers. They have had experience of teaching in different areas of the UK, in other countries and in a variety of institutions.

They have taught in UK schools under the Education Secretaries of Labour, Conservative and Coalition governments, ranging from Edward Boyle in 1962 to Michael Gove, the present incumbent in 2012.

Their research interests and writing over a number of years have ranged across school and college leadership, creative governance, education policy, nursery education and classroom management. These activities have contributed to their insight into the influence of the Education Secretaries and of their policies.

LIST OF ABBREVIATIONS

AEC	Association of Education Committees
ALI	Adult Learning Inspectorate
APU	Assessment of Performance Unit
AQAC	Assessment, Qualifications and Curriculum Authority
BCU	Birmingham City University
BEC	Business Education Council
Becta	British Educational Communications and Technology Agency
BSF	Building Schools for the Future
BTEC	Business and Technology Council
CACE	Central Advisory Council for Education (England)
CPD	Continuing Professional Development
CRB	Criminal Records Bureau
CSE	Certificate of Secondary Education
CSG	Curriculum Study Group
CTC	city technology college
DCSF	Department for Children, Schools and Families
DES	Department of Education and Science
DfE	Department for Education
DfEE	Department for Education and Employment
DfES	Department for Education and Skills
EAZ	Education Action Zone
E-Bacc	English Baccalaureate
EMA	Education Maintenance Allowance
EPA	Educational Priority Area
ERA	Education Reform Act 1988
ETS	Educational Testing Services
FE	Further Education
FEFC	Further Education Funding Council
FTE	full-time equivalent
GCE	General Certificate of Education
GMS	Grant Maintained School
GNVQ	General National Vocational Qualification

GTC	General Teaching Council
HMI	Her Majesty's Inspectorate
ICT	Information and Communications Technology
ITB	Industrial Training Boards
LEA	local education authority
LMS	local management of schools
LSC	Learning and Skills Council
MSC	Manpower Services Commission
NAHT	National Association of Head Teachers
NCC	National Curriculum Council
NCSL	National College for School Leadership
NCVQ	National Council for Vocational Qualifications
NEET	'not in education, employment or training'
NFER	National Foundation for Educational Research
NQT	Newly Qualified Teacher
NUT	National Union of Teachers
NVQ	National Vocational Qualification
Ofsted	Office of Standards in Education
PFI	Private Finance Initiative
PSHE	Personal, Social and Health Education
PLTS	personal, learning and thinking skills
QCA	Qualifications and Curriculum Authority
RE	Religious Education
ROSLA	raising of school-leaving age
SACRE	Standing Advisory Council for Religious Education
SAT	Standard Assessment Task
SCAA	School Curriculum and Assessment Authority
SCCE	Schools Council for the Curriculum and Examinations
SEAC	Schools Examination and Assessment Council
SEU	Standards and Effectiveness Unit
SSAT	Specialist Schools and Academies Trust
SSEC	Secondary School Examination Council
STF	Standards Task Force
TA	Teacher Assessment
TDA	Teaching and Development Agency for Schools
TEC	Technician Education Council
TGAT	Task Group on Assessment and Testing
TTA	Teacher Training Agency
TVEI	Technical and Vocational Education Initiative
UCE	University of Central England
UTC	University Technical College
YOP	Youth Opportunities Programme
YTS	Youth Training Scheme

INTRODUCTION

This book had its origins in a series of conversations between the three authors who had worked together for a number of years in the Institute of Education at the University of Warwick. Our working experience as teachers and researchers ranged across higher education, further education, and secondary, primary and nursery schools over a period of fifty years. Obviously even before that we had been children in schools so it was perhaps inevitable that education policy would feature as part of the conversations.

As we shared our experiences it became clear that during our time 'at the chalk face' there have been comparatively few occasions when we had time to stand back and think about how education policy was being formulated at the highest level. Yet that policy had impacted enormously on our teaching lives and the lives of children/students in our care.

Among other things we had worked with two-year trained emergency teachers who in some cases had fought in the war; we had experienced the upheaval when comprehensive education had been introduced into our schools; seen teaching becoming a 'degree only' profession; taught classes in secondary modern schools when the school-leaving age was raised in the 1970s; read and implemented the newly published Plowden and Warnock Reports; seen teacher strikes; experienced Ofsted inspections; and been working when a National Curriculum was instituted. At a later stage we saw Academies and Free Schools introduced and we engaged with 'Teach First', a very recent method of teacher training which owes much to its American roots.

Indeed all of us had eventually been employed preparing aspiring teachers for a career teaching in schools and colleges and working with experienced teachers on their professional development.

As we talked reference was frequently made to those people who had formulated the policies which we had implemented. Thus we remembered the Education Secretaries (or whatever they were titled at any particular time), their ideologies and the governments of which they were part.

- What did we recall of the likes of Edward Short, Kenneth Baker and Shirley Williams, or know of Michael Gove – their backgrounds, legacies, feelings and convictions when they were in power and afterwards?
- And what of the others – many others?
- How were their policies developed within the political context and what was the context of the schools/colleges in which they were implemented?

This led to the realisation that in our experience the present generation of trainee teachers has little idea of *how* many aspects of the present state education system in schools and colleges have developed – and *why* they have developed in particular ways.

- Was there really a time when teachers were broadly in charge of the curriculum and politicians would never have dared to dictate what was taught?
- What happened when there was no formal inspection system, or league tables of schools?
- Why are local education authorities so much involved with some schools but hardly at all in others?
- How did it come about that that there are grammar schools in some areas of the country and 'bog standard' comprehensive schools in others?
- And how did the rather demeaning term 'bog standard comprehensive' arise?

These are the sort of questions which we found being asked by many students studying for initial and higher degrees in education, as well as students on the multitude of modular courses which include aspects of the history and development of our education system. Included among these are many courses studied by foreign students seeking to gain insights with which to inform education in their own countries.

The answers can only really come from reference to the development of education policy over the whole postwar period.

Research into the existing literature revealed that although there were some relevant texts about particular periods, and that some pertinent articles had been written at various times, our suspicion about the apparent lack of an overall text focusing on policy and on Education Secretaries was justified.

More formal discussions with a number of colleagues, ex-colleagues and students substantiated this view. A text which particularly looked at the development of education policy since 1945 and took account, as far as possible, of the insights of the Education Secretaries – with reference to their writings and the remarks of their contemporaries and later commentators – would be a valuable addition to existing literature.

It further became clear that such a text would be much enhanced by the addition of responses to interviews carried out with as many Education Secretaries as possible. These up-to-date interviews would give the benefit of hindsight to the participants and enable the whole to be written up taking account of the political context and school/college context at the time.

Consequently, when the project was given formal support by colleagues in several university departments across the country, a list of education secretaries was compiled and invitations to interview were dispatched.

Kenneth Baker, Ed Balls, David Blunkett, Michael Gove, Alan Johnson, Ruth Kelly, John MacGregor, Estelle Morris, Gillian Shepard and Shirley Williams all indicated their willingness to participate and were interviewed over a period of two years. Many of these were still in political office and were interviewed in the House of Commons or the House of Lords, while others were interviewed privately. The interviews were designed to be flexible but nevertheless to follow roughly the same pattern and enable the interviewee to make individual points. Interviewing senior politicians created a number of issues and we soon discovered how difficult Jeremy Paxman's job actually is! However, all the interviewees were generous with their time, open about their period of time in office and relished the opportunity to talk about what for many of them had been the most important job in their political career. The interviews were recorded and the resulting insights used as the basis of the text of the book.

The writers hope that the result is a text which will help students, researchers, teachers, policy-makers and other interested parties to understand the development of education policy in the postwar years.

We wish to thank everyone who has helped with this project and in particular the Education Secretaries who agreed to be interviewed, Caroline Parker who was responsible for much of the secretarial work with the text and those at Sage Publications who supported the work.

We, of course, take responsibility for any errors in the final text.

1945–1979: THE POSTWAR CONSENSUS

Preamble

The end of the Second World War marked a period of massive social reforms in the creation of the welfare state which was established to end the absolute poverty and depression of the 1930s. It also marked the beginning of a huge increase in the role of the state in terms of the extension of state planning and collectivism, and the 1942 Beveridge Report introduced momentous changes in welfare, health and education which were aimed at reducing poverty. Although this was also a period of traumatic economic and social change there were high expectations of a new welfare world after the war and a great deal of optimism in all sectors of society. Between 1944 and the mid-1970s the differences between the two major political parties on educational policy were comparatively small and there was agreement that in order to reduce poverty and improve health, housing and education there needed to be full employment and significant improvements in welfare provision.

It was the Labour Party, in office from 1945 to 1951, that had the responsibility for implementing the programme of social reform and reconstruction. The Conservative Party, which was in office for 13 years from 1951 to 1964, made no serious attempts to reverse the Labour policies of 1945–51.

From 1945 to 1979 there were 20 Ministers of Education (later, in 1964, to become Secretaries of State for Education) representing the two main political parties (for a full list see the Appendix at the end of the book) and they each played their part in defining the postwar consensus on the purpose of education.

During this period the volume of educational reform is reflected in the large number of significant education acts, reports, circulars and initiatives that were instigated by the Ministers of Education and the Secretaries of State. These in turn reflect the dominant issues that were being debated and discussed by educationalists, sociologists, the media and the political parties. They also reflect the sets of values that informed these debates and discussions. Some of the key reforms focused on 'secondary education for all', the tripartite system, educational inequality and 'educational opportunity for all', selection and streaming, 'wastage of talent', comprehensivisation, the curriculum and the public schools.

The 1944 Education Act was one of the most important pieces of legislation in the twentieth century and it emerged from the consensus between the major political parties, the churches and the education service. It provided a framework for the education system until the whole-scale reforms introduced by the 1988 Education Reform Act.

Following the 1944 Act there was unprecedented expansion across all phases of education with many more pupils in primary, junior and secondary schools, more young people and adults using further education, more teachers recruited and trained, and an ambitious school building programme – all of which inevitably needed considerable state funding.

However, during the period under review there were economic, social and political events, such as slumps and economic recession, overseas competition and the oil crisis in the early 1970s, which all affected the proportion of Gross Domestic Product spent on education, and it is clear that Ministers of Education almost always had to fight battles with the Treasury to secure adequate funding to implement change and reform.

Through the 1960s arguments about the comprehensive reorganisation of secondary education and the end of selection continued, and there were as Chitty (2009: xiii) points out: 'local political battles over comprehensive schooling in the 1950s and 1960s'.

The 1960s witnessed substantial changes in important questions associated with the curriculum: the nature and organisation of the curriculum, approaches to teaching and learning, assessment and issues around motivation and teacher and pupil identities. For the first time, challenges to the control of many of these issues came from the government and from a growing number of educational pressure groups.

While access to education broadened overall during the 1960s and 1970s, there were still considerable inequalities suffered by working-class pupils compared to their middle-class counterparts. The private system was relatively untouched by developments in the state sector, and consequently the public schools continued to confer advantages on their pupils.

The 'Black Papers', a collection of right-wing articles published between 1969 and 1977, were significant because they attacked 'the associated concepts of comprehensive education, egalitarianism and "progressive" teaching methods' (Chitty, 2009: 28). The 'Black Papers' added to the general feeling 'in the country' that education in England and Wales was increasingly characterised by a fall in general standards, ill-discipline and inappropriate progressive teaching methods.

The 1970s were a period of transition and change within the education system against a turbulent economic, social and political background. There was a definite shift from the relatively consensual discourse about the role and relationship of education and the economy, articulated emphatically in Callaghan's 1976 Ruskin College speech and to some extent in the 'Great Debate' about education. Key concerns about the autonomy of teachers, the relationship between the teachers' unions, local education authorities and central government, the purposes and construction of the curriculum, and the relationships between parents and schools, were irrevocably changed during this period.

Victory by the Conservatives in the 1979 election presented opportunities for the 'free market' approach to education which challenged the taken-for granted assumptions of the postwar democratic consensus.

CHAPTER ONE

1944–1960: THE POSTWAR CONSENSUS: EDUCATION FOR ALL?

- The religious question
- Private schooling
- The role of the state, the LEAs and the teaching profession
- The eleven plus, selection and streaming
- The drive towards comprehensivisation

Introduction

Following the end of the Second World War there was a desire by all political parties not to return to the problems of the 1930s and to introduce widespread social and economic reconstruction. The 1944 Education Act recognised the importance of education in raising living standards and enhancing social mobility. Secondary education to 15 was made compulsory, and free school meals and milk were introduced with a range of other welfare services. Children were segregated at the age of eleven by ability and aptitude into grammar, technical and modern schools. However, education was accepted by Labour and Conservative politicians as a major feature of the welfare state.

This chapter, which will focus on the period 1944–60, will examine that postwar consensus and also some of the tensions that started to appear during this period. McCulloch (2002: 35) provides an appropriate summary of the main focus of this period: '. . . a period during which an initial experiment with a so-called "tripartite" system of different types of secondary schools eventually gave way to a model of a single type of school designed for all abilities and aptitudes, the comprehensive school.' As well as discussing the drive towards comprehensivisation, this chapter will also consider some key issues relating to key reports and publications, with a main focus on the contributions of Education Secretaries (Ministers until 1964). The issues that will be discussed include: the 1944 Education Act, the different phases of education and 'secondary education for all', the drive towards comprehensivisation, the end of selection, the religious question and private schooling. There will also be references to the relationship between central government, the local education authorities and the teaching profession.

Context

Political, social and economic

The end of the Second World War marked a period of massive social reforms in the creation of the welfare state which was established to end the absolute poverty and depression of the 1930s. It also marked the beginning of a huge increase in the role of the state in terms of the extension of state planning and collectivism. This was a period of traumatic economic and social change but there were high expectations of a new welfare world after the war and a great deal of optimism in all sectors of society. Carr and Hartnett (1996) in their discussion of postwar reconstruction note how the increased demand for improved public education came to be embedded in the commitment to the right to employment, family allowances, improved old age pensions, health, housing and education as enshrined in the 1942 Beveridge Report, *Social Insurance and Allied Services*. In the Report which received widespread support, Beveridge outlined in principle the concept of the welfare state and one of the five 'giant evils' in society, Ignorance, would be combated by the 1944 Education Act.

The period 1944–60, in retrospect, might be described as a fairly lengthy era of uneven growth and opportunity characterised, as Kogan (1978: 27) suggests, in terms of three interwoven themes:

- the rise of expectations as to how the 'Opportunity State' would offer widened educational chances as part of the good life;
- the related expansion of the economy and changing distribution of its products;
- demographic pressures and fluctuations.

Initially, however, Britain was only just beginning to recover from the war efforts and despite a postwar boom in some industries and the growing service industry, as Jones (2003) argues, there was a lack of investment compared to other European countries and competition from these countries. Britain was also heavily reliant on American loans to fund the new welfare state. Thus, in terms of the realities of instigating ambitious changes and reforms, Barber (1994: 188) notes, for example, that 'the Labour Government of 1945–51 had to work on a mass of competing priorities with strictly limited resources.' The following section identifies the some of these priorities.

Labour in office 1945–51

Labour came into government with a landslide majority. There were enormous challenges within the education system (Hughes, 1979). During the war years there had been considerable debate about the purposes and structure of postwar Britain, and there was profound agreement on the need to remodel post-primary education, raise the school-leaving age to 15, provide free school meals and milk, implement a system of part-time education beyond the statutory leaving age and provide adequate health and welfare services for schoolchildren. Within these key priorities the government also had to develop strategies for dealing with the desperate shortage of school buildings and teachers to cope with the expansion of the system. For example, the Emergency Training Scheme was introduced which brought for the first time into schools on a large scale young men and women with experience of life outside school or college. The scheme which ran between 1945 and 1951 provided 35,000 additional teachers who qualified after just one year's training. At the same time a special 'Huts on Raising of the School Leaving Age' plan was initiated using temporary accommodation in an attempt to cope with the parlous state of school buildings. This might explain why the Cabinet was keen to postpone the raising of the school-leaving age in order to save money on an extensive and new school building programme and the costs of additional teachers' salaries.

However, as Fieldhouse (1994: 287) notes: 'Despite the 1945 Labour Government's commitment to social reform, it did not have a very radical education policy beyond its determination to implement the 1944 Education Act and raise the school-leaving age to fifteen.'

Schools and colleges

In the following sections the origins of the Act and its passage into legislation are briefly described and key issues such as the 'religious question', private schooling and the relationship between the state, the local education authorities (LEAs) and the teaching profession are discussed.

The 1944 Education Act and related issues

The Second World War brought to a halt a number of reforms which had been developed in the 1930s, for example the raising of the school-leaving age from 14 to 15 due to be implemented in 1939, the reorganisation of elementary education as proposed in the 1926 Hadow Report, and the 1938 Spens Report on the secondary curriculum. There were increasing demands recognised by the Board of Education from the public and the media for significant changes in the education system in the postwar period.

In 1939, the majority of children in England and Wales attended a 5–11 school and then transferred to a senior elementary school or the senior department of an elementary school to complete the final three years of compulsory education, or they attended an 'all-through' elementary school. Barber (1994: 1) suggests that '80 per cent of children received no further formal education after the age of fourteen' when they left to join the labour market.

It should be noted that a small minority of elementary school pupils (just over 14 per cent in 1938) had been given the opportunity to transfer to secondary schools at the age of 10 or 11.

It was very different for middle- and upper-class children, admittedly a minority of the overall school-age population, who attended fee-paying day grammar schools or else had access to the separate public school system. The issue of public school education was a major issue for the incoming Labour government of 1945 and will be discussed later in this chapter.

The types of schooling, which served different classes or groups in society, in existence in the immediate postwar period, are identified by Chitty (2009: 20–1) as follows:

- the so-called public schools;
- the direct grant grammar schools;
- the grammar schools;
- a small group of technical, 'central' and other types of 'trade' schools;
- the new 'secondary modern' schools;
- the old, unreorganised 'all-age' elementary schools.

Reference is made to each of these 'types' in the following discussion.

In 1941, a detailed document which became known as the Green Book was produced: *Education After the War*. This took the form of a memorandum from the Board of Education and was circulated confidentially to a variety of organisations to canvass opinions about educational reforms. Chitty (2009: 114) notes that the Green Book 'contained many of the proposals which were first presented to Parliament in 1943 and eventually became the 1944 Act.' R. A. Butler became President of the Board of Education at the Prime Minister's (Churchill) request in 1942 and began the massive task of developing and steering an education bill through Parliament using the Green Book as a foundation upon which to act.

The Education Act of 1944 emerged out of a democratic consensus between the coalition wartime government, the churches and the education service (Tomlinson, 2005). It marked the beginnings of what was to become the most comprehensive and expansionary phase in English education since the 1870 Education Act and introduced widespread reforms across all sectors of education: primary, secondary, further and higher education. The Act followed the publication of a number of key policy and discussion documents.

At its heart, the 1944 Act introduced free secondary education for all, raised the school leaving age to 15 from 1947 (with a further rise to 16 at a later date) and established a tripartite system of education. It was clear that 'secondary education for all' would be part of a continuous process ranging from the primary sector, through the secondary sector and then into further or higher education.

Earlier, it was noted that the 1944 Act was based upon the 1938 Report of the Spens Committee and the 1943 Report of the Norwood Committee. The former had argued that educational provision post-eleven was inappropriate and its authors outlined a system based on a tripartite division into modern schools, grammar schools and technical high schools. It should also be noted that Spens Committee also recognised the importance of social and cultural background in pupils' gaining access through scholarships to the grammar schools and argued that 'parity of esteem' could be achieved between the different schools. Norwood focused on concerns about the organisation of secondary schooling and argued for a classification of pupils into 'types' with different aptitudes, interests and abilities: the 'secondary grammar' pupil who is 'interested in learning for its own sake'; the 'secondary technical' pupil whose 'interests lie markedly in the field of applied science or applied art'; and the 'secondary modern' pupil, who 'deals more easily with concrete things rather than ideas . . . He [sic] is interested in things as they are; he finds little attraction in the past or in the slow disentanglement of causes or movements' (Norwood Report 1943, cited in Ball, 1986: 19). The organisation of secondary schooling was influenced greatly by this delineation of types of pupil.

The 'religious question'

Throughout the nineteenth and twentieth centuries the 'religious question', that is to say the relationship between the state and religion and educational provision in society, had played an important if not central role in all of the major Education Acts 'quite out of proportion to its significance in the wider, largely secular society' (Carr and Hartnett, 1996: 111).

The 1944 Act marked a new stage in the balance between making voluntary schools viable with the help of public funds while allowing them to retain religious freedom. Butler turned to the 'intractable problem: the Dual System – the co-existence of the "voluntary" (Church) schools and the publicly provided system' (Barber, 1994: 38). With great skill and tremendous understanding he undertook a renegotiation of the place of religion and the churches in schools. Barber quotes the then General Secretary of the National Union of Teachers (NUT), Frederick Mander, who suggested the enormity of the 'problem' when he described how it 'lay like a tank trap across the highway to educational advance' (Barber, 1992: 31).

The Anglican and Catholic churches in particular had huge religious influence and involvement in the school system and ran almost half the schools in the country (Benn, 2011a: 40), thus the government – and in particular Butler and his chief civil servant, Chuter Ede – came under huge pressure in the negotiations which took place from the early 1940s until the passing of the Act. Indeed, it has been argued that Butler gave much more time and attention to the churches than to any other interested parties.

With great difficulty Butler agreed a settlement, the key features of which were increased funding for church schools (which had to opt for voluntary aided or voluntary controlled status) coupled with increased state control, and new legislation on the place of religion in state schools. There were fraught discussions with representatives from the Anglicans, Roman Catholics and Nonconformists. Butler eventually found a compromise which secured the backing of the Church of England which was keen on reform to the education system, the Nonconformists and the teaching profession. The Catholics, who faced the most difficulties in financial terms, were left with no alternative than to accede to Butler's political manoeuvring in order to avoid being isolated (Barber, 1994; Sharp, 2002).

It should be noted that there were some forthright contributions from key players such as the Archbishop of Canterbury, William Temple, who welcomed the Bill as 'a notable contribution to social justice, to fuller national fellowship and to growth in religious knowledge' (cited in Barber, 1994: 80). It was Temple who published *Christianity and Social Order* in 1942 which advocated a higher school-leaving age and contributed to left-wing theories of equality in education (Sanderson, 1987).

The 1944 Act made a requirement that there should be religious instruction and a daily act of collective worship with an agreed syllabus for religious instruction in local authority schools. There appeared to be no serious opposition to this provision which changed only with the 1998 Education Reform Act.

Private schooling

At the beginning of Labour's first administration there were polarised views about the Party's and the government's position on the public schools. It is significant that the 1944 Education Act made no serious attempt to deal with the sensitive issues of the public schools which, as Barber (1994: 10) points out, had 'provided education not only for virtually all Conservative MPs, and many in other parties too, but also for almost the entire senior ranks of the Civil Service, including those at the Board of Education.'

At this time, there was growing criticism of the public schools and they were at their most vulnerable towards the end of the Second World War (Benn, 2011a). There were fears amid the private sector that it would be difficult for the public schools to survive. Indeed, Simon (1991) suggests that public schools had been under fire for many years from a range of individuals and organisations – culminating in a wide popular move against these schools and their hold on access to positions of power and responsibility. It is therefore not surprising, as Tomlinson (2005: 14) notes, to see '. . . private schools, keeping a low profile during the post-war Labour Government'.

The Fleming Committee had been set up in 1942 to report on the public schools question with the brief 'to consider the means whereby the association between the public schools . . . and the general education system of the country could be extended and developed' (Board of Education, 1944) – a device perhaps to keep a problematic question off the political agenda. Not surprisingly, the committee did not report until the 1944 Act had been approved and its main recommendation was that independent schools reserve at least 25 per cent of their places for children from grant-aided primary schools. However, no national policy was adopted and LEAs infrequently applied these recommendations. The Labour Party at this time seemed to take little interest in the Fleming Committee proposals and it was not until Anthony Crosland was Education Secretary in power from 1965 to 1967 that the debate about private schooling was reopened.

As Butler (1971: 120) stated afterwards, perhaps in self-congratulation: 'the first class carriage had been shunted onto an immense siding', thus, a unique opportunity to unify the country's education system was destroyed. McCulloch (2002: 40), in his succinct overview of secondary education in the period, notes that: '. . . the independent schools had survived virtually unscathed from the debate over secondary education' and '. . . they remained a separate system, comprising an alternative form of provision based on parental fees'.

It is not surprising therefore that having survived this threatening situation, the public schools underwent a striking upturn during the late 1940s and, as Lowe notes (1988: 51), 'a public school education began to seem particularly attractive to the growing number of parents who could consider the expense'.

The role of the state, the LEAs and the teaching profession

In this section, the critical relationship sometimes referred to as the 'Golden Triangle' between the state, the local education authorities (LEAs) and the teaching profession (Dale, 1989) is briefly discussed. Each had areas of responsibility throughout the education system which amounted to a balance of control between central and local powers. This is a theme which, because of its importance in education policy-making and the roles of key players in that process, will also be examined in Chapters 2 and 3.

This balance has been explained by Bogdanor (1979: 157, cited in Dale, 1989: 97) who argues that, following the 1944 Act, 'power over the distribution of resources, over the organisation and context of education was to be diffused among the different elements and no one of them was to be given a controlling voice'.

Thus the 1944 Act stipulated that LEAs were required to provide secondary education, and schools would 'not be deemed to be sufficient unless they are sufficient in number, character, and equipment to afford all pupils opportunities for education offering such variety of instruction and training as may be desirable in view of their different ages, abilities and aptitudes' (Lawson and Silver, cited in McNay and Ozga, 1985: 282). It is important to note that while the LEAs built, staffed and maintained institutions it was teachers at this time who were largely in control of the curriculum and teaching methods. Ranson (1985) cites Briault (1976) who describes the system of educational decision-making as a 'triangle of tension, checks and balances'.

Barber (1994: 119) argues that the 1944 Act was 'perceived as a centralising measure'; 'it increased the power of the state' and, consequently, the idea of a 'national system locally administered' proved highly durable and adaptable.

The LEAs were given a greater degree of control than ever before while at the same time the Ministry of Education was also able to exercise a great deal of influence over the LEAs, far more than the its predecessor, the Board of Education (Barber, 1994).

The eleven plus, selection and streaming

The postwar state education system, although frequently referred to as 'the tripartite system', was more accurately a 'bi-partite system' because the third element, the secondary technical schools, were never fully endorsed by LEAs or by the governments of the period. Sanderson (1987: 20) argues that the failure to develop the technical schools was '. . . perhaps the greatest lost opportunity of the twentieth century education system' since they could provide valuable education and training which had a direct relevance to the scarce skills which industry needed. In the postwar system children were assessed during their final year of primary education and then allocated through the eleven plus to a grammar school or a secondary modern school. The latter, described by Kynaston (2009: 160) as 'the defining life event', was a universally accepted method of selection and was based on a number of assumptions: that intelligence was fixed and could be measured and that abilities could be measured at the age of eleven and would be fixed for life. Once it was accepted that children could be ranked according to their ability or 'intelligence', then, ranking the schools according to the tripartite system or organising groups of pupils into streams by 'ability' was easily justified.

However, during the 1950s and early 1960s those ideas and practices which had dominated educational thinking and planning for many years were criticised by mounting evidence from sociologists, psychologists and educationalists which showed that relatively few working-class children compared to middle-class children 'passed' the eleven plus. Evidence also revealed regional disparities in the provision of grammar school places thus making it more difficult to pass the eleven plus in some areas than in others. There was also evidence that girls were frequently discriminated against in the allocation of grammar school places.

In the critique of the existing system, the work of Vernon, Yates and Pidgeon (cited in Crook, 2002) demonstrated that both the rationale and methods of so-called 'objective' psychometric testing were severely flawed, particularly when used to predict future performance. It was recognised that such early selection resulted in a wastage of ability and the assumption that working-class children and their families were responsible for their own 'failure' was challenged. The negative effects of the eleven plus on the upper primary school curriculum were evident in the need for widespread streaming and coaching for the examination.

According to Kogan (1971) studies in the late 1950s also showed that as many as 15 per cent of pupils were allocated to the 'wrong' schools and there were limited transfers between the secondary modern and technical schools and the grammar schools at the age of 13.

A key factor which was important in the movement to end the eleven plus was the introduction in 1951 of the General Certificate of Education (GCE) in England and Wales. Gradually, secondary modern schools started to allow some of their pupils to stay at school until 16 in order to take the new GCEs, and the achievement of those schools in terms of good examination results proved to be a further indication of the fallacy of selection at eleven.

Primary and junior school education and nursery education

The 1944 Act recognised the importance of a primary stage of education through which all children should pass before moving on to secondary schooling and thus ended the old distinction between elementary and secondary education that had persisted since the eighteenth century. It was agreed that transition between the two phases would take place at the age of eleven.

The situation facing the Labour government as regards primary and junior education immediately after the war is comprehensively described by Cunningham (2002: 18) who refers to 'the scandalous neglect of the primary school building stock'. In the first years after the war major gains were made through the provision of free school meals and free milk for all pupils, and despite the need for cutbacks in expenditure initially, new buildings did begin to appear.

In terms of teaching and learning there were important developments in what might loosely be termed 'progressive' education – a theme which will be explored in Chapter 2. Some teachers working in newly built schools equipped with specialist teaching areas and classrooms, with libraries and access to new technology (Cunningham, 2002) were introducing new approaches to the curriculum and pedagogy. The diverse and complex movement called 'Progressivism' emphasised the importance of child-centred and activity-based learning and the freedom of the teacher (Jones, 2003). Not all pupils experienced these new approaches and continued to be educated in substandard buildings with inadequate resources. At this time too, many schools adopted strategies that maximised their success and their pupils' success at the eleven plus examination. As a result many schools streamed their pupils and there was much coaching especially for the 'A'-stream pupils who were more likely to gain a place at the local grammar school. Simon (1991: 153), in his study of education in the period under review, suggests that the nature of education within the primary school became 'dominated by the requirements of the selection examination which in most areas by this time took the form of so-called "objective" tests in "intelligence", English and arithmetic'. Thus what was occurring in the upper levels of the system affected junior and primary school pupils' experiences and ran counter to official ideologies focused on progressivism.

Research by sociologists, educationalists and psychologists, as has been indicated, pointed to the enormous pressures that many junior school pupils and their parents were subjected to, and highlighted the fact that selection at eleven was becoming the flashpoint of educational criticism.

Lowe (1997: 210) argues that the failure to accomplish educational reconstruction during this period when progressive educational ideology was quite dominant meant that: '. . . the new primary education was unable to shake off many of the characteristics of the old elementary schooling, and some were even reinforced because of the greater emphasis on streaming because of the eleven-plus'.

As late as 1951, according to Lowe (1997), there were still some one million pupils in all-age schools and some authorities believed that it was necessary to exclude children of statutory age from schooling for want of facilities.

With regard to nursery education, the 1944 Act seemed to herald a new dawn for nursery education too. Clause 8(2)(b) of the Act instructed the LEAs to plan for the needs of pupils under five while phasing out the all-age schools (Lowe, 1988: 21). It was anticipated that LEAs would follow this advice and would begin to phase out all-age schools and thereby extend the benefits of education to the growing number of under-fives. Lowe (1988: 22) notes: 'It was a revolution that never took place' – an example once again of the complicated relationship between policy provision and policy enactment.

Further education

After 1945 both Labour and Conservative governments began to recognise the importance of technical and commercial education and training as a key issue in the nation's economic success.

The 1944 Act had made clear references to further education and recommended compulsory part-time further education: 'All young persons from 15 to 18 will be required to attend an appropriate centre part-time unless they are in full-time attendance at school' (White Paper (1944) cited in Barber, 1994: 67). Although the number of students in further education increased dramatically during the period under review, there were growing concerns about the influence of social class on access to further education.

In 1954 the Gurney-Dixon Report *Early Leaving*, the terms of reference of which had been to consider what factors influenced the age at which boys and girls left secondary school at the minimum school-leaving age, reported that there was considerable 'wastage' of talent in these groups of young people. It drew attention to the 'neglected educational territory' (McKenzie, 2001: 191) of pupils who left school at 15 to follow a craft or a technical rather than an academic career. The Report recommended maintenance allowances for needy children staying on at school beyond 15.

The White Paper on Technical Education published in 1956 was important because it recommended an expansion in technical education in further education, this once again recognising the importance of investment in science and technology education for the wealth of the nation.

Fieldhouse (1994), in a review of the Labour government's further education policy 1945–51, argues that the Minister of Education (Ellen Wilkinson) and her civil servants were keen to expand and reform further education (FE) and in 1947 published a detailed national plan for FE. The plan placed a heavy emphasis on vocational education and its most far-reaching aspect was the proposal to introduce compulsory part-time education and training up to the age of 18 for all those who had left school, to be provided in the new county colleges. However, this proposal was overtaken by deepening economic crises faced by the government in the later 1940s and was not implemented.

Voluntary part-time vocational education and training did expand considerably but in a much more limited form than was originally envisaged. At the same time there were quite ambitious plans for non-vocational further and 'liberal' education to be provided through a partnership of the LEAs and other local providers such as universities and the Workers Educational Association. Inevitably, although there was fairly significant postwar expansion, this was uneven and often depended on the commitment and drive of the LEAs (Fieldhouse, 1994), and the worsening economic situation severely limited funding for this provision. The development of further education is further examined in Chapter 2 with particular reference to the 1959 Crowther Report *Fifteen to Eighteen*.

The drive towards comprehensivisation

The growing body of evidence referred to in the section on the eleven plus and streaming was used to demonstrate that the 1944 Education Act was not promoting 'equality of opportunity', had done much less than anticipated for working-class pupils, and was used increasingly by advocates of comprehensive schools. Carr and Hartnett (1996: 105) in their discussion of 'Secondary Education for All' provide a succinct summary of the problem when they argue that: '. . . it was no longer self-evident that a meritocratic system of education was any more democratic than the class-based aristocratic system that it had replaced.'

There were some pioneers of the comprehensive school from as early as 1945 in Anglesey and the first purpose-built comprehensive school, Kidbrooke, was opened in London in 1954. LEAs began to think about alternatives to the tripartite system – for example, London County Council had planned a scheme of partial comprehensive organisation in 1944 and issued its London School Plan in 1947. Crook (2002: 247) describes the postwar drive for comprehensive education as 'a grassroots initiative', which both began to challenge the 'orthodoxies of tripartism and bipartism' and thus 'paved the way for officially non-selective experiments during the following decade'.

Furthermore, Limond (2007: 342) comments: 'It was a desire to achieve economies of scale rather than ideological fervour that prompted various rural authorities to invest in early comprehensive schemes.' In this context, Simon argues that these 'experiments' in the 1950s provided the background to what he calls the 'breakout' of the following decade when the move towards comprehensivisation became more firmly established across the country.

The Labour government, as will be shown in the discussion of the contributions of the two Labour Ministers of Education in the period under review, was slow to adopt comprehensivisation, although the Labour Party had successfully passed a resolution calling on the government to implement the Party's policy on comprehensive schools in 1950.

In 1951, in the pamphlet, *A Policy for Secondary Education* published by the Party, there was a clear statement of the Party's full support for the introduction of a comprehensive system. However, as Lowe (1988: 130) observes, the electoral defeat in 1951: 'committed the Party to a lengthy period of introspection, during which internal dissensions severely weakened its power to promulgate clearly defined polices.' Chapter 2 explores how the move towards comprehensivisation became a majority concern and was at the forefront of educational debate during the 1960s.

The next section looks at policy through the contributions of the Ministers of State in the Labour and Conservative governments of the period.

The Education Secretaries and policy development

(*Note*: The Ministry of Education was reorganised as the Department of Education and Science in 1964, and the Minister became known as the Secretary of State for Education and Science.)

In the period under review there were nine Ministers or Secretaries of Education who each came into office bringing a range of abilities, successes, experiences, strengths and personal characteristics. The range included the public school and Oxbridge-educated Conservatives and the working-class and socialist Labour Party members. It is important also to note that Ellen Wilkinson (Labour, 1945–7) was the first female Minister of State for Education and Florence Horsbrugh (Conservative, 1951–4) was the first female Conservative member of the Cabinet. Chapter 3 describes how another female gained the post of Secretary of State for Education and Science: Margaret Thatcher.

The Ministers during the period 1945–60 were:

Richard Law 1945	(Coalition)
Ellen Wilkinson 1945–7	(Labour)
George Tomlinson 1947–51	(Labour)
Florence Horsbrugh 1951–4	(Conservative)
Sir David Eccles 1954–7	(Conservative)
Viscount Hailsham 1957	(Conservative)
Geoffrey Lloyd 1957–9	(Conservative)
Sir David Eccles 1959–62	(Conservative)

In the discussions focused on these individuals, there will be references to the Minister's main achievements and the influences of the Treasury, the Cabinet and the Party. The Minister's relationship with LEAs, civil servants and the teaching profession, and reference to the Minister's own values and philosophy and own educational experiences, will also be considered when appropriate. Each of the factors, to a greater or lesser extent, influenced the thinking and actions of the Ministers who held office in the period under review.

Before looking at the Labour and Conservative Ministers, however, the contributions of R. A. Butler, Minister in Churchill's Coalition government, and Richard Law, Minister for a short period in 1945, are reviewed.

R. A. Butler

R. A. Butler played such an important part in steering the 1944 Education Act through Parliament. This section begins with a review of his achievements.

R. A. Butler was educated at Marlborough College and then won an exhibition to Pembroke College, from where he then obtained a fellowship at Corpus Christi College, Cambridge. Marriage led to financial independence and enabled him to embark on a parliamentary career. He had a comfortable victory in the general election of 1929 when he became MP for Saffron Walden, holding this seat until his retirement in 1965.

Butler held posts in the Foreign Office and a period as parliamentary secretary at the Ministry of Labour gave him a useful acquaintance with the depressed areas and with mass unemployment. Butler spent several years at the Foreign Office, but in July 1941, after nine years as an under-secretary, he became president of the Board of Education. Even further removed from the war than the Foreign Office, education was nevertheless seen to be a major challenge for the Board of Education.

That Butler played a formidable role in postwar reconstruction (he was also Chancellor of the Exchequer after Education) cannot be denied. He also played a significant part in influencing and shaping Conservative policy in the postwar period, although he was generally opposed to drastic change and contributed to the political consensus and bipartisanship in the period under review.

In 1941 Butler founded the Conservative Post War Problems Committee. Its educational subcommittee reported in 1942 and emphasised the importance of national education in developing a strong sense of patriotism (Sanderson, 1987). The experience of working with the Committee served him well and later in 1941 Churchill appointed him President of the Board of Education. Chitty (2009: 19), in his review of educational policy at the time, comments that Butler was positive about the opportunity to 'harness to the educational system the wartime urge for social reform and greater equality' (cited in Butler, 1971: 86). As Barber (1994: 119) argues, '. . . like almost everyone else in his time, [he was] inspired by the idea of a democratic, liberal education system for all.'

All Butler's formidable diplomatic and political skills were needed to secure the agreement of the churches as well as the acquiescence of Churchill and Conservative backbenchers, whom Butler thought 'a stupid lot'. The 1944 Education Act, which Butler believed would 'have the effect of welding us into one nation – instead of two nations as Disraeli talked about' (Timmins, 1996: 92), was Butler's greatest legislative achievement and was deservedly called after him.

In his study of the making of the 1944 Act, Barber (1994: 36), details how Butler had to use all of his skills' repertoire to secure widespread support for the Board's main proposals. He was particularly adept in promoting the reforms in a way which left most of the interested parties believing that they had indeed received a considerable proportion of what they had asked for. For example, as Lawton argues, he had to negotiate a path that allowed him to give in to Conservative pressure to retain the selective direct grant schools and, simultaneously, he had to work closely with belligerent Labour leaders and persuade the Treasury that education reforms would not cost too much money.

Butler's indefatigable work in dealing with the 'religious question' has already been discussed in an earlier section. However, it can be emphasised again that Butler's role in securing the passage of the 1944 Education Act through a democratic consensus between the wartime government, the churches and the education service was formidable (Tomlinson, 2005).

A final comment summarises Butler's achievement: 'The Act was an achievement for Butler who was also pleased that he had safeguarded his Party's interests: diversity and variety among the state schools, the place of religious instruction, and the autonomy of the Public Schools' (Jeffereys, cited in Lawton, 1994: 24).

Richard Law, 'a little known Tory' (Simon, 1991: 77) who replaced Butler as Minister for Education in Churchill's caretaker government but not as a

Cabinet member, was soon replaced by Ellen Wilkinson. A brief entry in the *Oxford Dictionary of National Biography* by J. Enoch Powell (2004) says of Law: 'When Churchill scraped the ministerial barrel to form a "caretaker government" after the coalition was dissolved in May 1945, Law became Minister of Education; but after six weeks he lost both office and seat.'

The Labour Ministers, Ellen Wilkinson and George Tomlinson, held office between them from 1945 until 1951 and contributed to the monumental task of reconstruction and of implementing the 1944 Education Act. Their respective ministerial careers are examined next.

Ellen Wilkinson

Ellen Wilkinson was born in 1891 in Chorlton, near Manchester, to a socially upwardly mobile family. After a higher elementary school education, she became a pupil teacher and also taught in elementary schools. She won a scholarship to Manchester University and there her interest in politics was firmly established. After a spell in the Communist Party she won the Middlesbrough East seat for Labour in 1924. She was an active and respected Parliamentarian but lost her seat in 1931. She fought back, however, and in 1935 was elected as Labour MP for Jarrow, having led the famous Jarrow Crusade in 1933.

Although she had not had experience of educational planning and policy she saw education as a critical area for the postwar Labour government and approached Attlee to ask for the Ministry (Lowe, 1988). Attlee, according to Wilkinson's biographer, showed the importance he attached to this office when offering her a seat in the Cabinet, despite her reputation for being something of a radical left-winger at the time. Wilkinson, became the first female Education Minister of any political party (Vernon, 1982: 201), and thus at the Ministry's head for the first time was a woman educated within the state system.

On coming into office, Wilkinson claimed, according to Lowe (1988: 38), that her two guiding aims were: '. . . to see no boy or girl is debarred by lack of means from taking the course of education for which he or she is qualified . . . and to remove from education those class distinctions which are the negation of democracy'. Her immediate successes were to almost single-mindedly persuade Parliament to avoid postponing the raising of the school-leaving age to 15, despite great opposition from her colleagues who preferred to see funds directed at the postwar housing programme, and to introduce free school milk in 1946. Her success in securing the raising of the school-leaving age has to be tempered against the fact that in the then economic climate the secondary modern schools, far from achieving parity of esteem, were guaranteed inferior staffing and accommodation.

Her former Parliamentary Private Secretary, Billy Hughes (1979: 158), argues that during her brief office she also attacked educational privilege by reducing the number of direct grant schools from 232 to 166 and she oversaw the introduction of university scholarships so that no one qualified should be deprived of a university education for financial reasons.

Wilkinson had to operate at a time when there was a desperate shortage of buildings and teachers, and she succeeded in increasing the education budget in a very difficult period where the Treasury controlled the 'purse strings' very tightly. She had also wanted to raise the school-leaving age to 16 and to provide universal free school meals. Both were ruled out on the grounds of cost.

It should also be emphasised that the new Labour administration (and the Party itself) had no clear policy on how to implement the 1944 Education Act and certainly had no coherent policy on comprehensive schooling, so all of Wilkinson's activities have to be judged against that background and context. Inevitably, her own educational experiences influenced the rationale for the educational policies that she pursued. 'What truly stirred her', Tomlinson (2005: 152) notes, 'in the wake of the 1944 Act, was the prospect of a new generation of bright, self-motivated, self-improving working-class children going to traditionally elite middle-class grammar schools and using this experience as a platform for future advance and fulfilment.' Wilkinson, of course, in her own educational career, had benefited from this kind of experience.

Hargreaves (1985) argues that the Labour government, with Wilkinson at Education, missed a unique opportunity for the radical reform of the education system because it endorsed the tripartite system and postponed large-scale comprehensive reorganisation for almost two decades (cited in McNay and Ozga, 1985: 79).

In a more sympathetic vein, Rubenstein (1979: 167) argues that Wilkinson's actions as Minister have to be understood in the context of her own origins and experiences, her advisers and her period as Minister. Nevertheless, he suggests that: 'However worthy her motives, she delayed and attempted to prevent a crucially important reform at a crucially important time.' Her failure to support comprehensivisation and hence her support for the tripartite system, and her failure to deal with private schools, were actions that were followed through by her successor, George Tomlinson, whose contributions are discussed below.

George Tomlinson

George Tomlinson was appointed as Minister of Education in 1947 following the sudden death of his predecessor, Ellen Wilkinson. He was born in 1890 in the industrial village of Rishton in Lancashire, and after elementary school worked full-time in the local mill. He joined the Independent Labour

Party and began to establish himself in local politics, eventually becoming Vice-President of the Association of Education Committees. He became an MP in 1945 and was given the post of Minister of Works by Prime Minster Attlee.

As Minister of Education, a post he held for four and a half years, he acted with enthusiasm and application following the direction laid down by Wilkinson (Dean, 1986). Coming into office he stated that his job was '. . . to implement the 1944 Education Act for a generation. What I shall do is to secure the fullest co-operation between all Local Authorities, without whose help the scheme will fail' (Blackburn, 1954: 177). He had to deal with a number of key issues in his first years of office, in particular the school building programme, an increase in school places and the recruitment of teachers, each of which resulted from the pledge of 'secondary education for all', the postwar 'baby-boom' and the raising of the school-leaving age to 15. Although educational expenditure continued to rise during this period, Britain was still having to deal with enormous financial problems, and according to Dean (1986: 116) 'caution rather than innovation became the Government's guideline'. Nevertheless, Tomlinson was successful in increasing the number of new school places and ensured a rapid increase in the number of trained teachers.

Tomlinson has been criticised for his position on the comprehensive movement and on private schooling. His biographer, Blackburn, argues that: '. . . he was naturally interested in the idea of the comprehensive schools, but he took the line that he was going to give them every chance to prove themselves and was not going to use his powers to force their adoption anywhere' (1954: 193). Not all critics accept this interpretation. Kynaston (2007: 576) argues that he did little to encourage those backing comprehensive or 'multilateral' schools, and 'he either blocked, delayed or watered down various proposals that came across his desk'. Tomlinson is on record as saying that: 'The Party are kidding themselves if they think that the comprehensive school has any popular appeal' (Kynaston, 2007: 576). He also supported the official view on private schooling (the Labour Party and government were, on the whole, fairly silent about private education at this time) arguing that: '. . . I personally do not see the sense in getting rid of something that is doing a useful job of work, or making everything conform to a common pattern. I am all for variety, especially in the field of education' (Blackburn, 1954: 193). He, like many at this time, did not see the massive growth in the divide between middle-class and working-class pupils in their different schools.

On the issue of selection and the grammar schools, he seemed to follow the Party line at this time. Grammar schools were still seen to carry enormous prestige both locally and nationally, and were thought to act as an escalator for the talented and hard-working. This was a rationale which would ring true in Tomlinson's case, as someone who through effort and application had himself 'made the grade'. He believed in 'parity of esteem' and thought that this could be achieved through the tripartite system (Carr and Hartnett, 1996).

Ill-health forced him out of politics and he died in 1952.

The Conservatives in power 1951–59

The Conservative government came into power in 1951 and would remain in office for a further 13 years. During the first period in office the Conservatives pursued much of the reforms that the previous Labour administration had set in motion (Dean, 1992).

The key politicians of this period – Churchill, Butler, Eden and Macmillan – had all had experience of the wartime Coalition government and, according to writers such as Dean (2006) in his analysis of the Conservative government from 1951 to 1955, 'this made it difficult for them to challenge the reforms instigated in this period.' Initially, this may have had some inhibiting influence on the actions of the Conservative Ministers of Education with only Sir David Eccles seemingly having the strength and confidence to act independently.

In what follows the policies pursued by the Conservative Party are examined through the contributions of the Ministers of Education of the period: Florence Horsbrugh, Sir David Eccles, Viscount Hailsham, Geoffrey Lloyd and Sir David Eccles in his second term of office.

Florence Horsbrugh was the Education Minister from 1951 to 1954 in the Conservative government led by Churchill. As senior minister, however, she remained out of the Cabinet until 1953 when she became the first woman to achieve a Cabinet position in a Conservative administration. Dean (2006) argues that her omission from the Cabinet weakened her standing with her partners in the educational world and, for much of her period in office, R.A. Butler was seen as the education spokesman.

In 1950–51 she had been chair of the Conservative parliamentary committee on education and having had a long and loyal career serving the Party, was seen to be a safe appointment in 1951.

Writers such as Hennessy (2006) and Dean (2006) argue that Horsbrugh spent much of her time struggling against the Treasury which was determined to squeeze the education budget. She seemed to be caught in a difficult position, having to make economies to satisfy the Treasury while angering many important interest groups and powerful political allies of the government (Dean, 2006). At this time, health and education seemed to lose out to expensive programmes in other priority fields such as defence and housing because the government was committed to the Cold War and reconstruction, albeit in an uncertain economic climate. Ironically, it was

R. A. Butler, who as Chancellor declared a moratorium on the school-building programme, something he had fought for during his steerage of the 1944 Act through Parliament. Thus Horsbrugh was forced to implement economies which reduced the school-building programme and consequently she found herself open to attacks about overcrowding and inadequate classrooms.

She had to deal with the possibility of lowering the school-leaving age to 14, to consider again charging fees for all secondary school pupils and restrict the numbers of children receiving education aged under five (Lowe, 1988).

Horsbrugh, according to Kynaston (2009: 114), 'although a conscientious Minister, lacked clout and charisma' and in Kogan's estimation was 'a dreary and disliked Minister who was brought only late into the Cabinet, who never fought for and never received an adequate educational budget' (cited in Lawton, 1994: 26).

Simon (1991: 162) is of the opinion that 'she gained a reputation as a cheese-paring Minister during her term of office', but despite her attempts to meet the economies demanded by the Treasury, Churchill remained dismissive and doubtful towards Horsbrugh and, in Simon's words, she was 'unceremoniously dropped and replaced by a very different character, Sir David Eccles, who would serve two terms in office' (Simon, 1991: 161).

According to Lawton (1994: 26), Eccles, alongside Butler and Boyle, is often seen as a modernising Conservative Education Minister and a Minister who was fascinated by educational policy-making and the school curriculum and examination system. He was successful in extracting money from the Treasury and this ability contrasts so starkly with that of his predecessor Florence Horsbrugh.

It must be recognised, as Kogan (1978: 34) aptly does, that at this time there was continuing optimism about economic growth and more resources for education were made available through Eccles's negotiating skills. Eccles held office during a period when, according to Chitty (2009: 24), 'education policy at national level was becoming increasingly "non-partisan" and even almost "bipartisan".'

At an NUT conference in 1955, he outlined his five working rules on secondary education (Gosden, 1983: 31, cited in Lawton, 1994: 26) and these, in Kogan's (1978) opinion, express clearly his 'optimism and opportunism':

1. A new range of 15–25 per cent for grammar plus technical school places.
2. New technical schools would be approved where there was a very strong case.
3. Modern schools would be encouraged to develop extended courses and to strengthen their links with grammar and technical schools, and with further education.

4. Transfers should be made as early as possible to put right glaring mistakes in the eleven-plus examination. Otherwise the time for transfers – and more should be arranged – should be 15 or 16.
5. Comprehensive schools would be approved as an experiment when all conditions were favourable and no damage was done to any existing schools.

(Lawton, 1994: 26)

Eccles was one of the first Ministers to talk about quality and standards and he argued that education should be seen as a national investment rather than a burden on the taxpayer – a position which is examined in Chapter 2 which discusses Eccles second period in office (1959–62) under Macmillan. It has to be noted that both Labour and Conservative Governments had to curtail drastically expenditure (and hence investment) on education because of the worsening international and national economic situation.

He was able to secure additional the funding for the FE building programme in one year from £5 million to £30 million. Boyle, who built up the system that Eccles did so much to create, and whose term of office is discussed in Chapter 2, referred to Eccles in the following way: 'I regard David Eccles as still by far the most under-rated figure who held office during the thirteen years of Conservative rule' (Gosden, 1983: 20, cited in Lawton, 1994: 29).

Evidently, Eccles remained a staunch supporter of the grammar schools but also recognised that existing secondary modern schools provided an impoverished education for four out of five children (Kynaston, 2007). He believed, however, that the grammar schools gave parents 'choice' and that the secondary modern schools should develop specialisms. At the same time he argued that 'no modern school pupil should be deprived of the opportunity of entering for the examination for the GCE if the school or his Headteacher thought that they had the necessary ability and persistence.' Eccles did acknowledge that frequently the aspirations behind 'secondary education for all' were not being fulfilled for all children (McCulloch, 2002). The importance of secondary modern pupils in being allowed to take GCEs has already been noted for its importance in the wastage of talent arguments in the 1950s.

Kynaston (2009: 411) has written about Eccles' defence of the grammar school: 'My colleagues and I will never agree to the assassination of the Grammar School', and in the same year, addressing a National Union of Teachers (NUT) conference, he directly attacked the comprehensive school as 'an untried and very costly experiment'. Later that year he blocked attempts by LEAs in Manchester and Swansea to open comprehensive schools, although later, as Crook (2002: 249) argues, Eccles was to show 'a more even-handed policy allowing the establishment of new comprehensives and county complements in both purpose-built accommodation and amalgamated premises'. He also approved of comprehensive schools in new towns and other locations that did not displace existing grammar schools.

Eccles left the Ministry in 1957 when the new premier, Harold Macmillan, whom he greatly admired, sent him to the Board of Trade. However, after an unhappy time there, he was asked to return to Education after the general election in 1959.

Following Sir David Eccles' departure, Viscount Hailsham was asked to join the Cabinet as Minister of Education and in his brief tenure (eight months in office) he could do little to influence the existing state of the education system. According to Lawton (1994: 29), 'he confesses that this was not a position he had sought and he seems to have had little interest in it'. In the brief time he spent at the Ministry he did lengthen the training period for teachers and, according to Cretney in an article in the *Oxford Dictionary of National Biography* (2005), he believed that he had restored the morale of teachers and others professionally involved by convincing them that a Conservative Minister could equal and even surpass politicians from any other Party in enthusiasm for improvement.

Geoffrey Lloyd, who succeeded Viscount Hailsham and held office for two years in the Macmillan government, is described by Lawton (1994: 30) as the first man of a technological bent to occupy the post of Minister of Education and that he had done much to enhance the standing of technology, although this was a subject that was still a long way from receiving academic approval in schools.

Like many Conservative Ministers of Education he had been to a public school and possessed little or no knowledge of the state system.

Dean (1992) says that he used 'public relations' effectively to secure funds for education, especially after the success of the Russian Sputnik in the space-race.

Lloyd was also impressed by some American ideas on education, but after his return from a study tour in the USA he was still intent on preventing the kind of sweeping comprehensivisation common in the USA and supported by the Labour Party. No one has suggested that he made any significant contribution to educational policies or ideas.

The Conservatives were re-elected for a third term in 1959 and it was once again Sir David Eccles who took over as Minister of State for Education. His period of office is discussed fully in Chapter 2.

Conclusion

The period from 1945 to 1959 ends with the Conservatives still in power after having been re-elected for their third term of office and Sir David Eccles is Minster for Education.

The system which evolved after the 1944 Education Act, despite the increasing demands for 'equality of educational opportunity', saw the tripartite system firmly established in the 1940s and 1950s.

Inevitably, economic and administrative considerations played a major part in developments during this period. The economic situation after the war was difficult, different types of schools already existed and it was no doubt easier to use these rather than plan radical reorganisation.

However, during the period under review, experience of the tripartite system in practice stimulated debates about equal opportunity and this influenced the demand for comprehensive education.

Opposition to the process of selection at eleven grew during the period. The ranking of pupils according to the notion of 'ability' was thoroughly discredited, although grammar schools still remained popular with middle-class and working-class parents. The private sector, almost wholly ignored by Labour in office, began to thrive in the 1950s and the 1960s.

Teachers in primary schools created opportunities to develop a 'progressive' and child-centred curriculum, while at the other end of the educational spectrum there was some expansion in further and higher education.

The important partnership between local education authorities, central government and the teaching profession continued to flourish and for most of the period under review the broad consensus between the two major parties continued to be upheld.

These issues will be explored further in Chapter 2. The contributions of both Conservative and Labour Ministers of Education to education policy in the 1960s will be examined as will the major reports and Acts that were introduced by both governments.

Further reading

Aldrich, R. (ed.) (2002) *A Century of Education*. London: Routledge Falmer.

Carr, W. and Hartnett, A. (1996) *Education and the Struggle for Democracy*. Buckingham: Open University Press.

Chitty, C. (2009) *Education Policy in Britain* (2nd edn). Basingstoke: Palgrave Macmillan.

Jones, K. (2003) *Education in Britain 1944 to the Present*. Cambridge: Polity Press.

Simon, B. (1991) *Education and the Social Order 1940–1990*. London: Lawrence & Wishart.

CHAPTER TWO

1960–1969: A DECADE OF SOCIAL AND LEGISLATIVE INNOVATION

- Comprehensivisation
- The Newsom Report
- The Plowden Report
- Educational priority areas
- Curriculum

Introduction

In this chapter we will examine some of the tensions that have remained at the forefront of the education debate in England and Wales. The 1960s saw a continuation of the postwar consensus in education policy and practice, but tensions began to emerge, particularly with the widespread discontent with the process of selection of children at age 11, streaming, particularly in primary schools, the inadequacy of a 'secondary modern' education and the 'creaming' off of bright and more able pupils by the grammar and independent schools. The negative influences of social class and neighbourhood on attitudes to schooling, aspiration and achievement gradually entered the discourses about equality of educational opportunity. Circular 10/65 issued by the Labour government established comprehensive schools as a priority and requested all local education authorities to present plans for the reorganisation of secondary education on comprehensive lines. This decade saw a growing difference between groups who favoured traditional methods in education against those who favoured more progressive approaches, especially in primary education with the publication of the Plowden Report in 1967. By the end of the decade the consensus had started to break down and a number of questions were being asked about the role, function and purpose of education, with opportunities for new approaches and continued expansion.

The 1960s witnessed an increased role and greater strength of central government in education and training across all sectors in England and Wales. Ministers too played a more interventionist role in education, for example through decisions about comprehensivisation and in dealings with the pay and conditions of teaching professionals. There was an increased concern with national economic needs, the underprivileged and manpower resources, and a focus on education principles, philosophy and practice. The use of evidence from sociologists and educationalists heavily influenced the provision and practice of education. A number of important reports covering primary education, public schools, less able children, the universities, the recruitment of scientists and the youth service were published. For example, the Crowther Report in 1959, the Plowden Report in 1963, the Newsom Report in 1963, the Robbins Report in 1963, and the Haslegrave Report in 1969. During this period the Ministry of Education was reconstituted, educational priority areas were designated, new provision to parallel higher education was established (the binary system) and the National Schools Council was formed. Equality of educational opportunity was a major issue, particularly in relation to the development of comprehensive schools which dominated the decade.

The 1960s saw two governments in power. The Conservatives, after having been in power for 13 years, lost the 1964 election to Labour, led by Harold Wilson, who then continued to govern until defeated in the 1970 general election.

The key areas that will be discussed in more detail in this chapter are:

- the contributions of the Ministers of Education (later to become Secretaries of State for Education) to education;
- primary education, which during the 1960s, as Simon (1991: 342) notes, 'was put firmly on the map', becoming a major and largely distinct sector of the national system of education;
- the Newsom Report;
- the Plowden Report on primary education;
- the move towards comprehensive education;
- streaming and the end of selection;
- the curriculum and the contribution of research by sociologists and educationalists which forced politicians and policy-makers to listen and act informed by this evidence;

- changes in the relationships between key players in the education system: central government, the local education authorities and teachers' representatives.

Political, social and economic context

The backdrop to the 1960s reveals major social, political, economic and cultural changes which had repercussions for society as a whole. The early-to mid-1960s, on the whole, were a period of general economic prosperity and relatively low unemployment, although there were problems with the balance of payments which affected educational expenditure and investment.

Dale (1989), for example, draws attention to the fact that during the 1960s there was an increasing emphasis placed on education as an instrument of national interest and inevitably education was under pressure to justify its potential contribution to national economic development through the identification and preparation of skilled personnel.

Nevertheless, there continued to be expansion in the economy and consequently in all sectors of the education system – primary, secondary, further and higher – built on a consensus about the nature and direction of education policy which was still largely consensual between the two major parties. Kogan (1987: 37) summarises the general situation when he writes: 'Educational politics were largely consensual in their belief and in their expectation.' For example, a number of Ministers, such as Eccles and Boyle (both Conservative) and Crosland (Labour), contributed significantly to the broad consensus about the direction and pace of educational change, although this changed as consensus politics broke down and were replaced by a new educational settlement.

Tomlinson, in her analysis of the period, argues that two key factors are important in understanding the changes in educational policy and practice: 'the principle that a democratic society should educate all its young people rather than selected elites' and 'modern economies needed more and better educated people' (2005: 20). Tomlinson is commenting on the fact that there was agreement, in general terms about key policy rationale between the Labour Party and the Conservative Party.

During the Labour government's term of office (1964–70), as Gillard (2011) notes, there were significant changes which liberalised many areas of society and helped to reflect and contribute to a more open society: capital punishment was abolished (1965), homosexuality was decriminalised (1967), abortion was legalised (1967), theatrical censorship was abolished (1968) and divorce law was reformed (1969).

In the 1960s immigration, the growth of feminism, changes in the family, marriage and sexuality, and the appearance of youth cultures, each contributed to changes in the 'traditional' ways of life, and some of these changes inevitably affected the structure, organisation and content of schooling. Ryder and Silver (1970: 352) argue that 'changes in the family, in authority relationships in the community as a whole, and particularly in the status and cultural identity of young people, had an important impact on the work of schools, weakening traditional goals and structure.'

The decade under review can also be seen as a time of innovation in terms of teaching and learning, of growth in educational, training and work opportunities for young people, and an expansion of further and higher educational opportunities. With an increased number of stakeholders in education, there was concomitant growth in expectations at all levels of society in the role that education and training should provide for its children and young people.

Education Secretaries and the development of policy

In an interview with Peter Ribbens in 1997, Mark Carlisle (his work as Secretary of State for Education is examined in Chapter 4) comments: 'The life expectancy of Secretaries of State for Education up until the mid-1980s was very short – about two years' (1997: 77). In the 1960s no one Minister or Secretary held office longer than two years. It is therefore interesting to note the number of important Education Acts, reports and papers that were produced in this decade, all of which were significant in terms of education policy-making and reform and changes in education ideology, provision and practice. The period in which these changes took place has been described as one in which 'Education policy was largely based on a social democratic consensus that Governments should regulate and resource education to achieve redistributive justice, and provide equal opportunity' (Tomlinson, 2005: 3). From the time of Boyle's appointment as Minister of Education in 1954 until the general election in 1964, when Labour secured victory, government education policy was mainly non-partisan and almost bi-partisan.

During the 1960s, there were three Ministers of State and four Education Secretaries in office (the Ministry became the Department for Education and Science in 1964): three from the Conservative Party and four from the Labour Party. They were Sir David Eccles (Conservative, 1959–62), Edward Boyle (Conservative, 1962–4), Quintin Hogg (Conservative, 1964), Michael Stewart (Labour, 1964–5), Anthony Crosland (Labour, 1965–7), Patrick Gordon-Walker (Labour, 1967–8) and Edward Short (Labour, 1968–70).

Sir David Eccles

Sir David Eccles (Conservative) was educated at Winchester and Oxford, and worked in the City before taking up a post in the Ministry of Economic Warfare. He became an MP in 1951 and after a posting as Minister of Works he was moved to Education following the resignation of Florence Horsbrugh in 1954. His achievements in that post from 1954 to 1957 were described in Chapter 1.

During his second period in office from 1959 to 1962, which was a period of continuing prosperity and economic growth, he was associated with a relatively long list of achievements including:

- reducing class sizes in primary and secondary schools;
- raising the qualifications of teachers;
- initiating the Curriculum Study Group (which became the Schools Council for the Curriculum and Examinations in 1964);
- introducing the Certificate of Secondary Education qualification.

Kogan (1978) credits Eccles as being the first Minister to employ economic arguments in favour of increasing expenditure on education. As has already been noted, his attitude towards comprehensivisation was pragmatic in that, as Minister, he stated that he would approve comprehensive plans as an experiment where favourable conditions existed.

The setting up of the Curriculum Study Group (CSG) was a most interesting initiative because it marked, for the first time, the government's intention to question 'ownership' of the curriculum which had always been in the hands of local authorities and teachers. For Eccles the CSG would act as a small 'commando-like unit' that would intermittently intervene in curriculum matters. Eccles was frustrated that the government had no key to the 'secret garden of the curriculum' and wished to change this state of affairs. Chitty, in his discussion of the CSG, cites Manzer who sees the CSG as 'marking a definite departure in the Ministry's conception of its role in the formulation of an important area of educational policy' (1970: 91–2).

However, there was inevitably a strong resistance by teacher unions to this seeming 'take-over' by the state and Edward Boyle, who succeeded Eccles, was forced to seek a compromise, establishing the Schools Council for the Curriculum and Examinations (SCCE) as an alternative to the CSG. The Schools Council, according to Chitty, was an independent organisation whose purpose was 'to undertake research and development work in all aspects of the curriculum and examinations in primary and secondary schools' (2004: 148). The Schools Council developed many initiatives to make the curriculum more flexible, more imaginative and more enjoyable for pupils, and was conceived as 'a hopeful act of reconciliation between central and local government and teachers' (Paskow, cited in Chitty, 2004: 148).

Edward Boyle

Edward Boyle (Conservative) was educated at Eton College and Oxford and entered Parliament as MP for Handsworth in 1950. He was a junior Education Minister under Macmillan and gained a Cabinet post as Minister for Education in 1962. He was to all intents and purposes demoted in 1964 from Minister of Education to Minister of State when the reorganisation of the Department of Education and Science took place. Kogan (1971) identifies Boyle's main achievements during his office as: commissioning the major study by the National Foundation for Educational Research (NFER) into the effects of streaming in primary schools (1962); establishing the Ministry of Education's Curriculum Study Group; establishing the National Advisory Council Report on the Training and Supply of Teachers; and reconstituting the English and Welsh Central Advisory Councils for Education 'to consider primary education in all its aspects and the transition from primary to secondary school' – the Plowden and Gittins Committees. Boyle also published the 1963 Newsom Report, *Half Our Future*, and supported the creation of the Schools Council for the Curriculum and Examinations to replace the Secondary School Examination Council (SSEC). It was Boyle also who announced the raising of the school-leaving age to take place in 1970–1.

Boyle is credited with pursuing a policy of expansion at Education and because of this, Lawton, for example, argues that Boyle was 'out of step with his fellow Conservatives in some aspects of education' (1994: 30). Boyle was the first Conservative Education Secretary who declared that he would not stand in the way of plans for local comprehensives. Yet, in Crook's (2002) opinion, while Boyle was interested in developing comprehensive education, he was a staunch believer in academic standards and therefore could not accept the demise of the grammar school. However, Boyle's position on the 'liberal' wing of the Conservative Party became untenable and he became a scapegoat attacked by right-wing backbenchers and constituency activists (Chitty, 1996: 259).

Lawton (1994) argues that Boyle left politics at a time when Tory opinion on education was moving to the Right – his own views on questions such as comprehensives schools, teaching methods and curriculum, remained essentially pragmatic and intellectual and that he decided to leave the political field.

When discussing Boyle's distinctive contributions to education in terms of policy between 1962 and 1964, Kogan (1991) observes: 'At that time he was responsible for accepting or approving or promoting policies which seemed both momentous and endurable.' And a former Parliamentary Secretary Christopher Chataway writes that: 'In the two years from 1962 to 1964 [during Boyle's term of office] important advances were made in curriculum development, teacher supply, the modernisation of old schools and the development of further education' (1991: 11). Boyle's pragmatism in terms of his role in educating the Conservative Party to accept change is noted by Simon in his detailed analysis of the 1960s when he writes that Boyle recognised 'the force of the movement for secondary re-organisation, and [was] increasingly sympathetic to its objectives' (1991: 274). Boyle's departure from politics was a further sign of the fact that the 'uneasy cross-party alliance on a number of welfare issues was beginning to fall apart' (Chitty, 1996: 258) thus undermining the partnership that had paved the way for comprehensive reform.

Quintin Hogg

Quintin Hogg (Conservative), who later took the title Lord Hailsham, also held office briefly in 1957. Hogg had attended Eton College and Christ Church, Oxford, where he was President of the Oxford University Conservative Association and the Oxford Union. He became a Prize Fellow of All Souls in 1931.

In 1964, after reorganisation, the Ministry of Education became the Department for Education and Science and Hogg became the first Secretary of State for Education. Lawton suggests that Hogg '. . . contributed nothing to policy ideas during his two terms in office, but he was concerned about the low standards of some aspects of the service, and did his best to improve its organisation and funding, seeing education as an investment for industrial survival' (1994: 29).

In Simon's (1991: 203) opinion, Quintin Hogg, who was in post for only eight months in 1964, continued 'Eccles' policy of obstructing the move to comprehensive education. Hogg's view that it was unnecessary to try to educate the mass of children is exemplified in the following citation which is a clear testimonial for secondary-modern schooling:

> In a speech attacking Labour MPs for their support of compre-hensivisation in January 1965, Conservative MP Quintin Hogg declared that secondary modern school pupils were happy 'banging metal and sawing wood'. These boys and girls were getting 'an education tailor-made to their desires, their bents and their requirements'. (Hansard, House of Commons, Vol. 705, cols 423–4, 21 January 1965, quoted in Chitty, 1989: 20–21)

Michael Stewart

Michael Stewart, who succeeded Quintin Hogg as Education Secretary when Labour won the 1964 general election, won a scholarship from his elementary school to Christ's Hospital, Horsham, and another scholarship to Oxford. Like Edward Short, he too was an educational practitioner and taught at Merchant Taylors' School and Copper's Company School until he was elected Labour MP in 1945 after war service. He held a number of junior posts including that of Shadow Minister of Education (1955–9) and then as Shadow Minister of Housing and Local Government (1959–64). Stewart fully supported Labour's commitment to comprehensive reorganisation and argued that the transition to a predominantly comprehensive system could be achieved within five years (Crook, 2002: 251). He was succeeded by Anthony Crosland who oversaw the implementation of Circular 10/65.

Anthony Crosland

Anthony Crosland (Labour) was educated at Highgate School and was a classical scholar at Oxford. After active war service, he returned to Oxford to become a lecturer and then a fellow in economics. He was elected MP for South Gloucestershire in 1950 but lost an election at Southampton in 1955. He published a seminal work in 1956, *The Future of Socialism*, which was extremely well-received and identified education as a way of increasing opportunity to the point that 'occupation and destinies no longer corresponded to their social origins' (cited in Jones, 2003: 50). Kogan (1991: 98) notes that Crosland published his views on many educational issues before reaching office and 'had a clear belief in strengthening the planning system within the DES'. Kogan also argues that Crosland's fundamental assumption about education which informed his thinking and hence many of his actions, was that 'the school system in Britain remains the most divisive, unjust and wasteful of all the social aspects of inequality' (2006: 75).

Crosland re-entered politics in 1964 and after a very short stint at the Department of Economic Affairs was asked to become Secretary of State for Education. He remained at Education for over two years. Kogan notes: 'His time as Secretary of State for Education and Science was relatively short, from January 1965 to August 1967, but he had prepared himself for it intellectually and in working through the underlying values issues' (2006: 72).

The key achievements of Crosland in office are noted by Kogan (1971) who lists his achievements as: the stewardship of Circular 10/65; the establishment of the Public Schools Commission under John Newsom to 'advise on the best way of integrating the public schools with the state system of education'; the creation of the Planning Branch of the DES; and the championing of the Educational Priority Areas initiative (examined later in this chapter). Crosland was transferred from Education to become President of the Board of Trade in 1967.

Patrick Gordon-Walker

Patrick Gordon-Walker (Labour) was educated at Wellington College and after winning a scholarship to Oxford became a history tutor at that university. He entered Parliament in 1945, rose rapidly through the ranks and by 1950 was a Cabinet minister and a Privy Councillor. He was made Foreign Secretary at the 1964 general election but resigned in January 1965 after losing a bi-election in a supposedly 'safe' Labour seat. Prime Minister Harold Wilson made Gordon-Walker Minister of Education but he was removed in a Cabinet reshuffle after less than a year in office. During his very short tenure of office, he oversaw some of the steps being taken to implement Plowden including an improvement in teaching supply, the accelerated school building programme and some action on environment and curricula issues. However, a reduction in the Education budget following post-devaluation cuts meant that he had to suspend the raising of the school-leaving age to 16 which led to substantial delays in the school building programme intended to assist comprehensive reorganisation.

Edward Short

Edward Short (Labour) graduated from Durham University and after war service was head teacher at Blyth School, a secondary modern school in Northumberland. He entered Parliament in 1951 as MP for Newcastle Central. He held a number of government offices before becoming Secretary of State for Education in 1968. Short supported the government's commitment to secondary reorganisation but reacted against the 'softly softly' approach with LEAs and began targeting recalcitrant authorities that had not responded to Circular 10/65. Crook argues that this action and Short's determined attempt to legislate for compliance was significant because they '. . . marked a watershed for central and local government relations in Education and ended the DES's cordial relationship with the Association of Education Committees (AEC)' (2002: 253). The latter, a powerful pressure group, was the chief organisation for education authorities from the time of the 1944 Education Act until its dissolution in 1977 and comprised the chairmen of all local authority education committees. Short, according to Crook, was adamant that LEAs should not frustrate national policy.

Comprehensivisation

Chapter 1 described the postwar developments that led to the move towards a system of comprehensive education and referred to postwar attempts to make education more accessible to working-class children. The evidence for these inequalities in education found parallels also in health, housing and the social services. By the early 1960s there was a growing body of research-based evidence from psychologists, sociologists and educationalists about the validity of intelligence testing in selection procedures in the eleven plus examination, about the relationship between social class and academic achievement, and about wastage of talent among working-class boys and girls. For example, the work of Jackson (1964) on streaming demonstrated that working-class children, compared with their middle-class counterparts, were extremely disadvantaged by streaming processes, and work such as this emphasised the influence of inequality and social class on a child's educational potential.

In 1961 the Labour Party published *Signposts for the Sixties* which argued the need for education to provide greater equality of opportunity, and during the 1960s the movement towards comprehensive education was one of the dominant themes in educational policy and practice. When Labour came to power in 1964, the Party had embraced the comprehensive principle and had called for an end to selection at the party conference in the previous year. Labour also wished to accelerate the existing trend for comprehensive reorganisation, which was well under way at the local level in many areas. The Party recognised the importance of comprehensivisation as a means of ensuring social justice and equality of opportunity.

At this time, however, there was rigorous debate within the Party and outside focused on Labour's position with regard to the grammar schools, with many still keen to retain the grammar school tradition and ethos, and in particular to retain the grammar schools which had afforded opportunities for some working-class pupils. Chitty (2002b) describes how Labour presented their proposals for secondary reorganisation and widening opportunities through the notion of 'grammar schools for all'. The latter, according to Chitty, 'appealed to the growing demands for a more "meritocratic" system of secondary education; and it dispelled the fears and misgivings of those working-class and middle-class parents who still had enormous respect for the traditional grammar-school curriculum.' The idea of 'grammar schools for all' was a much vaunted aim in the 1964 general election campaign won by Labour.

By the mid-1960s there was a great diversity in how local education authorities were approaching comprehensive reorganisation and the pace of reorganisation was very different in local authorities across the country. Indeed, Haydn (2004) describes the ad hoc manner in which comprehensives were introduced and Chitty (2002b) refers to the fact that there was no blueprint for a successful comprehensive school in the 1960s.

Reorganisation had been well under way for years, particularly in Labour-led authorities, for example, in Birmingham, London, Leicestershire and Yorkshire. Some Conservative authorities too, were, according to Manning and Pischke (2006), committed to ending selection in favour of comprehensive schooling. Comprehensivisation, as has been shown in Chapter 1, had also progressed among the Conservative Party during its years of government, with some senior Conservatives giving tentative support to comprehensive reorganisation, and this probably would not have ended had Edward Boyle continued as Education Secretary in 1964.

In some localities Conservatives were content to support the removal of the eleven plus in order to facilitate the development of carefully planned comprehensive schemes (Crook et al., 1999: 12). For example, Dale, in his discussion of political and education change, notes that 'with no central guidance, already 10 per cent of pupils were in comprehensive schools before 10/65 was issued' (1989: 101), evidence of the willingness of even Conservative LEAs to adopt a pragmatic approach when necessary.

The issuing of Circular 10/65 (DES, 1965) while Crosland was at Education, which requested rather than required LEAs to reorganise secondary schools in order to allow the creation of comprehensive schools catering for all abilities, proved to be a watershed in the movement towards comprehensive education. In terms of this example of policy-making, Crosland in an interview with Kogan (1971: 189) refers to the fact that there was 'a great deal of internal consultation within the Department' and 'there was a lot of consultation with the outside educational and teachers' representative bodies'. The circular stated that it was the government's intention to end selection at eleven and to eliminate segregation in secondary education. Kogan suggests that Crosland was keen to move policies quickly and in defence of the decision to 'request rather than require', he argues that for Crosland: 'It was fundamental to his view of democracy that reform would be more lasting if it could be achieved voluntarily' (2006: 78).

The importance of the power relationships between central government and local authorities during comprehensive reorganisation is discussed by Ranson (1985) who suggests that this was an example of the way in which important policy initiatives are often made by local rather than central government. He sees the role of the Education Department 'not so much as a policy-maker as a promoter and catalyst of policies around which there is a growing consensus' (1985: 108). It might be argued that the government did not legislate for comprehensivisation but rather, by issuing

Circular 10/65 which, it believed, rested on consensual beliefs about the way forward, created a position which avoided too much opposition and conflict. It should also be pointed out that Labour had a tiny majority at this time in the Commons (six MPs). There had been considerable discussion within the DES as to whether Circular 10/65 should require or request the local authorities to prepare plans for comprehensive reorganisation (Chitty, 2002a). To illustrate this point Marsden (1973: 126) argues that Crosland may have hoped that slow changes at the local level would provoke less hostility and permit time for the education of the public to support comprehensive reorganisation. Fogleman suggests that Crosland 'was a firm believer in the power of persuasion, rather than an arm-twister, and he was part of a Cabinet which felt distinctly ambivalent towards the comprehensive ideal, particularly if it meant abolishing the grammar schools' (1999: 9, cited in Sumner, 2010).

Indeed, later, when Edward Short attempted to persuade Cabinet to pass legislation to compel LEAs to 'go comprehensive', the dominant response was to favour persuasion over compulsion. As Chitty comments, Circular 10/65 'was the means chosen by the first Wilson Government for securing a *smooth* implementation of its declared policy of reorganising secondary education on comprehensive lines' (2002a: 64).

It was stated earlier that there was no clear blueprint for comprehensivisation but LEAs were offered a number of possible models for reorganisation and they could choose the form that suited their individual circumstances in terms of social, economic, demographic and school-specific variables (Crook, 2002). For example, Leicestershire had pioneered a system of middle schools and this was popular with Conservatives because it allowed them to retain their grammar schools. In practice, however, the dominant model for comprehensive reorganisation involved 11–16 or 11–18 schools (Manning and Pischke, 2006).

In his study of Local Authorities and comprehensivisation, Crook (2002: 257) argues that 'The drive for comprehensive education in England and Wales was a "bottom up", rather than a "top down" initiative', and this seems to describe well, the way in which the Labour government failed to act decisively by compelling LEAs to provide fully comprehensive education for all.

It must be pointed out that there was still significant opposition and protest, along established lines, to complete comprehensive reorganisation. Opponents argued that by eliminating the grammar schools (and their reputation for academic excellence) and the right to a choice of schools, comprehensive education undermined the democratic freedom of the individual. Simultaneously, the continued existence of private schools and grammar schools in many areas meant that the secondary system never became fully comprehensive. Benn and Chitty (1996) pointed out, perhaps not unsurprisingly, that many LEAs and politicians did not see any contradictions in having grammar schools and comprehensives coexisting in one area. The Labour leadership seemed prepared to live with the coexistence of private schools and grammar schools despite their distorting influence on the very principles of comprehensive education. However, the political consensus between the two parties, which had existed since the Second World War, began to break down, with disputes focusing upon Labour's commitment to comprehensive as opposed to Conservative support of selective education and what was seen as Labour's ineffectual attempts to challenge the influence of the independent, 'public' school sector.

There were many different types of comprehensive school and there were serious issues relating to the internal organisation and structure of these schools (Carr and Hartnett, 1996). There were, for example, different policies on streaming, setting, banding and mixed-ability teaching. Some schools, particularly those in middle-class areas, offered a viable and acceptable alternative to a grammar school education, and schools were very different in terms of the quality of the academic ability and social background of their pupils and in the resources and facilities available. Lowe has argued that the development of comprehensives in inner-city areas appeared to offer 'no more than an alternative secondary modern for the working classes' (1997: 148). There were also obstacles to reform (Kogan, 2006) in the fact that although schools were becoming better housed and equipped at this time, there were limits on the amount of funding available for reform and professional challenges relating to the preparation and training of teachers who would be staffing the new schools.

The ad hoc manner in which comprehensive schools were introduced also meant that some comprehensive schools had academic sixth forms and some did not. McCulloch (1998: 14) argues that, where secondary modern schools were re-designated as comprehensive schools, 'the underlying continuities were often readily apparent, especially as the buildings, facilities, teachers, and pupils were the same as before. They also retained their former status in the community, and their previous status was often an encumbrance.'

It could be argued that because of the continued existence of private secondary schools, and some grammar schools in many areas, the secondary system never became fully comprehensive and therefore could never realistically fulfil the aspirations of the comprehensive philosophy. However, and despite these issues, by the beginning of the 1970s there seemed to be, in Haydn's words, 'a sea-tide in favour of the comprehensive model and LEAs of all political persuasions deluged the DES with a range of diverse models of providing comprehensive schooling' (2004: 418).

The Secretary of State Edward Short moved a motion in Parliament which, by virtue of the Conservative majority in the House of Commons, was agreed:

> That this House, conscious of the need to raise the educational standards at all levels, and regretting that the realisation of this objective is impeded by the separation of children into different types of secondary schools, notes with approval the efforts of Local Authorities to reorganise on comprehensive lines which will preserve all that is valuable in grammar school education for those children who now receive it and make it available to more children; recognises that the method and timing of such reorganisation should vary to meet local needs; and believes that the time is now ripe for a declaration of national policy. (DES, 1965)

Chapter 3 will explain that, although comprehensive reforms had promised to increase the educational opportunities of working-class pupils, in reality the expansion in such opportunities was primarily taken up by the children from middle-class families. Chapter 3 will also examine the fact that by the mid-1970s the educational debate increasingly became concerned with the decline in the British economy, the rise in unemployment, the massive rise in inflation and unprecedented industrial unrest. As Carr and Hartnett imply:

> Against the background of the failures to translate the comprehensive principles successfully into practice, the democratic values and assumptions that had influenced official educational policy since 1944 began to be questioned by the mid-1970s. (1996: 106)

In the sections that follow attention will be given to several of the key reports that had a major transforming effect on education at primary, secondary and further and higher education levels.

Newsom Report (1963)

The Newsom Report of 1963, *Half Our Future* was a government report which stimulated the need to understand the education system's failure of non-academic pupils and the increasing concerns about selection. It looked at the education of average and below average children and was one of the earliest investigations into 'underachievers'. Its brief was 'to consider the education between the ages of 13 and 16, of pupils of average or less than average ability who are or will be following full-time courses either at schools or in establishments of further education. The term education shall be understood to include extra-curricular activities' (Ministry of Education, 1963a: xv).

The welcoming of the report by the Minister of Education, Edward Boyle, is important because it offers insights into the consensus politics of the time with the emphasis on meritocratic principles: 'All children should have an equal opportunity of acquiring intelligence, and developing their talents and abilities to the full' (Ministry of Education, 1963a: v).

Newsom argued that the future of the country depended on better education for those of below-average ability. There had been increasing concern over the very large numbers of young people who left school with few or no qualifications. As the Report noted:

> Our pupils constitute, approximately, half the pupils of our secondary schools; they will eventually become half the citizens of this country, half the workers, half the mothers and fathers and half the consumers. (Ministry of Education, 1963a: xiii)

The Report made a number of key recommendations, including the raising of the school-leaving age to 16 (this did not happen until 1972), an experimental school-building programme which would allow schools to 'to try out different forms of school organisation and teaching methods in buildings designed for the purpose' (McKenzie, 2001: 201) and a more stimulating and demanding curriculum. As part of the curriculum reform following Newsom, the introduction of the Certificate of Secondary Education (CSE) examination in 1965 meant that the 'Newsom' child now had an examination route to follow where before there were no opportunities for these learners to gain qualifications.

The results of one of the Newsom Committee's commissioned surveys showed that many pupils at this time were taught in overcrowded, under-resourced and poorly equipped schools, particularly those in slum areas. These schools were also characterised by high staff turnover and low expectations and consequently were in need of major reform. Tomlinson (2005) notes that despite the redistribution of spending towards average and below-average ability pupils and a more stimulating curriculum in secondary modern schools to give a wider choice of courses, including some 'broadly related to occupational interests', others concerned with personal and social development, and 'imaginative experience through the arts', girls were still directed to domesticity and boys to the labour market.

The Plowden Report (1967)

Throughout the late 1950s and early 1960s there were, as has been explained in Chapter 1, growing concerns about eleven-plus selection and the impact that this had had on primary school organisation, pedagogy and curriculum matters. The fact that successive governments were showing an interest in comprehensive education, as were certain sections of the general public, was also important in raising the profile of primary education. In 1963, Edward Boyle, the Conservative Minister for Education, recognised the need for a major enquiry and gave a new remit to the Central Advisory Council for Education, chaired by Lady Plowden, to 'consider primary education in all its aspects and the transition to secondary education'.

The Committee sat for three years eventually offering 197 broad policy proposals. It focused research and discussion into investigations which looked at the child's physical and intellectual development, the family and neighbourhood, and finally reviewed the organisation of school and the curriculum. There were also investigations into teacher training, staffing and the general status and government of primary education and highlighted best practice in all aspects of primary school education.

Kogan refers to the composition of the Plowden Committee as 'a strong and powerful team constructed to subject the hot knowledge of the practitioner and practical administrator to the informed critique of the sceptical philosopher and professional social scientist' (1987: 13).

By the time the report was returned to the Ministry of Education in 1967, it was Gordon Walker, who as Secretary of State for Education, finally introduced the report *Children and Their Primary Schools* with 'an immediate and general welcome for its general tenor and philosophy' (Simon, 1991: 373).

A significant criticism of the Plowden Report is noted by Cunningham who writes that 'its insufficient and partial research into classroom practice, and pedagogical debates emerging from Plowden revealed a dearth of knowledge about how primary school teachers taught' (2002: 21). Plowden, it should be noted, stimulated a groundswell of research by educationalists, psychologists and sociologists which offered evidence-based outcomes to inform pedagogy and practice.

It could be argued that although many of its recommendations were not acted upon, nevertheless the Plowden Report had a profound effect on the way both professionals and parents viewed primary education.

The context for the Plowden Report is important. Cunningham suggests that Plowden's philosophy 'reflected a prevailing spirit of the time, an optimism about the ability of society to secure general social improvement and the prospect of technology delivering an ever-increasing standard of living' (2002: 20). Similarly, Simon notes that Plowden reported 'at a time of relatively full employment and the economy was fairly stable and was predicated on a perspective of continuous economic growth, full employment, enhanced affluence and an egalitarian view of society' (1991: 365).

The Plowden Committee was extremely supportive of the notion of compensatory education, educational priority areas, the expansion of nursery education and the development of community schools in areas of high deprivation throughout the country.

In its recommendations, Plowden exemplified a commitment to raising standards in education for all, and focused on three approaches to achieving this goal.

The first, to which the Committee itself gave priority, were the proposals relating to educational priority areas (EPAs) where a policy of positive discrimination led to greater resources and assistance being given to specific areas. Secondly, Plowden proposed a massive expansion of nursery education, and thirdly, Plowden proposed that community schools should be developed in all areas and especially in EPAs. Of all the recommendations, those relating to EPAs and to nursery education were to prove the most important in terms of future policy developments.

Comprehensive reforms, particularly in relation to curricula and pedagogy (Gillard, 2011), had a direct effect on the nation's primary schools in which the Plowden Report advocated new kinds of teaching and learning. Plowden focused on child-centred education and activity-based teaching and reflected and influenced practice to such an extent that Bernstein and Davies called it 'the semi-official ideology of primary education' (cited in Jones, 2003: 80).

Exploiting the results of extensive research by educationalists and sociologists, Plowden also explored key concepts such as streaming, selection, cultural deprivation, parental attitudes and equal opportunity in its championing of a child-centred philosophy: 'At the heart of educational progress lies the child' (DES, 1967: 7).

Issues such as learning by discovery, an integrated curriculum, individualisation, ethnicity, special educational needs and relationships with the school's local community, although at the heart of Plowden's recommendations, were heavily criticised by Conservatives who saw individualisation as an obstacle to economic growth since it did not allow for the development of the necessary skills in a rapidly changing economy. There were also arguments, to be developed in the 'Black Papers' and by the Conservative government of the 1970s that focused on educational accountability and appropriate investment in education.

The writers of the 'Black Papers' and their followers criticised much of what the primary schools were doing and blamed the Plowden Report –

at least in part – for what they saw as undesirable trends. Some of these criticisms are taken up in Chapter 3 in a discussion of the influence of the 'Black Papers' on New Right thinking within the Conservative Party.

Educational priority areas and compensatory education

As has been noted, one of the major recommendations of the Plowden Committee was the commitment to 'educational priority areas' (EPAs) as a response to the inequalities of educational opportunity associated with schools in relatively deprived areas. This recommendation received immediate and widespread support from all parties. Plowden recalls earlier reports such as Crowther (1959) and Robbins (1963) which also emphasised the importance of the relationship between home and social background, the primary school and academic achievement. In this context, Lawson and Silver (1973: 349) discuss Douglas's (1964) longitudinal study *The Home and the School,* which examined the relationships between family size, health, poor housing, home–school relations and a range of social class differentials, all of which were identified as characteristic of areas classified as EPAs.

The Plowden Committee believed that positive discrimination through the development of EPAs was justified by the fact that, 'as the homes and neighbourhoods from which the children come provide little support and stimulus for learning, the schools must provide a compensating environment' (DES, 1967: 57).

At the same time the need for a new distribution of educational resources was noted, and Anthony Crosland, the Secretary of State for Education and Science, successfully persuaded the government to accept the proposal that national policy should adopt the principle of positive discrimination. This was one of the key actions taken by the government to implement the Committee's recommendations. A sum of £16 million for EPAs was secured and in Crosland's view: 'It was almost the last thing that I did at Education and one of the things that gave me most satisfaction' (Kogan, 1971: 197). It is interesting to note that Crosland recruited two sociologists, Young and Halsey, to organise a nationwide study of slum schools in a major collaborative effort to collect evidence-based theory for government and local government action to raise standards of schooling in deprived area (McKenzie, 2001).

In Britain, as in the USA with the Headstart programme, educational priority areas, involving the provision of additional resources to schools in deprived areas, could be seen as one of the most conspicuous attempts at educational compensation at the regional level.

EPAs were set up in parts of London, Liverpool, the West Riding of

Yorkshire and Birmingham in order to raise the educational performance of children, improve the morale of teachers, increase the involvement of parents in their children's education and increase the 'sense of responsibility' for their communities of the people living in them (Halsey, 1972).

Through positive discrimination, Plowden recommended policies for pre-school and primary education, which included better pupil–teacher ratios, better salaries for teachers in EPA areas and teacher education focused on the needs of disadvantaged children such as raising literacy standards, better buildings and resources. The new forms of school organisation such as the 'community school', the exploration of new curricula and the development of different teaching approaches all resulted from Plowden and the EPA initiatives and helped to create new kinds of relationships between teachers, pupils, parents and the wider community.

The EPA initiatives were not without their critics and there was considerable controversy about the meaning of the concept of compensatory education which made operationlisation and evaluation difficult. As critics have pointed out concepts like cultural deprivation can be confused with the notion of difference and some cultures, that is to say working-class culture, can be assumed to be inferior and inadequate compared with middle-class culture.

Other critics such as Bernstein (1970) argued that 'education cannot compensate for society' because the massive economic and structural inequalities which caused poverty could not be countered by initiatives such as the EPAs. Ball (1986) has also argued that compensatory education schemes operated with a 'deficit' model that influenced policy-makers and appeared to blame working-class parents for their supposed inability to support their children's education. This was a theme taken up by the emerging 'New Right' thinkers in the first Black Papers published by Cox and Dyson in 1969 who argued that some working-class families were unable to contribute to their children's education because their culture, compared to the implied middle-class culture of schooling, was inferior and inadequate. Despite the initial enthusiasm and interest the EPA programme faltered and was gradually absorbed into more general aid programmes for deprived areas.

However, the Labour government retained its belief in the value of compensatory education and in 1968, despite a declining economic situation, made considerable funds available (£20 million) for inner-city improvements through the Urban Aid Programme, much of which was funnelled into additional pre-school provision in poor areas.

Ethnicity

Governments in both the 1950s and 1960s did not appear to pay much attention to the educational and social welfare of children from different racial and ethnic groups, although by the 1960s the education of these children began to be a serious policy issue. It is estimated that there were in 1961 about 46,000 children from ethnic minorities in primary schools in England and by 1966 this number had increased to 100,000 (Ryder and Silver, 1970; McKenzie, 2001). Often these ethnic groups were to be found in areas of relatively high deprivation and were often seen as 'problems' by many schools at a time when local authorities provided additional support on an ad hoc basis. There were no national policies to meet the needs of racial and ethnic minority children and their schools apart from some funding provided by the 1966 Local Government Act.

Plowden (1967) recommended that there should be greater attention paid to the children of immigrant parents but it was not until the 1970s that the government and local authorities acted more coherently to develop strategies to deal with the multi-racial and multicultural realities that presented challenges to schooling. The contributions of politicians such as Enoch Powell and psychologists such as Jensen (1973) and Eysenck (1964) contributed to racist discourse. These were welcomed by some sections of the community because the arguments of the former about inherited levels of intelligence and differential education attainment between whites and blacks fitted racial stereotypes of many communities at the time. For example, Tomlinson makes the comment that: 'The hostility of some white parents to their children being educated alongside racial and ethnic minorities was an issue from the 1960s' (2005: 184). And it was not until the 1970s that more comprehensive research focused on ethnic minorities began to emerge and act as a catalyst for change. Watts, in her study of the experiences pupils and students, notes that following the publication of research evidence: 'The black and Asian community groups who challenged racism in education from the 1960s were motivated partly by reactions against the high proportion of black children, especially Afro-Caribbean ones, who were put in schools for the educationally sub-normal' (2002: 151).

Until the mid-1960s central government had no policy on the education of immigrant children. The main concerns were to teach English to non-English speakers and to disperse immigrant pupils, partly to prevent individual schools having to cope with large numbers of them and partly to facilitate their assimilation into British society.

Towards the end of the 1960s, 'assimilation' was replaced by 'integration' in policy statements which began to refer to diversity, tolerance and equal opportunity and attempted 'to give at least some recognition in schools to the backgrounds of ethnic minority children' (Swann, 1985: 191).

In the sections that follow a number of key areas relevant to educational change are highlighted and briefly discussed: gender, the curriculum, further education and the relationship between central government, local education authorities and the teacher professions. Some of these areas are examined in more detail in Chapter 3.

Gender

Throughout the 1960s educational opportunities continued to improve in general, but as McKenzie notes, 'the different opportunities for boys and girls had barely been acknowledged' (2001: 209).

By the 1960s, there was, despite evidence that girls achieved more when educated separately, a strong belief in the superiority of mixed-gender education as providing better training for 'real life'. This led many of the remaining girls' schools (both state-run and privately owned) to close, to amalgamate with boys' schools or to open their doors to boys. Girls were offered a similar core curriculum but were still expected to study cookery and needlework while boys learned metalwork and woodwork and to play separate sports.

In the 1960s, boys achieved results that were on average 5 per cent better than girls and until the mid-1980s, boys outperformed girls at all levels of the education system, with the exception of performance in the eleven plus examination. This data was used as 'proof' that girls were less intelligent than boys and indeed that boys were late developers and would catch up and then outperform girls. These issues are explored in more detail in Chapter 3.

Watts provides a succinct summary of the position of many girls in this period:

> The needs of many working-class girls were most sharply differentiated from boys. Girls received limited technical education, while in educational debate they were either ignored, or despite some acknowledgement of change, placed largely in a domestic, 'feminine' setting, as a series of influential reports, Norwood in 1943, Crowther in 1959, and Newsom in 1963, stressed. (2002: 145–6)

In a review of the Newsom Report, Watts cites Newsom's rather narrow conception of girls and their educational potential: 'females are uniquely suited for a single social role' underlay official policy for secondary modern schooling for girls (cited in Watts, 2002: 146).

Tomlinson points out that even the Central Advisory Council for England in its 1963 report promoted a different curriculum for boys and girls: 'Girls know that whether they marry early or not, they are likely to find themselves eventually running a home' while a boy 'is usually excited by the prospect of a science course' (Ministry of Education, 1963a: 142).

However, although there was relatively little research into gender and education during this period, some sociological research was becoming available that provided evidence that girls were achieving better results in, for example, primary schools (Douglas, 1964). Inevitably this raised questions about the ways in which girls might be subject to discrimination at eleven plus compared with boys. Girls thus were denied full educational opportunities and at this time, the general attitude was that social class was more iniquitous than gender in equality of opportunity in education. Nevertheless, the expansion of comprehensive schools did have significance for the development of girls' education because of the coeducational nature of many of the comprehensive schools.

It was not until the 1970s that more attention would be paid to girls' education as a result of changing societal attitudes, changes in legislation in key areas such as equal pay and sex discrimination, and the influx of gendered sociological research.

Curriculum

Reference has already been made to changes in the rationale for new curricula and new approaches to pedagogy in the classroom. The 1960s witnessed substantial changes in important questions associated with the curriculum: the nature and organisation of the curriculum, approaches to teaching and learning, assessment and issues around motivation, and teacher and pupil identities. For the first time, challenges to the control of many of these issues came from the government and from a growing number of educational pressure groups. Reference has been made in the previous chapter to David Eccles' earlier attempts in 1960 to give the government greater opportunity to direct change in curriculum definition and teacher autonomy, for example by trying to gain entry to 'the secret garden of the curriculum'. But in 1962 when the Ministry of Education did set up a 'Curriculum Study Group' as a 'relatively small, commando-like unit making raids into the curriculum' to consider curriculum issues and pedagogy, the opposition from teachers' organisations and local authorities was so fierce that it had to be abandoned because the political climate of the time was too hostile and it was felt that the balance of power between central government, LEAs and teachers was not being maintained. It was replaced, during Edward Boyle's period of office, by the Schools Council which, according to Jones was 'dominated by representatives of teachers and it was teachers – through their organisations and as individuals – who had a leading influence on curriculum change' (2003: 52–3). The Schools Council did create a legitimate institutional location for debate about curriculum and legitimised a long-established pattern of informal relationships among teachers and central and local administrators in the area of curriculum development.

The significance of the work of the Schools Council has been summarised by Lowe: 'Perhaps the key agent of this "golden age" of teacher autonomy in terms of curriculum definition at secondary level was the Schools Council' (1997: 58).

Further education

The 1960s were a time of massive expansion in higher education (HE) with the 1963 Robbins Report being the catalyst for significant changes in numbers accessing higher education, in building programmes and in the creation of new universities. Hoggart has argued that the expansion of HE 'confirmed that there was far more talent in the country than we had guessed or were willing, out of class-and-culture meanness, to recognise' (1996: 42). Similarly, Benn points out that the Robbins Report 'rejected the idea that only a select number of children had talent worth cultivating' (2011a: 49). However, during the 1960s, the picture was very different in terms of the focus given to further education colleges which became the fastest growing sector of education despite the fact that there was no official policy guiding and monitoring this development. Evans (2012) succinctly summarises the national situation at this time:

> England still lacked the necessary critical mass of a well-trained, skilled and adaptable workforce at all levels of industry. Real evidence was emerging of our continuing low levels of productivity, declining industrial competitiveness, skill shortages and industrial poaching within the small stock of competent, experienced and qualified workers.

In response to the problems identified by Evans, and the increasing threat of overseas competition from countries such as Germany and Japan, there were a number of Acts and Reports in the late 1950s and 1960s. These had significance for the post-compulsory education and training sector, and which reflected a change from the indifference towards scientific and technical education and training which had characterised English politicians' and employers' attitudes.

The important Crowther Report of 1959, *Fifteen to Eighteen*, looked at different educational and training needs in a changing technological world, particularly for boys and girls between the ages of 15 and 18, and especially school-leavers, who were 'incurably tired' (Neary, 2002: 5) of school. At this time almost 60 per cent of 15–17 year-olds received no daytime education or training and over 40 per cent of LEAs had no technical schools. At this time, many school-leavers still entered jobs which offered no formal training, and those who did receive training embarked on apprenticeship programmes.

Crowther (1959) argued that education and training should be more closely integrated. The Report pointed out that technical education and vocational training in other countries was much better coordinated and integrated with other sectors of the education system. The Report also noted that successive governments remained distant from direct involvement in technical education and training that allowed employers, if they wished, to take decisions unhindered by any government policy.

The White Paper of 1961, *Better Opportunities in Technical Education*, supported the development of new courses for technicians, craftspeople and operatives, reflecting the instrumental view of politicians and employers. The main aims of the Paper were:

- to broaden the education received by students and provide continuity between school and college;
- to ensure that provision at college be matched by the needs of industry and to urgently improve facilities for technicians, to increase the range of courses to suit the needs and ability of the students and to tackle the high rate of failure and wastage rates experienced by students.

The 1964 Industrial Training Act established Industrial Training Boards (ITBs) which were meant to raise the volume and quality of training and thereby tackle the problem of craft and skills shortages. The ITBs were administered by employers and trade union representatives. A compulsory levy ensured that costs of training were fairly shared between firms, as Bailey says (2002): 'an attempt to ensure that if only for a brief period employers had to take some responsibility for the training of their employees' (2002: 62). Initially successful, by the end of the decade there were 27 ITBs covering employers with some 15 million employees, although their autonomy was curtailed by the incoming Conservative government from 1970. The ITBs marked a significant shift towards preparation for employment in further and higher education institutions and simultaneously, in Lowe's words, 'sounded the death knell of the apprenticeship system which was at its peak in the mid-sixties' (1997: 34).

The Haslegrave Report of 1969, *Technical Courses and Examinations*, had a significant impact because it rationalised examinations for technicians in business, commerce and technology. It created the Technician Education Council (TEC) and the Business Education Council (BEC) to oversee courses and examinations. These were later amalgamated to form the Business and Technology Council (BTEC).

Each of these interventions helped to support significant growth and change in post-16 education and training, although as Bailey (2002) points out there was no evidence of official policy underpinning these developments.

According to Bailey it was during this period that colleges of further education were establishing themselves 'as multi-purpose institutions and providers of an increasingly wide range of courses for the communities they served' (2002: 66).

Further education colleges became the fastest growing sector of education in the 1960s despite the contemporary trend for more students to stay at school. Bailey argues that public policy did not account for all developments in the sector, and it was employers, the colleges themselves and the parents of young people who also contributed to this growth. Local authorities also played their part, albeit there were often differences in the amount of funding and levels of support, particularly when the local authority was mindful of competition from its own sixth-forms.

The golden triangle: central government, the local authorities and the teaching profession

During the 1960s, the relatively cosy relationship between central government, the local education authorities and the teachers' unions began to show signs of fragmentation and rupture as the former intervened to wrestle power and autonomy from powerful local education authorities and an increasingly militant teaching profession.

Since the Second World War there had been the commitment to the concept of 'a national system of education, locally administered'. The tripartite partnership acted as a system of checks and balances which ensured that no one 'player' had the monopoly of power. While there had been a relatively stable economy the partnership was able to cope with major changes to the system, with comprehensivisation being a key issue. But the relationship began to break down in the late 1960s and early 1970s as the economy moved into recession, the political climate became more heated and antagonistic, and there was increasing emphasis on the need for accountability in terms of educational expenditure and performance. Thus the stage was set for government and the Secretaries of State to wrest power from the local authorities, heads and teachers (Plowden, the Schools Council and the introduction of the CSE examination had all traded power to these players) and assert their influence.

Conclusion

The 1960s witnessed a significant number of major changes and positive achievements, including the transformation of the secondary education system into a non-selective system, a new emphasis on primary education, some modest changes in curriculum development with the setting up of the Schools Council for Curriculum and Assessment, and the establishment of EPAs. There were the major reports by Newsom and Plowden which were extremely influential for primary and secondary education. In further and higher education there were significant developments that increased the number of students benefiting from post-16 education and training.

The decade ended, as Tomlinson observes, 'with a general expectation of an expansion of non-selective secondary education, further innovation, and higher levels of expenditure on education' (2005: 23).

There were, however, as Simon notes, a number of setbacks – 'postponement of the raising of the school leaving age, economic cutbacks and the public schools fiasco' (1991: 388) – which served to undermine the status quo and set the education scene for radical change through the power and actions of central government.

The next chapter picks up these issues and explores their development and growth in the 1970s.

Further reading

Aldrich, R. (ed.) (2002) *A Century of Education*. London: RoutledgeFalmer.

Chitty, C. (2009) *Education Policy in Britain*. Basingstoke: Palgrave Macmillan.

Kogan, M. (1971) *The Politics of Education*. Harmondsworth: Penguin Education Specials.

Lowe, R. (1977) *Schooling and Social Change 1964–1990*. London: Routledge.

Simon, B. (1991) *Education and the Social Order 1940–1990*. London: Lawrence & Wishart.

CHAPTER THREE

1970–1979: THE BREAKDOWN OF CONSENSUS

- Comprehensive education
- Teachers and reform
- The Education Black Papers (1969–77)
- Youth unemployment and the raising of the school leaving age and the MSC
- The Ruskin College speech

Introduction

This chapter will describe and examine the range of educational policies and issues prominent during the 1970s and will consider the contributions to education policy and practice of the Secretaries of State who held office from 1970 to 1979. Contributions from the four Secretaries of State – Margaret Thatcher, Reginald Prentice, Frederick Mulley and Shirley Williams – were extremely variable and reflected the length of office served by each, the agendas that each had to work with, and the demands of party, career and office.

Context

The economic problems of the 1970s provided the background to the final fragmentation of the postwar consensus described in earlier chapters. This chapter will address the end of that postwar consensus and the polarisation of political views on education. Arguments about the comprehensive reorganisation of secondary education and the end of selection continued, but a new range of issues emerged as economic recession, the result of rising oil prices and widespread industrial action, led to rising widespread debate about the relationship between education and the economy.

Debates about standards, the curriculum, 'progressive education' and the status of the teaching profession all took centre stage and were given national prominence when, in 1976, the Labour Prime Minister Jim Callaghan instigated the 'Great Debate' about education in a speech at Ruskin College. This speech questioned the fundamental nature and purpose of the education system. However, before this debate could be concluded, a radical Conservative government was elected in 1979.

Political, social and economic background

The decade began with Edward Heath installed as Prime Minister after the general election in June 1970 with key economic policy objectives focusing on inflation, the balance of payments, unemployment and deteriorating economic growth rates. National and international economic crises following the Arab–Israeli War (1973) and the subsequent dramatic rise in oil prices – for example, oil prices increased by 70 per cent and there was 7 per cent inflation – were the backdrop against which many governments had to provide a rationale for developing educational and training policies which could be used to counter the effects of recession and restrain public sector spending.

This period sees a change in the debate about the role of education and training as unemployment reached over one million, the growth in youth unemployment continued to rise, industrial disputes increased and the 'three-day week' was introduced, and recession struck home.

Galton et al. (1980: 41, cited in McKenzie, 2001) suggest that the recession 'provided a rationale for economic cutbacks in education not only in England but in most advanced western industrial countries'.

Schools and colleges

Education, although it did not feature as a major issue in the 1970 election campaign, nevertheless allowed each party the opportunity to identify the key areas of policy which they regarded as important to secure a prosperous and stable long-term future.

The manifestos of each of the three main political parties (Bell et al., 1973) each talked about growth, expansion and investment as key elements of their policies in all phases of education and highlighted the issues facing government and local education authorities as they prepared for the challenges of the new decade.

The Conservative Party, while acknowledging the major problem of resourcing, advocated growth in nursery and primary education, particularly in areas of social handicap, and stated that children 'should be able to develop their abilities to the full' and that this was recognised as 'not only right in itself but a vital national investment in the future'.

While making reference to the growth in comprehensive provision and noting 'Labour's attempt to insist on compulsory reorganisation on rigid lines' as 'contrary to local democracy and the best interests of the children', they argued for the rights of local authorities to 'decide what is best for their area' and even recognised the fact that the age of eleven was too early to make final decisions which might affect a child's whole future: 'Many of the most imaginative new schemes abolishing the eleven-plus have been introduced by Conservative council.' They also committed to raising the school leaving age to 16.

Labour recognised the importance of education as a means of furthering social equality and the need to widen and extend the education system: '. . . the best preparation that we can make for our people and our country for the world of tomorrow'. Labour stated their commitment to ending selection 'under which 80 per cent of our children are, at the age of eleven, largely denied the opportunity of a broad secondary education with the chance of higher education beyond'. They were committed, at this time, to legislate to require the 'minority of Tory education authorities who have so far resisted change to abandon eleven plus selection in England and Wales'. Like the Conservatives they too advocated offering more resources to expand nursery and primary provision, and talked also of commitments to raising the school leaving age, to putting more resources into teachers, and to bringing parents and teachers into closer partnerships. Finally, Labour promised a review of further and higher education with the intention of expanding provision in all areas.

The Liberals too placed emphasis on giving children the 'best start in life' through improvement of primary schools and the provision of nursery schools. They were against selection but did not wholly embrace comprehensive schooling.

These manifestos taken together identify the key issues facing all governments during the 1970s.

The Education Secretaries and policy development

During the period covered by this chapter, four education secretaries held office: Margaret Thatcher (Conservative: 1970–4), Reg Prentice (Labour:

1974–5), Fred Mulley (Labour: 1975–6) and Shirley Williams (Labour: 1976–9).

The backgrounds, formative influences, philosophies and achievements of each will be referred to in what follows in order to gauge their contributions to education and training in the 1970s and to identify the key legacies of their time in office.

Margaret Thatcher (Conservative: June 1970–February 1974)

Margaret Thatcher had been in Parliament for ten years as MP for Finchley and Friern Barnet and had under Edward Heath's sponsorship held several posts within the Shadow Cabinet. She was appointed in October 1969 as Shadow Education Secretary, replacing Edward Short who was the Secretary for Education and Science in Harold Wilson's Labour government. Margaret Thatcher ceased to be Education Secretary in 1974 when the election was lost, having held office for almost four years, but returned as Prime Minister in 1979.

She was an enthusiastic supporter of private education although she attended a state school as a child. She had a degree in chemistry. While Education Secretary she showed herself to be rather dismissive of some aspects of state education and attracted controversy when attempting to stop 'free school milk' to children over seven. She was attempting to save money in order to increase expenditure on nursery education and on raising the school leaving age to 16 (Thatcher, 1993).

The main issue Margaret Thatcher had to deal with as Education Secretary was with regard to expanding the number of comprehensive schools. Edward Heath had committed his government to continue the move towards comprehensive schools. While in office Margaret Thatcher accepted and reluctantly approved over two thousand proposals for such 'comprehensive' schemes submitted by local authorities.

A year after Harold Wilson's Labour Party returned to office in 1974 Margaret Thatcher was installed as leader of the opposition and worked with Keith Joseph to set up the Centre for Policy Studies. Their intention was to carry out a wholesale revision of the economic and social policies of her party ready for a return to power (Ball, 2008).

Reginald Prentice (Labour: March 1974–5)

After serving in the Second World War, an experience which turned him into a convinced socialist, Reg Prentice studied at the London School of Economics and while still a student became a Labour borough councillor. After graduation he joined the Transport and General Workers' Union and by 1957 he was elected as MP for East Ham in a by-election. He was Minister of State at the DES under Michael Stewart and Anthony Crosland and won 'golden opinions' from both. An unusual accolade from the opposition came in Margaret Thatcher's private note to the economist and educational adviser, John Vaizey (7 March 1974): 'I am delighted that Reg Prentice is the new Minister. He and the Department will work very well together.'

Reg Prentice became a member of Wilson's Cabinet in 1967 as Minister for Overseas Development. When Labour was unexpectedly returned to office in 1974, Reg Prentice was appointed Secretary of State for Education and Science. He was in office for a relatively short period – 15 months – from March 1974 to June 1975 and in October 1977 he crossed the house to join the Conservative Party after a series of increasingly outspoken interventions on wider and more controversial issues outside his education brief.

As Secretary he followed the party line and continued the push towards comprehensivisation. Kogan (1978: 147) notes that the decision to compel local authorities to conform was made by Edward Short and put into effect by Prentice, Mulley and Williams.

As part of this strategy Prentice began to phase out direct grant schools in 1975, although the outcome was that the majority became independent. Prentice announced that he intended to legislate to end selection for state secondary schools. He described Circular 10/74 as a 'tough document' (Simon, 1991: 443) and one which he believed would, with the cooperation of local authorities and voluntary bodies, 'make the fastest possible progress to a fully comprehensive system'.

Reg Prentice has been criticised (Morris and Griggs, 1988) for his refusal to restore the huge educational cuts instigated by the Conservative Chancellor Anthony Barber, for following 'a continuous policy of restricted expenditure' (also supported by Mulley and Williams) and also for not honouring Labour's pledge in opposition to cut class sizes to thirty and improve the situation regarding the deplorable state of the nation's school buildings. Indeed, the 1975 budget drew up plans for cuts of over £500 million. Reg Prentice vowed to maintain the core of the service, that is to say provision for those aged five to 16, but other parts of the education service, the youth service and further and adult education were sidelined.

Fred Mulley (Labour: 1975–6)

Fred Mulley was a bright, working-class child unable to go to university because his father was unemployed – similar in fact to George Tomlinson, the Minister of Education from 1947 to 1951. However, he gained a BSc in economics and qualified as an accountant while a prisoner of war in Germany, 1940–5. He did get to Oxford and became a research fellow, and by 1950 he became MP in Sheffield and was called to the bar in 1954. Fred

Mulley was one of the few people of working-class origin who achieved Cabinet status in Labour governments and survived the course. He was trusted by Prime Ministers Wilson and Callaghan. He became Secretary of State for Education in 1975 and was immediately critical of the severe public expenditure cuts proposed by the then Chancellor Healey, arguing that it was not the sort of thing that a Labour government should be doing. He is quoted by Tony Benn as saying: 'If this is the way it's got to be, let the Treasury and the Think Tank run the country' (Benn, cited in Dell's brief online biography).

According to Barber (1996) Jim Callaghan became convinced that Fred Mulley was not the right person to lead on Education and shifted him to Defence in favour of Shirley Williams. This was after Jim Callaghan had invited Cabinet ministers to identify key priorities for their departments in the face of the severe economic crisis. Simon (1991: 432) refers to Fred Mulley as the 'forgotten minister, chiefly memorable for his complaint that he had no powers to act'. In his brief term of office, he continued the drive towards comprehensive reorganisation and in 1975 introduced an Education Bill that required local education authorities to submit proposals for complete reorganisation. Mulley's proposals for mandatory legislation were rejected in the courts and the DES policy was less forceful (Kogan, 1978: 105). The Bill was not given royal assent until the following year by which time Shirley Williams was in post.

Shirley Williams (Labour: 1976 –9)

After being educated in the USA and the UK, Shirley Williams began her career as a journalist with the *Daily Mirror* and *Financial Times*. She was General Secretary of the Fabian Society from 1960 to 1964, and was first elected to Parliament in 1964. She held junior ministerial appointments 1964–70 (she was a Junior Minister to Anthony Crosland in the 1960s) and appeared to have a smooth rise up the ministerial appointments ladder serving at the Ministries of Labour, Education and Science, and Home Office. When Labour was returned to power in 1974, she joined the Cabinet as Secretary of State for Consumer Protection and two years later, Prime Minister Jim Callaghan asked her to take up the role of Secretary for Education and Science. Shirley Williams is remembered for her key role in orchestrating Callaghan's 'Great Debate' and for her involvement in comprehensivisation.

The next section explores the key issue of comprehensivisation in the 1970s and highlights the contributions of the four Secretaries of State.

Comprehensive education

The previous chapter described how the secondary education system in England and Wales in the 1950s and 1960s underwent a period of quite radical reorganisation, moving gradually from an essentially tripartite system which was highly selective to a comprehensive system based on mixed-ability schooling.

These changes were informed by evidence from sociologists and educationalists about inequities in the system and were explored fully in Chapters 1 and 2. This section focuses on how successive governments attempted to deal with the moves to end selection and implement comprehensive reorganisation.

Both Conservative and Labour governments issued Circulars and Acts either to drive or to forestall the move towards comprehensive reorganisation which had grown momentum after the introduction of Circular 10/65 discussed in Chapter 2. The complex issue of comprehensive organisation and the end of selection dominated educational politics for many years in the 1970s. The period, it could be argued, also marks a significant change in the relationship between central government, the LEAs and teachers' unions – the 'golden triangle' referred to in an earlier chapter – and the demise of the alleged postwar consensus. Chitty argues that the 1960s, characterised by a sense of hope and optimism, were followed by the 1970s, characterised by cynicism and defeatism. Similarly, Carr and Hartnett (1996: 105) describe a 'time of partnership, consensus and relative optimism about the future development of education' but suggest that the emerging demand for comprehensive education and the call for the end of selective education marked a significant turning point in this belief in change and progress.

During the 1970s, both the Conservative and Labour governments continued to deal with comprehensivisation through legislation and exhortation, although it should be noted that the arguments for the end of selection and the introduction of comprehensive education were by no means universally accepted at the beginning of the 1970s. It was evident that policy-makers at national and local levels were not totally committed to reorganisation. LEAs during this period had relatively high levels of autonomy in determining educational policy at grass-roots level and subsequently many LEAs developed reorganisation schemes that allowed for the coexistence of comprehensive schools and grammar schools and did not see any contradictions in this situation (Benn and Chitty, 1996; Kerckhoff et al., 1996). During this period, it could be argued too that the relationship between central government, the local authorities and teachers were forced into question by all parties and that the 1970s saw significant critical changes in what had been a generally genial relationship characterised as 'the golden triangle'.

At the same time, both the pace of change and the actual shape of reorganisation varied greatly within and between LEAs. Haydn (2004: 421), in a discussion of educational policy-making, refers to 'the ad hoc manner in which comprehensives were introduced meant that there were different forms of "comprehensive school . . ."' Chitty (2002b) reinforces this description with his statement that: 'To be fair, there was no blueprint for a successful comprehensive school in the 1960s', and it could be argued that this situation continued to exist because the new comprehensives inherited and assimilated the old grammar school and secondary modern curricula. There seemed to be a 'general complacency regarding issues of curriculum and pedagogy' (Arblaster, cited in Chitty, 2002a). These issues were taken up by both the Black Paper writers and by the Labour Prime Minister Jim Callaghan in his 1976 Ruskin College speech.

It was apparent that comprehensive reorganisation with the move to mixed-ability schooling did not remove ability segregation within schools as many continued to stream students into different classes on the basis of perceived ability. The existence of selective-entry grammar schools coexisted with the comprehensive schools, 'creaming off' the most able students and thereby diminishing the drive towards a fully comprehensive intake by ability. The comprehensives could only take students from the bottom 80 per cent of the ability distribution. The situation is summarised succinctly by Haydn (2004: 421): 'The continued existence of the private secondary schools and some grammar schools, meant that, in most areas, the secondary school system never became fully comprehensive.'

When Margaret Thatcher came into the DES in 1970 she began very quickly to deal with the important and sensitive issue of comprehensive reorganisation. Indeed, after only three days, Circular 10/65 (requesting local education authorities to submit plans for reorganisation of secondary education) which had been introduced by Labour, was withdrawn. Circular 10/70 released LEAs from their obligation to have comprehensive plans and stated that only proposals for individual schools to 'go comprehensive' would be considered. Thatcher held the flag for those Conservatives who were firmly committed to maintaining the grammar schools and selection and fought for the maintenance of the direct grant schools.

Thatcher appeared to do all she could to delay and prevent comprehensive schemes. Simon (1991: 429) summarises her position as follows:

Although Margaret Thatcher tried, and failed, to deflect Local Authorities from comprehensive reorganisation, she did succeed, through controversial use of her powers as Secretary of State, in braking the rate of change, and above all, in deliberately preventing many Authorities from developing genuinely 'comprehensive' systems by ensuring the survival of over 100 selective (grammar) schools within those systems.

Thatcher, despite her opposition to moves towards comprehensive education, nevertheless presided over a huge increase in the number of LEAs who submitted plans for reorganisation, as Haydn (2004: 419) observes: 'Mrs Thatcher was to preside over more comprehensive school designations than any of her predecessors or successors.' During her period in office, comprehensivisation became more of a reality for school children in England and Wales. At the same time, her actions as Secretary of State, according to Woods (1981: 59), 'broke the consensus in education and in doing so both reflected and gave impetus to the wider movement within the Conservative Party to return to traditional principles.' Above all, Margaret Thatcher had to some extent succeeded in allowing the grammar schools to coexist with comprehensive schools and had raised the debate about principles and choice that would be fought over in all periods up to and including the present.

Woods (1981: 51) does point out that although Thatcher was involved in reforms that were often controversial, she nevertheless did 'gain a considerable reputation for fighting for resources to preserve the primary school building programme, the raising of the school leaving age and the Open University in the face of Antony Barber's (Conservative Chancellor) demands for expenditure cuts.' He also argues that the 1972 White Paper which she introduced was 'an achievement of high order' (Woods, 1981: 51).

But when Labour returned to power in 1974 (having won both the February and October elections) Reg Prentice, committed to the drive to comprehensivisation, issued Circular 10/74 which overturned the previous Conservative Circular. He also abolished the direct grant schools in 1975 in the hope that they would go comprehensive. Not surprisingly, the majority seized the opportunity to take on independent status.

In an interview in 2010 Shirley Williams makes an interesting observation about the fact that Circulars 10/65 and 10/74 left her, as Secretary of State, with no real powers to deal with reluctant or unwilling LEAs: 'The whole thing was a negotiating relationship. It was not a relationship of mandatory power at all. I wanted to work through the Local Authorities.' This, she notes, was particularly important when having to work with some LEAs which were Labour but 'were passionately against comprehensive education'.

It is clear that during the 1970s the tensions surrounding the debate about the achievements and purposes of comprehensive reform focusing on curricula and pedagogical issues, the power of the local education authorities, youth unemployment and post-16 education, and parental power were increasingly questioned by a range of key stakeholders, including politicians, employers, parents and educationalists.

A number of key issues relating to these debates were brought to the public's attention and are discussed in the following sections:

- the Black Papers (1969–76);
- the William Tyndale 'affair' (1975);
- the 1976 Ruskin College speech.

Teachers and reform

In the postwar period, as has been described in earlier chapters, teachers had maintained a relative autonomy over pedagogy and control in the classroom (the notion of the curriculum as a 'secret garden' was referred to in Chapter 2 in the discussion of the contributions of Sir David Eccles as Minister of Education (1954–7)) and there had been little public debate over the role and status of the teaching profession. The politicians' attitudes are seen to be exemplified in the following statement made by the Labour MP George Cunningham in the House of Commons November 1976:

> We have never clearly addressed ourselves in modern times to the question of who should decide matters of curricula and teaching methods in our schools.

When reviewing the role of the LEAs with regard to curriculum policies in the postwar period, Chitty (2002a: 263) writes:

> No one seemed to care overmuch, for example, that the majority of Local Education Authorities were failing to exercise even a nominal control over curriculum policies of their primary and secondary schools.

And, in 1977, when the then Secretary of State Shirley Williams asked LEAs for basic information about their curriculum policies, many of the replies were politely worded 'nil returns' (Maw, 1988, cited in Chitty, 2002a).

On reflection, Shirley Williams (2009) suggests that in her experience the partnership between the local authorities and the Department of Education and Science worked well, arguing that Secretaries of State in those days were rather like American presidents – they operated by persuasion. To get anywhere, they had to carry powerful partners in the shape of the local authorities and the teachers' unions.

During the postwar period it could be argued that typically it was head teachers and teachers who had controlled the content of the curriculum, with tacit permission from governing bodies. However, changes were imminent and a series of events each contributed to significant changes relating to teachers, curriculum control and the relationships between LEAs, schools and unions.

Taylor (2008: 292), discussing the James Report of 1972 (see below), writes: 'During the late 1960s, however, teacher education came to attract systematic professional, public and political attention and criticism.' By the time Margaret Thatcher was Secretary of State it was clear that the relative freedom that teachers had enjoyed when deciding what should be done in the classroom was beginning to be questioned, such that by the end of the decade, following a series of events and interventions which were given full exposure in the media, teachers were, for the first time, under serious public and official scrutiny and often viewed with suspicion by government, representatives of industry and business, parents and the media. The decline in the British economy, the rise in unemployment and the huge rise in inflation created a context/site where key questions were being posed concerning not only the 'position' of teachers, but the role of education and its relation to economic well-being and prosperity.

Teachers, their trade unions and the local education authorities during the 1970s had had to respond to a range of initiatives and criticisms focused on the curriculum, teacher training, standards and key questions about the nature and purpose of the education system. There was, inevitably, pressure placed on the 'golden triangle' – the relationships between central government, the local authorities and the teachers' unions which had been relatively harmonious in the postwar period – for change. Political, social and economic factors combined to place teachers and the profession under the spotlight of public scrutiny and various criticisms were to emerge.

The popular perception of teachers at the time in the press and in the Conservative Party was that teachers were often left-wing activists bent on indoctrinating children with liberal propaganda. The teachers' unions had been opposed to some of the policies that Margaret Thatcher had introduced as Education Secretary. These included, famously, scrapping free milk for primary pupils over seven years old in 1971, the move that led her to be nicknamed 'Margaret Thatcher, milk snatcher'.

The Callaghan years were marked by a view that the teachers' unions, especially the National Union of Teachers, played a significant part in the difficulties governments had in effecting change in educational matters, in general, and curriculum matters in particular.

It was felt that teachers had to be controlled and this could be tackled by reviewing teacher training procedures and key parts of the curriculum. Lawson and Silver (1973: 458) suggest that: 'The future pattern of teacher education was one of the most prominent problems at the beginning of the 1970s . . .' and this concern resulted in Margaret Thatcher establishing the James Committee (1972) on teacher education and training – the first major review following the rapid expansion after 1944. However, despite the Committee's call for a radical reorganisation of teacher training, there was strong opposition from teachers and their unions, and consequently not many of the proposals were implemented. The James Committee, nevertheless, focused attention on teachers and can be seen as one of several 'tipping points' during this period which set in motion debates about the nature and purpose of the education system and the role and status of teachers in society. These included: The William Tynedale 'affair', the Black Papers, youth unemployment, the Ruskin College speech and parentocracy, which are dealt with in the next sections.

In 1974 the DES established the Assessment of Performance Unit (APU) which began to examine critically approaches to assessing and monitoring children's performance, thereby emphasising the notion of teacher accountability – an issue which became dominant throughout the 1970s and 1980s and was much to the fore in the controversial William Tyndale 'affair' discussed in the next section.

The William Tyndale 'affair'

Several of the key issues which have been referred to in this chapter were highlighted by the events which were reported on by the national press in 1975 at the William Tyndale Primary School in Islington, North London.

Simon (1991: 444) describes 'the whole extraordinary story of the Tyndale saga' where staff and the head teacher basically implemented an 'extreme version' of the child-centred philosophy as propounded in the Plowden Committee Report. A range of issues relating to the 'affair' are identified by Cunningham (2002: 20) who argues that Tyndale raised the visibility of primary education, the anxiety of parents, and the tensions between governors and the local education authority. In Shirley Williams' view, 'the events at Tyndale fed into the picture of trendy, irresponsible left-wing teachers who got away with anarchy while the Local Authority looked the other way.'

These issues were certainly seized upon by the media which turned local, albeit complex issues, into a national debate about the value of comprehensive schools and, implicitly, of teacher education.

Shirley Williams when interviewed in 2010 also picked up on the way in which the media appeared to successfully shape public perceptions: 'People somehow associate Tyndale with comprehensive. They always forget that it wasn't a secondary school.'

Such was the perceived outcry over the William Tyndale 'affair' that a report was set up by the Secretary of State, Reg Prentice. The Auld Report (1976) was heavily critical of teachers, governors and managers and these criticisms were seized upon by certain sections of the Conservative Party as ammunition to support the intensifying critique of progressive education, and in particular progressive teaching methods and curricula. And, as will be argued, the Black Paper contributors were able to use this 'affair' to scapegoat progressive methods and teachers and indirectly to criticise the Labour government.

It was, as Simon (1991: 445) suggests, as if a 'relationship was made, in the public eye, between "progressivism" and the left'. This issue, Shirley Williams observed when interviewed in 2010, was used by the Black Paper authors who 'brilliantly managed to somehow imply that Tyndale was a perfect example of a disastrous comprehensive school'.

The William Tyndale 'affair', it could be argued, marked a significant turning point in thinking about these issues and forced a new discourse about education, the role of parents in their children's schooling, Her Majesty's Inspectorate, the LEA and governors, and introduced a new vocabulary focused on concepts such as standards and accountability. The 'debate' also highlighted the developing discourse about the autonomy of teachers, about their ownership and control of the curriculum, their professional responsibilities and the relationship between education and the economy. Chitty (2009: 149) refers to 'a powerful shift in the dominant metaphor of informed educational discourse: from "partnership" to "accountability".'

Shirley Williams does suggest some implicit criticism of some aspects of state education at the time of the Tyndale 'affair': 'It was really shocking that youngsters from deprived backgrounds should be treated in a way that gave them no opportunities at all' and indeed highlights some of the issues raised in the Black Papers (1969–77) and the Ruskin College speech of 1976.

The Education Black Papers (1969–77)

From the early 1970s onwards the education-led consensus about educational policy and practice began to come apart. The political forces of the Right began to articulate their objections to the liberal values they saw embodied in the education system, and especially the pursuit of egalitarian principles represented by the comprehensive school. The Black Papers, the fall-out from the Tyndale enquiry and, above all, the sustained attack on education by the popular press had the effect of bringing education to the forefront of critical public attention.

The five Black Papers which were written by right-wing (not always) educationalists and politicians and published between 1969 and 1977 identified a number of themes relating to an 'attack' on teachers, progressive teaching methods and educational philosophy which allegedly led to a decline in standards. These polemical attacks on progressivism and on contemporary educational developments suggested that child-centred teaching methods led to a decline in discipline and, subsequently, reports of violence and drug abuse in schools, especially in the popular press, were used as evidence of the failure of such methods.

It should be noted that the Black Papers were published at the end of the 1960s, following widespread student unrest in a society that was still coming to terms with the 'permissive '60s' and of an emerging educational agenda which began to focus on gender, ethnicity and special needs education, each of which required rethinking about key pedagogical and curricular issues.

Accusations were made that teachers were indoctrinating their pupils with radical, anti-establishment ideas. Rhodes Boyson, a former head teacher and a soon to be education spokesman in the Thatcher government talked in a flamboyant way about the infiltration of London comprehensives by Marxists and Maoists (Tomlinson, 2005). This kind of speech chimed with the enormous press interest following, for example, the William Tyndale 'affair', in describing all schools as undisciplined, badly managed and contributing to societal discontent through inappropriate curricula, progressive teaching methods and lack of standards and accountability at all levels: classroom, school and local authority.

Another theme, widely accepted in an increasingly difficult economic climate, suggested that teachers were deliberately persuading school-leavers to reject work in industry and commerce and at the same time blamed teachers for the lack of a basically trained and competent pool of recruits to industry because of the anti-capitalist sentiments promoted by some teachers. These themes were eagerly picked up and reinforced by Prime Minister Callaghan in his Ruskin College speech and later played an important part in the 1979 general election.

The Black Papers, despite their lack of evidence and substantiation, seemed to reflect a good deal of public opinion and by the end of the 1970s their claims about the adverse effects of 'equality', about the need to maintain 'standards' and about the need to preserve 'excellence' begin to dominate the educational debate (Carr and Hartnett, 1996).

Youth unemployment, the raising of the school leaving age and the MSC

One of the consequences of the oil crisis was unemployment, and youth unemployment in particular was a growing problem during this period. Both Conservative and Labour governments recognised opportunities to reduce youth unemployment would be provided by raising the school-leaving age.

The discussions about the raising of the school-leaving age in 1972 had been acknowledged as far back as the 1938 Spens Report on Secondary Education, had been recognised by the 1944 Act, re-emphasised by the 1959 Crowther Report on education for 15–18 year olds and championed by the Labour government, who actually postponed it for economic reasons in 1968. It was implemented eventually in 1972. Simon (1988) suggests that it was widely welcomed as it provided the opportunity to introduce a full five-year secondary course bringing higher level skills to a wider range of abilities and would provide a response to increasing criticisms that comprehensive education was failing to provide the much-needed recruits for a skilled and modern workforce. By 1974 there were some 10,000 young people classified as unemployed but this had risen to over 240,000 by 1977 (Tomlinson, 2005). A number of other initiatives were introduced to attempt to deal with unemployment in general and some schemes were targeted specifically at young people. For example, the Manpower Services Commission (MSC) was established by Margaret Thatcher following the Employment and Training Act of 1973, an Act which was given support by both sides of the House. The MSC became operational on 1 January 1974 and introduced the Youth Training Schemes (YTS) alongside measures such as Job Creation Programmes and the Youth Opportunities Programme. However, these were seen as being reactive 'stop-gap measures' and ineffective (Lowe, 1997).

The new Labour government which came into power in March 1974, with Reg Prentice installed at the DES by Prime Minister Harold Wilson, did not result in a change in policy. One of Reg Prentice's first tasks was to deal with cutbacks in the education budget in order to cope with massive inflation, a confident trade union movement and world recession. Ironically, those very services which were in a key position to attempt to deal with school-leavers and young adults, the youth service and further and adult education, had to cope with severe cuts to their respective budgets.

Dale (1989: 96) suggests that the it was working-class youth and especially young black people in this period who were most severely hit by increasing unemployment thus 'exacerbating the problems for an economic system which requires a basic level of social harmony, and for an education system expected to contribute in major ways to achieving that harmony'.

With hindsight it is possible to describe these measures, developed by successive governments, as pilots or experiments in which other government departments were able to intervene and have direct influence over what was previously Department for Education and Science territory. As Lowe (1997: 37) comments: 'The events of the 1970s had shifted the debate on schooling and the economy away from what went on in school towards what happened to school leavers.'

During this period, civil servants at the Treasury and the Department of Industry as well as some sections of the DES began to put together an educational policy which gave greater emphasis to the contribution which education could make to the economy, and in particular to the 'employability' of young people. These were issues relating to changes in the boundaries of education policy that featured strongly in Jim Callaghan's Ruskin College speech which is examined in the next section.

The Ruskin College speech

The Ruskin College speech can, in several ways, be seen as a turning point in postwar education drawing together a number of key issues that had risen or were rising to the top of the education agenda for the government, the DES, local authorities, teachers, pupils, parents and industry. It was an opportunity for the government to begin to restore public confidence in education that was perceived as being on a downward spiral. Barber (1996) suggests that it can be seen as 'an obvious attempt by the Prime Minister to simultaneously address public concern over Tyndale and shift public attention from the parlous state of the public finances'. (Only a month before the then Chancellor Denis Healey had, through a much-criticised deal with the International Monetary Fund, 'rescued' the country from bankruptcy.)

Following advice from the head of the Downing Street Policy Unit, Bernard Donoughue, that he should have education as a major policy focus (Chitty, 2009), Jim Callaghan had asked his Education Secretary, Fred Mulley, who had gone on record as identifying education as 'a key to our industrial regeneration', to pick out four key areas of public concern relating to education. These focused on the appropriateness of the curriculum in comprehensive schools, especially the teaching of science and mathematics – Callaghan was very interested, as Sharp (2002: 106) points out, in 'a basic curriculum with universal standards', and expressed anxiety that 'school-leavers appeared to be inadequately equipped to enter work'. Callaghan was also concerned about the teaching of the three 'Rs', the appropriateness of existing assessment schemes and education and training for 16–19 year olds. These issues featured prominently in Jim Callaghan's speech along with those of accountability, effectiveness and the complex relationship between government, industry, teachers and parents (Barber, 1996).

Prior to the Ruskin College speech, two other events should be noted. Firstly, Jim Callaghan gave a speech to the Labour Party Conference in September which, as Chitty (2009: 40) says, was a 'curtain-raiser' to the Ruskin College speech. Secondly, only weeks before Ruskin, a briefing paper (the Yellow Book) from the DES caused substantial debate as it argued that the DES should be giving a stronger lead on what went on in schools, particularly with regard to standards and efficiency and value for money.

Morris and Griggs (1988: 6) suggest the 'notorious' Yellow Book gave the Prime Minister 'a distorted picture of schools and teachers and of the Schools Council whose efforts to reform and democratise as well as broaden the secondary school examinations it undermined'. The work of comprehensive schools was heavily criticised as was pedagogy in the primary sector. Underpinning many of the criticisms were the central issues of standards and performance – two key concepts which would feature prominently in the Ruskin College speech.

These issues featured, as has been noted in an earlier section in this chapter, in the Black Paper publications and in calls for greater intervention into the 'secret garden of the curriculum'. The media, not surprisingly, took the opportunity to scapegoat public sector schools for failing to address the economic needs of the nation. It is not surprising therefore that Jim Callaghan argued, as Jones notes in his discussion of the Ruskin College speech that:

> Education policy should be guided by economic imperatives; students should be prepared for the world of work; existing classroom practice should be subject to critical scrutiny and central influence over education change asserted. (2003: 73)

The scene was thus set for increased state intervention to address all educational issues in the light of 'economic needs' and the changes necessary to meet them. As Tomlinson suggests:

> . . . many of the criticisms voiced by Callaghan gave weight to industrialists who were arguing that the comprehensive system was not serving the needs of British industry, thus setting the scene for greater links between education and industry. (2005: 25)

It is clear that the speech carefully highlighted issues which had been brought to the public's attention by the mass media: the fall-out from the William Tyndale 'affair', the publication of the Black Papers, fears about standards and control of the curriculum, and the relationship between education, industry and the economy.

Thus, it can be argued, Jim Callaghan seized upon an opportunity for a public debate on education against a backdrop of challenging political, social and economic problems. This was a significant direct intervention by a prime minister in educational issues and the political control of education – and although the Great Debate was initiated by a Labour prime minister, it was in tune with much of the thinking of the New Right and subsequent Conservative governments.

Barber (1996) suggests that the speech made a huge impact at the time and raised issues that were to be at the forefront of public interest in education for many years. Chitty emphasises the importance of the Ruskin College speech for the following reasons:

> It marked the end of a period of educational expansion; it called for a re-definition of educational objectives involving the more skilful use of limited resources; it marked a shift by Labour towards policies which would facilitate greater control of the education system; and it was aimed to construct a new educational consensus around a more direct subordination of education to what were the perceived needs of the economy. (2009: 44)

Following the Ruskin College speech, Callaghan appointed Shirley Williams to lead what was to become known as the 'Great Debate' (referred to rather disparagingly by Lawton as 'not a debate, not very great' (Lawton, cited in Tomlinson, 2005: 25). There were, as part of the Great Debate, eight regional conferences (invitees only) in January and February 1977. She was also asked by Callaghan to produce a Green Paper covering the issues raised in the Ruskin College speech. Callaghan had moved Williams to the DES believing that Fred Mulley was not the right person to deliver his agenda.

In her 2010 interview she recalled:

> Jim Callaghan suggested that there should be a great debate on the subject [. . .] conducted in every region of the country, to which representatives of industry, trade unions, parents and local authorities should be invited – an early example of what would later become fashionable – consultation with the users of public services. (Interview, 2010)

On reflection during an interview in 2010 Williams stated that she felt that the press were predictably sceptical and educational experts disdainful about the value of the debate. Interestingly, Simon, although often critical of Williams' own performance, nevertheless argues:

> The Great Debate, irrespective of its content, simply as a means of intervening in education, helped to change the political context in which educational issues were discussed bringing together as it did, for the first time, a range of stakeholders including parents and educational and industrial organisations. (1991: 471)

Shirley Williams (interview, 2010) believes that the regional conferences were useful and they showed strong support for comprehensive schooling, coupled with concern about the wide differences between the curricula followed in different schools. In her view the public conferences provide evidence that there was also a strong undercurrent of worry about the mastery of basic literacy and numeracy, shared not only by parents, but also by employers. These concerns prompted the first tentative steps into what was called 'the secret garden' of the curriculum.

In 1977 Williams introduced a Green Paper, *Education in Schools: A Consultative Document* (DES, 1977c), and this covered many of the issues raised by Callaghan's Ruskin College speech.

In her interview in 2010 when discussing this document Williams emphasised that the Green Paper for the first time proposed that there should be a core curriculum of fundamental subjects, and that the core curriculum should take up around half the time children spent in school. Importantly, she reflects, the local education authorities were asked to review curricular arrangements with their teachers. However, she states that there was not enough time to implement this proposal before the 1979 election and a Conservative government – and eight years later Margaret Thatcher and Kenneth Baker would introduce the 'draconian' National Curriculum which would lay down in detail what should be taught in almost the whole of the school year.

Chitty (2009: 45) describes the Green Paper as 'reaffirming a strictly utilitarian view of education and training' because it argued that the performance of the manufacturing industry should be improved and that the whole range of government policies, including education, should contribute as much as possible to improving industrial performance and thereby increasing national wealth.

This period is one in which there were momentous changes in the structure and direction of the education system and the Ruskin College speech, the Great Debate and the 1977 Green Paper combined to lay the foundations for the equally great changes to be instigated by the incoming Conservative Party.

Parentocracy

In the last 50 years there have been great changes in the relationship between the home and the school but in the periods under review any changes in this relationship were gradual and at times almost imperceptible. The 1970s saw some movement wherein expectations about the 'home–school' relationship began to change. There was no great groundswell from parents demanding their right to be involved in curriculum matters, to have greater access to information about the achievement of their children or to have access to data about schools' performances. Nevertheless, by the end of the decade, there were important changes in the parents' power and in the way in which the state and schools perceived their roles and responsibilities.

Brown (1977: 394) describes a movement, 'the ideology of parentocracy, involving a major programme of educational reform under the slogans of parental choice, educational standards and the free market', which had its foundations in several initiatives and interventions in the 1970s which have been discussed in previous sections: the William Tyndale 'affair', the Bullock Report, the Taylor Report, the Ruskin College speech and the comprehensive debate.

During this period a combination of factors led to a gradual change in the ways in which the roles, responsibilities and rights of both parents and professionals were perceived in terms of home–school relationships and the educational system. It could be argued that by the end of the 1970s there had been a change from the situation where parents were, on the whole, effectively excluded from any other than a fleeting relationship with teachers, the school and the local education authority to one where the relationship between the home and the school was becoming more parent focused (Bastiani, 1978; Torkington, 1986).

Jones, writing about the postwar period, suggests that:

> The [education] system, though universally provided, offered few points at which parental or community interests could become involved in discussion either about general educational purpose, or about the day-to-day running of the school. (1989: 12)

And Davies (cited in Brown, 1977: 260) refers to the 'the rigidity of the boundaries thrown up by the great majority of British schools against parents' in the 1950s and 1960s which were beginning to be eroded by the early 1970s. This is not to say that parents were universally excluded or indeed excluded themselves from greater participation in matters relating to the curriculum, relationships and school–community links. Kogan (1978: 71) cites, for example, the Confederation for the Advancement of State Education created in the early 1960s which attempted to get parental voices heard in the schools and also to get parents involved in the work of the schools more directly.

There were positive attempts to involve parents through a range of channels: through parent teacher associations, by encouraging parents to discover more about teaching methods and the curriculum and become more involved in the governing bodies of schools, and, inevitably, by giving parents more choice over where their children should be educated. As has been argued in earlier chapters, the changes in postwar home–school relations, based on particular assumptions of the roles of parents and teachers, developed away from an emphasis on 'compensation' where children from working-class backgrounds were seen to be less well prepared and less well supported by their parents in pursuit of educational values set by the school to an emphasis on 'participation'.

The Labour government in 1975 set up the Taylor Committee to look at school governance and the relationships between schools, parents and the wider community. The Education Act 1980, resulting from the Taylor Report is described by Sallis (1989: 34) as 'a diluted response'.

Shirley Williams was very interested in creating a climate more favourable to parents and, commenting on Taylor, says in her interview in 2010:

> That really grew very much out of the Great Debate because what became clear in the Great Debate was that parents, and for that matter teachers, felt cut off from the way in which schools were run.

She continues:

> They felt that they were divorced from the school in a way and they didn't feel the same responsibility for how well the school did and how it looked after its difficult students and that kind of thing as certainly I felt they needed to and so I set up the Taylor Commission.

She notes that the Taylor Committee 'broadened the social base of governing bodies and rooted local schools even more closely into the communities they served.' Williams also makes an interesting point when she considers the importance of parental support: 'I wanted to see diversity among schools as distinct from a selection-based pecking order – and believed that this kind of choice would strengthen support for comprehensive schools' (Interview, 2010). The Great Debate, organised by Shirley Williams, also gave parents the opportunity to voice their concerns along with industrialists, teachers and educationalists (Simon, 1991).

Parents' voices were also heard and in some cases amplified by the mass media in, for example, the Tyndale 'affair' (discussed above) which resulted in the media publicising a range of parental viewpoints and perspectives relating to their experience of primary schooling in their neighbourhood. This served to open up national debate about the curriculum and the roles and responsibilities of professionals and parents. The sense of anxiety and discontent felt by some parents may have been exacerbated by the media at this time but one positive outcome was that LEAs and schools began to pay more attention to the interests and demands of parents. These new orientations would become central to Conservative thinking in the 1980s.

Conclusion

The 1970s were a period of transition and change within the education system against a turbulent economic, social and political background. There was a definite shift from the relatively consensual discourse about the role and relationship of education and the economy articulated emphatically in Callaghan's Ruskin College speech and to some extent in the 'Great Debate' about education. Key concerns about the autonomy of teachers, the relationship between the teachers' unions, local education authorities and central government, the purposes and construction of the curriculum and the relationship between parents and schools were irrevocably changed during this period.

Carr and Hartnett, in their examination of politics and education ideas in the period under review, provide a succinct overview:

> The democratic values and assumptions that had influenced official educational policy since 1944 began to be questioned. By the mid-1970s the educational debate increasingly became concerned with decline in the British economy, the rise in unemployment, the massive rise in inflation and unprecedented industrial unrest. (1996: 106)

Conservative and Labour Secretaries of State each contributed to these changes but it was to be Margaret Thatcher who held office between 1970 and 1974 who, returning to government as Prime Minister in 1979, would ensure that education and training became firmly under the control of New Right thinkers and ideologues within the Conservative Party. Under the new Prime Minister's leadership, education and training were to be subject to direct political control as never before.

Further reading

Aldrich, R. (ed.) (2002) *A Century of Education*. London: RoutledgeFalmer.

Carr, W. and Hartnett, A. (1996) *Education and the Struggle for Democracy*. Buckingham: Open University Press.

Chitty, C. (2009) *Education Policy in Britain* (2nd edn). Basingstoke: Palgrave Macmillan.

Jones, K. (1989) *Right Turn: The Conservative Revolution in Education.* London: Hutchinson Radius.

Simon, B. (1991) *Education and the Social Order 1940–1990.* London: Lawrence & Wishart.

Conclusion to Section 1

Section 1 covered the period from 1945 to 1979 which was a time of innovation, progress and change in the education service in England and Wales, in the context of a postwar, social democratic consensus about the importance of education to economic advance and social welfare.

The starting point for the review of this period was postwar reconstruction, the creation of the welfare state and the major education reforms following the 1944 Education Act. The evolution of the tripartite system was examined in the light of the demand for 'free secondary education for all' and 'equality of educational opportunity'. The development of the drive towards comprehensive education was explained as were the key issues of selection at eleven, the grammar schools, streaming and assessment, and the changing curriculum.

However, tensions in the national system of education were noted during the late 1960s and early 1970s. The break-up of the postwar consensus was charted and the importance of the role of factors such as inflation, the balance of payments deficits, industrial unrest and overseas competition was highlighted in terms of the impact on the education system.

The significance of the publication of the 'Black Papers' between 1969 and 1977 was explored as the shift from egalitarian and innovative education policies manifested by the thinking of the 'New Right' became mainstream.

Debates about standards, the curriculum, 'progressive education' and the status of the teaching profession all took centre stage and were given national prominence when, in 1976, the Labour Prime Minister James Callaghan instigated the 'Great Debate' about education in a speech at Ruskin College.

Thus the stage was set for the introduction by the Thatcher government of market competition between schools and reductions in the power and influence of local authorities and the teaching profession on schooling. These 'innovations' were implemented to reverse the democratic and egalitarian policies of the 1950s and 1960s.

1979–1997: MARKETISATION AND COMPETITION

Preamble

Looking back at the history of electioneering in the later half of the twentieth century it is evident that 'education' has been a significant factor in the election campaigns of all major parties and in the perceptions of the electorate (Ranson, 1985; Roberts, 2001).

For some politicians 'education' was always seen as a way of signalling their political intent, for example improving 'social mobility', emphasising 'market forces', etc., while for the majority of the electorate it was simply a means of improving the lot of their children.

Clearly the policies put in place over the years have reflected the culture and ethos of the times, so that the Education Act of 1944 was set within a rather different context from the Education Reform Act of 1988 which figures significantly in Chapters 4, 5 and 6 making up Section 2. The period is that of the Conservative government under the Prime Ministers Margaret Thatcher (1979–90) and John Major (1990–7).

A 'free market' philosophy to enable competition guided all Conservative thinking during this era in an attempt to prioritise the economic well-being of the nation (Thatcher, 1993). There was an attempt to eradicate institutional inefficiency and bureaucracy and introduce market forces to take the place of government intervention in the public services (Ball, 2008). This philosophy was vigorously pursued by both Prime Ministers.

In the first two years of Margaret Thatcher's government the philosophy was applied specifically to economic policy but later to all areas of public life, including education. To enable the nation to compete in economic terms with competitor countries it was considered that schools and colleges must produce students who were well prepared for life in a commercially orientated world (DES, 1985; Baker, 1993; Thatcher, 1993). The Education Secretaries were responsible for putting this philosophy into practice.

For reasons that will be explored below, the 'free market' approach led to developments and ideas which were largely new to education in 1979. They significantly influenced education policy between 1979 and 1997 and, as set out by the present Education Secretary, Michael Gove, remain evident in the policies of the present Coalition government (see Section 3).

There can be no doubt that the years dealt with in Section 2 of this book were the most turbulent in education since the Education Act of 1944. Vigorous and speedy change was attempted – included in which was the Education Reform Act of 1988.

Between 1979 and 1997 there were six ministers in charge of Education who apparently drove these changes. In reality, however, they emanated from the whole Cabinet (Baker, 1993) and from the particular Conservative philosophy espoused by the prime ministers (Thatcher, 1993). However there was a good deal of agreement between the six Secretaries of State about the need for this philosophy to be implemented and for a wide range of legislation to be put onto the statute books. Hence there was real continuity from 1979 to 1997 in the process of 'reform'.

The principal ideals behind education policy in this period were:

• to increase parental choice;
• to reform the power structure within education;
• to enable the privatisation of some education services.

In this section use has been made of an imaginary 'conversation' conducted with Keith Joseph by Peter Ribbins and Brian Sherratt for their book published in 1997. The authors of that text point out that at the time Keith Joseph was seriously ill and could not undertake such an 'interview'. Using various sources an 'as if' conversation was undertaken using available information and it is that which is referred to in this text.

CHAPTER FOUR

1979–1987: THE INTRODUCTION OF COMPETITION INTO EDUCATION

- A 'free market' in education
- The redistribution of power from 'producers' to 'consumers'
- Control of the 'outcomes' of education
- The education of children with special needs

Introduction

Chapter 4 is concerned with the period from 1979 to 1987, ending just prior to the Education Reform Act of 1988. The chapter begins by setting out the political context within which policy was decided, and also the context within schools and colleges at the time. Subsequently there is a detailed consideration of the role of the Education Secretaries Mark Carlisle, Keith Joseph and Kenneth Baker who were in office during this time and of the development of education policy under their leadership. Kenneth Baker was interviewed for this book in 2010.

The main themes which dictated education policy between 1979 and 1987 are explored. These were the expansion of parental choice and the redistribution of power in education. Initiatives which would pave the way for some aspects of privatisation were also put into place.

Context

Political

A concern about the link between the economic and educational performance of the country was one of the main factors behind government
education policy after 1979. The new Prime Minister Margaret Thatcher
recorded that the economy was going through a difficult period.
Unemployment and the high price of oil were causing inflation and public
spending was increasing. At a Cabinet meeting in July 1980 it was felt that
local authorities were overspending and needed to be restrained, but that
nevertheless the government ought to accept an increase in the budget for
the Youth Opportunities Programme (YOPs) in order to help youngsters get
into work (Thatcher, 1993). The scheme was later boosted to almost half a
million places.

The purpose of YOPs was to help youngsters leaving school to find work.
In the early 1980s the Youth Training Scheme (YTS) and the Technical and
Vocational Education Initiative (TVEI) were set up with a similar intention,
though in spite of the fact that these schemes were 'educational' they were
not funded through the education budget.

Subsequently *Better Schools* (DES, 1985) was produced under the
guidance of Education Secretary Keith Joseph. It noted the need for schools
to promote enterprise and adaptability in children in order to enhance their
employment chances. The same document pointed out that education was
an investment in the nation's future and that the best possible returns were
needed from the resources allocated to education.

As will be seen in subsequent chapters this 'Thatcherite' philosophy was
continued throughout the Conservative government's time in office and
after the election of 1997 by 'New Labour' under the guidance of Tony Blair
and his Education Secretary David Blunkett.

From 1979 to 1981 the economy dominated the work of the new
government in which Mark Carlisle was Education Secretary. The imposition
of 'free market' economics enabling the pursuit of private gain encumbered
by minimal governmental intervention was the foremost priority (Joseph
and Sumption, 1979).

When Keith Joseph replaced Mark Carlisle in 1981 the political impetus
for change in education increased although education had not been seen as
a major factor in the concerns of the electorate. As Margaret Thatcher noted
in *The Downing Street Years* (1993) the main issues in the Conservative
manifesto prior to the 1983 election were jobs, health, pensions and defence.
After the triumphant Falklands campaign of 1982 it probably mattered little
that the manifesto was somewhat ambiguous with regard to education –
increasing choice of schools and giving vouchers or credits for education
did not seem to be major issues (Halcrow, 1989).

The Conservatives won a majority of 144 in 1983, the largest of any government since 1945. Between then and 1987, however, the government became less popular as issues like the miner's strike in 1984 polarised popular opinion in the country. Cabinet ministers were shuffled and Keith Joseph resigned as Education Secretary in 1986. Kenneth Baker moved from the Department of the Environment to take over the Department of Education and Science. The idea was to bring what Thatcher hoped would be a stronger 'public image' to education. She felt that education would be a critical feature in the 1987 election (Thatcher, 1993) with the core curriculum, testing and the opportunity for schools to 'opt out' being of great importance. Kenneth Baker backed that up in 2010 by recalling that the manifesto of 1986 had 'twelve pages setting out the Education Reform Act'.

After the election in 1987 the government majority in the House of Commons remained at over a hundred.

When Keith Joseph had replaced Mark Carlisle in 1981 the Prime Minister had begun to exert a much more powerful influence on education policy, an influence which she continued to wield until she left office in 1990. She felt very strongly that state education had largely catered for children in the middle range of potential rather than pursuing excellence. She supported selection, specialisation and competition in education with specialist schools in the arts, sciences, technology, etc. She felt that these schools ought to be able to control their entry criteria (Thatcher, 1993).

She was convinced that there was nationally a 'deep dissatisfaction' with the standard of education and that one way to improve education generally lay in enabling more parental choice. She also wanted to iron out some of the disparities in education provision across the UK (Thatcher, 1993).

Particularly towards the end of her period in office she suggested many of the policy initiatives which were introduced by her Education Secretaries, though Kenneth Baker noted in 2010 that on his appointment as Education Secretary in 1987 she did not give him an agenda to follow and that he felt that he was in charge. She did, however, study legislation in great detail and emphasises in *The Downing Street Years* (1993) that she had strong opinions for example about the English and History proposals for the National Curriculum and about taking control of education away from local authorities (Thatcher, 1993). In this respect she personified what Whitty (2008) saw as a tendency by the state to retain strategic control of outcomes when appearing to offer devolution, an almost inevitable consequence of the free market approach. Some of her views were opposed by her colleagues as well as by opposition MPs and some 'education professionals'. Nevertheless she continued to support 'reform'.

Schools and colleges

As has been pointed out in Section 1, prior to the election of 1979 money to be spent in education was largely devolved from government to local education authorities (LEAs). In addition there was very little published information with which to judge the quality of state schools or their results in public examinations, and many parents who could afford to do so sent their children to 'public schools' to be educated privately.

This situation continued during the early years of Margaret Thatcher's government with great disparity between the quality of schools depending on the population of their local catchment area, the local authority and local politics. The Inner London Education Authority was perceived by the government to personify the influence of politics on educational provision (Thatcher, 1993; Balen, 1994).

Faith groups also continued to hold power over some schools, related to funding processes and the curriculum. The lack of central control of the curriculum prompted the White Paper *Better Schools* (DES, 1985: para. 5) to note that there was a weakness in curriculum planning and implementation in the majority of primary and middle schools. Kenneth Baker pointed out when interviewed in 2010 that it was possible for children to study 'dinosaurs' three times in primary schools.

LEAs in the early 1980s offered a wide diversity of secondary provision which included comprehensive school provision. In some areas children took selection tests at eleven years of age (the eleven plus) which determined which pupils could go to grammar schools and hence follow an academic education – while the remainder attended secondary modern schools where they were taught a more vocationally orientated curriculum. In different areas of the country there was a disparity in the number of children able to attend the grammar schools depending on the number and size of schools and the density of population in that area. Other parts of the country had opted for comprehensive schools to which all pupils progressed at eleven and which were generally larger than the average secondary school in 'grammar/secondary modern' areas.

By 1980 only 20 per cent of children were subjected to a selection procedure and, although when in charge of Education in Edward Heath's government Margaret Thatcher had approved over two thousand comprehensive applications, she was very much against the continuation of the comprehensive ideal (Thatcher, 1993).

The 1979 Education Act removed from LEAs the obligation to consider comprehensive reorganisation plans and enabled them to revert to a selection process if they wished. However, the idea of comprehensive education was anathema to many Conservative politicians elected in 1979 and remains so to the present day.

Within all schools at the time there was considerable disparity of teaching methods – often dependent upon the philosophy of head teachers and LEA advisers. These philosophical differences had an impact on the teacher recruitment process which was carried out by LEAs in conjunction with head teachers and, in the primary sector, on the architecture of school buildings. New schools were still being built with an 'open plan' layout to enable teaching in large groups for 'topic work' – a system in which amalgamated classes were put together for input from a specialist teacher before being dispersed into smaller groups to be taught by other teachers.

In broad terms, probably the main differences in the primary sector revolved around whether 'child-centred' or 'curriculum-centred' methods were employed and to what extent formal 'testing' (usually internal and unreported) was seen as useful.

Even in the 1980s the Plowden Report (DES, 1967) was often seen as the most influential document among those who advocated a child-centred approach to teaching in the primary school. It advocated a philosophy in which children 'discovered' rather than 'were told' and maintained its influence well into the 1980s.

In the secondary sector the main discussions were about how classes of children should be organised to take account of the whole range of ability. In some schools in the 1980s classes were taught in mixed-ability groups whereas in others setting by academic ability was the preferred teaching style.

When pupils reached 16 they could leave school if they wished but most grammar school pupils were expected to stay at school to complete public examinations before leaving or going into a sixth form and then into higher education.

One choice for pupils leaving school in the early 1980s was to go into a publicly funded further education college in the locality. LEAs typically had some influence within the colleges, an influence which varied significantly between institutions. The curriculum of individual colleges was largely determined by the local employment market, so that, for example, courses in colleges in engineering and manufacturing areas were set up to help students get employment in those industries. Local business leaders were involved in course planning. Thus to a large extent the curricula of these institutions were driven by the needs of local business and of students, a fact that Kenneth Baker thought of as highly commendable.

By 1980 around 40 per cent of 16 year olds continued full-time education with 14 per cent studying part-time. This was much lower than the numbers in some other comparative countries and was seen as a factor which could hamper the economic development of the country.

This then was the context into which the new government wanted to introduce market forces and increase parental choice.

The Education Secretaries and policy development

It is clear from the various interviews with the Education Secretaries, from books written about their periods in office and from the autobiographies of Margaret Thatcher, John Major and Kenneth Baker that education policy throughout this period was driven by the 'free market' philosophy championed by Keith Joseph and Margaret Thatcher as the solution to the country's economic tribulations.

Three Education Secretaries were in office during the years covered by this chapter. They were Mark Carlisle (1979–81), Keith Joseph (1981–6) and Kenneth Baker (1986–9). Reference will be made to their backgrounds, their ideas about education, the policies they attempted to develop, the problems encountered and their feelings when looking back at their achievements.

Mark Carlisle (1979–81)

Mark Carlisle had trained as a lawyer in Manchester and became an MP in 1964. He was shadow Secretary of Education for two years while in opposition. He had no experience of the state education sector having attended a private school and having sent his daughter to a private school. His ambition in politics was to be Home Secretary, but he was asked to take on the role of Education Secretary after the 1979 election. He suspected that he was not Margaret Thatcher's choice, but that Willie Whitelaw (Deputy Prime Minister) had suggested him for the post. Indeed when Margaret Thatcher reshuffled her Cabinet two years later she replaced him with Keith Joseph, calling Carlisle left-leaning and ineffective (Thatcher, 1993). He remained in the Commons until 1987 when he became Baron Carlisle of Bucklow. He died in 2005.

Keith Joseph (1981–6)

Keith Joseph had been Margaret Thatcher's great ally in setting up the Centre for Policy Studies in 1975 and campaigning for a move to the right. In her book *The Downing Street Years* (1993) she notes her reliance on his radical ideas and general philosophy of wanting the Party to put its faith in freedom and free markets with which governments should not interfere. He was seen, as Kenneth Baker underlined when interviewed in 2010, as the intellectual 'driving force' of 'Thatcherism'.

Joseph had been educated in the private sector and after army service worked as a barrister. He was elected to Parliament in 1956, taking his first ministerial post in 1962 as Minister for Housing. He held various positions in the government including Secretary of State for Education from 1981 to 1986. When interviewed in 1997 he said that in 1981 he had been keen to take charge of Education after having been Secretary of State for Industry, although he refers to the education system as the 'bloody state system' with which government ought not to be involved (Ribbins and Sherratt, 1997).

By 1986 he was keen to leave the post, feeling that there were still lots of problems to sort out in education (Halcrow, 1989). He left Parliament in 1987, becoming Baron Joseph, and passed away in 1994 after a severe illness.

Kenneth Baker (1986–9)

Kenneth Baker was educated in the state and private sectors, before studying history at Oxford. He completed his National Service and then became a businessman. He was elected to Parliament in 1970 and took his first Cabinet role in 1985. He was appointed as Education Secretary in 1986 and later became Home Secretary. He had strong feelings against the comprehensive system, about the need to preserve grammar schools and about what he saw as fundamental problems with the curriculum. As will be seen later he set about dealing with these issues during his time at Education. After leaving the Education Department Kenneth Baker held various important offices including that of Home Secretary from 1990 until 1992. He left Parliament in 1997, becoming Baron Baker of Dorking, but as he argued in his interview in 2010 by his advocacy of University Technical Colleges he continued to be enthusiastic about the importance of teaching aspects of industry and commerce in schools (see Chapter 10).

Policy development

When one considers the varied opinions of three Education Secretaries during this period it is apparent that there were some differences between the philosophy of Mark Carlisle (1979–81) and the more interventionist views of Keith Joseph (1981–6) and Kenneth Baker (1986–9). These differences are exemplified in Mark Carlisle's attitude to teachers and his feeling about 'standards', both of which will be explored below.

Mark Carlisle and special needs

After his appointment Carlisle was responsible for backing ongoing legislation in relation to children with special needs which derived from a policy of the previous Labour administration. Nevertheless he was working within prevailing Conservative philosophy when introducing legislation with regard to the Assisted Places Scheme and overseeing LEA policies in relation to comprehensive schools. He had been appointed as Education Secretary to follow Shirley Williams. During his years in office there were comparatively few significant changes made in education compared with the plethora of activity in subsequent years. Nevertheless some of the major changes in policy which have come to characterise the years 1979–97 can be seen as having had their basis under his stewardship.

Carlisle believed that the teaching profession was mistakenly maligned and that it ought to be recognised as a profession in the same way as the legal profession, setting and validating their own standards and acting in a professional manner. He recognised the Professional Association of Teachers and was keen to set up a General Teaching Council, although his efforts were not well received by most teaching unions.

In the context of relations with the teaching profession it is clear that he inherited a difficult situation from Shirley Williams (see Chapter 3) who had been in conflict with the National Union of Teachers over pay and conditions. He was proud of the fact that during his period in office there was comparative calm (Ribbins and Sherratt, 1997) and that although his relationship with the teaching unions was never easy he managed, unlike his successors, to avert any strike action.

Unlike the Prime Minister he considered it his job to facilitate the context in which education could occur rather than tinker with the details. Kenneth Baker by contrast said that he became involved in the minutiae of education which he found fascinating (Ribbins and Sherratt, 1997). Mark Carlisle cared about the prospects of all pupils and felt that the background of pupils was important to their achievement (Ribbins and Sherratt, 1997).

In this and in other ways he recognised that he was not in line with predominant Tory Party thinking. Although he was in favour of parental choice and the drive to improve standards he was clear that there was no evidence that standards were falling (Ribbins and Sherratt, 1997). He did not try to privatise aspects of education. Rather he tried to work with the 'education establishment' – teachers, LEAs, etc. – and in this respect had views directly opposed to those of the Prime Minister who is on record as saying that she wanted to break the hold of left-wing teachers, teacher training institutions and LEAs on education in schools (Thatcher, 1993). She felt that in initial teacher training there was too much sociology and psychology with insufficient teaching practice. In schools children were not taught enough facts, standards were falling and child-centred education was too predominant.

Speaking in an interview in 1997 (Ribbins and Sherratt, 1997) Carlisle noted what he felt were the three most important pieces of legislation that were carried through in his time in office:

• First, the restoration to LEAs of the powers to decide about comprehensive reorganisation (Education Act 1979).

The Education Acts of 1979 and 1980 had given LEAs the opportunity to oppose the Labour ideal of comprehensive education and reintroduce selection, one of the most emotive aspects of Conservative education policy. However, selection at eleven years of age remained, and still remains, in only a minority of local authorities. Some conservatively inclined local authorities such as Solihull and Berkshire found that the majority of parents were enthusiastic about comprehensive schools and resisted any attempt to revert to grammar schools. Consequently the measure had less impact on the move to halt comprehensive schools than had been envisaged.

• Second, the initiation of the Assisted Places Scheme. This was set up to enable children from poorer backgrounds to benefit from public school education (see below).
• Third, the Education Special Needs Act of 1981.

It is possible with hindsight to say that Carlisle's acceptance of Special Needs legislation (Ribbins and Sherratt, 1997) may have been his most significant achievement.

In formulating the Special Needs Act Carlisle accepted the conclusions of the 1978 Warnock Report set up by Shirley Williams to look into Special Needs provision in mainstream schools. Prior to the Education Act of 1970 a small number of children were regarded as ineducable at school. The number was approximately thirty thousand in 1970. Health authorities had the obligation to provide training for these children who were typically looked after in special care units and training centres. After 1971 they were entitled to an education.

In 1978 Mary Warnock, one-time school teacher, headmistress and philosopher at Oxford, produced a report on Special Education in England, Scotland and Wales suggesting that most disabled children ought to be integrated into mainstream schools, although some would continue to attend special schools. The report also emphasised the importance of parental knowledge about their children and the necessity of using it in the assessment of the children's needs.

Legislation in 1981 came into force in 1983 and made it the duty of LEAs to educate these children in mainstream schools provided that their education could occur in those schools without adversely affecting the education of other children and that there were sufficient resources available. Kenneth Baker, speaking in an interview in 2010, said that Mary Warnock had later expressed the view that she had been mistaken in the main thrust of her report.

Problems began to occur as the process of assessing these children became very bureaucratic and drawn out and some professional and administrative resistance became apparent. These problems were highlighted ten years later when the Audit Commission and HMI criticised the system, with some LEAs taking a long time to complete what were often vague assessment statements and not providing adequate provision in mainstream schools. There was also evidence of poor accountability, including unprofessional inspection procedures.

In 1993 an Education Act gave an improved appeals process to parents, removing the appeals from the control of LEAs and setting a timescale for the process. As will be seen in Chapter 7 the New Labour government published an influential Green Paper to take this area of education forward.

While it might be possible to see the involvement of parents in the preparation of Special Needs statements after the Warnock Report as part of the Conservative movement towards increasing parental involvement in education, the report was 'left over' from the previous government and Mark Carlisle is on record as saying that he remembered little of the detail (Ribbins and Sherratt, 1997).

Keith Joseph and selection

Keith Joseph, who replaced Mark Carlisle in 1981, was strongly in favour of selection. He felt that secondary modern schools and comprehensives had tried to align themselves with grammar schools and taught an academic curriculum to children who were better suited to follow the courses of vocational training which he vigorously championed. He said that it had been wrong to raise the school leaving age to 16 in 1972 and that to keep children in school against their will was 'tyrannical' (Ribbins and Sherratt, 1997). He disagreed with the imposition of a National Curriculum and emphasised the importance of quality rather than quantity.

In an interview (Ribbins and Sherratt, 1997) he felt that he had made some mistakes in his period in office, for example in merging the GCE and CSE exams. He thought the resulting GCSE exam had become too broad. In addition he had been too optimistic in thinking that he could bring market forces to bear on education in the same way as they had been successfully applied to the housing market and industry (Ribbins and Sherratt, 1997).

Kenneth Baker and the free market

In 1986 Kenneth Baker was appointed to succeed Keith Joseph in the Department of Education and remained in post until 1989. He shared the 'free market' enthusiasms of Margaret Thatcher and Keith Joseph. He presided over some of the most significant developments in education which took place during a period of great change. During his time in office a National Curriculum within which politicians dictated what should be taught in schools became a reality. Some of the proposals which had germinated from Margaret Thatcher and Keith Joseph's view of 'marketisation' came to fruition. Kenneth Baker has said (1993) that he wanted to try to introduce schools that would represent a halfway house between private and state education. He used the introduction of free market forces into the housing market as an example. The sale of council houses had led to the elimination of the division between social housing and the private sector – a process which he felt could be replicated in education.

At the end of his tenure he felt that his Education Reform Act had led to significant social and educational reform (Ribbins and Sherratt 1997), a point he reiterated in the interview of 2010.

Analysis of policy development

An analysis of policy and its implementation between 1979 and 1987 suggests two main factors which were seen as essential to help schools and colleges increase the levels of performance of their pupils and contribute to the economic well-being of the country:

- an increase in parental choice by extending the variety of schools and colleges;
- a reform of the power structure in education.

Both themes include issues related to:

- selection;
- curriculum development;
- shifts away from child-centred education;
- accountability and testing;
- provision for children with special needs;
- taking power from LEAs and teachers' unions;
- changing the pay and conditions of teachers.

Further policy developments

Parental choice

Parental choice was one of the central tenets of the Conservative education policy and became part of the idea that the 'power' in education needed moving from the 'producers' to the 'consumers' (Baker, 1993).

One of the first initiatives to help increase parental choice was the Education Act of 1980 which the Prime Minister identified as a Parent's Charter (Thatcher, 1993). A variety of measures were introduced very quickly such as increasing the number of parents on school governing bodies in order to give parents more say in the activities of their schools and giving back to LEAs the opportunity to introduce selection.

Other initiatives which were developed with the same intention are set out below.

Information for parents

Keith Joseph wanted to increase the information about schools and the school curriculum which was given to parents. He felt that such information would help parents to decide which schools they favoured for their children.

The White Paper of 1985 *Better Schools* (DES, 1985) was followed by the 1986 Education Act which required schools to be more explicit about their curricula, encouraging schools to make close links with business and industry thus enabling children to be better equipped to meet the demands of working life. In his enthusiasm for a 'technology'-based curriculum Joseph was supported by Kenneth Baker, his successor, who in an interview in 2010 recalled talking to Joseph about 'Information Technology Centres' which 'turned pupils on' to education and needed to be extended throughout the country. Baker said that a curriculum based around science and technology would help pupils who were less academically inclined.

Vouchers

In giving choice to parents the government was attracted towards the idea of Education Vouchers – 'a shibboleth of Thatcherite radicals' (Halcrow, 1989: 168) – a scheme which would give parents the chance to have a voucher allowing them to spend a sum of money on their children's education using whichever school they preferred. This system did not come to fruition with regard to mainstream education because after discussion within and beyond the Conservative Party Keith Joseph decided that it was politically unworkable (Halcrow, 1989). Some members of his own party were against the idea but in any case he reckoned that in making choices consumers could not always be relied upon to make what he felt were sensible choices (Ribbins and Sherratt, 1997). Margaret Thatcher (1993) was satisfied, however, that her government was able to give parents choice in a number of other less contentious ways, for example through open enrolment and per capita funding (see below).

In relation to nursery education the idea of vouchers was developed significantly when Gillian Shephard was Education Secretary in John Major's government (1990–7). Details can be found in Chapter 6.

The Assisted Places Scheme

Mark Carlisle was responsible for the legislation in 1980 which established the Assisted Places Scheme to enable children from poor backgrounds to enter public schools provided that they came within the top 10–15 per cent of applicants in the school's entrance exam. It was hoped that this scheme would contribute towards 'social mobility' though subsequent evidence shows that, as in other similar attempts, it was unsuccessful (Roberts, 2001; Ball, 2008).

Kenneth Baker, speaking in an interview in 2010, was rather dismissive of a scheme that was only 'an adjustment on the side', although in the first five years of the scheme some 6,000 pupils were enabled to have a private education. It has subsequently been calculated that a large majority of these were the offspring of parents with professional jobs (Fitz et al., 1989).

The Assisted Places Scheme was planned to expand to over 30,000 places before the election of 1997 (Baker, 1993), but the Labour government of 1997 brought it to an end. Those children in the scheme in 1997 continued to be subsidised until they had completed their studies.

The Special Needs Education Act 1981

As has been discussed earlier the Special Needs legislation brought into effect in 1981 as a result of the Warnock Report allowed for more input from parents into the process of statementing children with special needs.

Types of school

One immediate corollary to parental choice was expanding the choice of type of school to which children could be sent – particularly in the secondary sector.

The notion of enabling wider choice was strongly driven by the ideas of Stuart Sexton and other 'Black Paper' authors of the mid-1970s who felt that parents should have a free choice of schools and that any schools that did not attract their quota of children would have to close (Gillard, 2011).

Kenneth Baker, the Education Secretary from 1986 to 1989, was enthusiastic to give parents the opportunity to choose between grammar, secondary modern and comprehensive, between single sex and co-educational, as well as between church and non-denominational schools (Baker, 1993). To help achieve this diversity he wished to develop some different types of school, e.g. grant-maintained schools (GMS) and city technology colleges (CTCs) (see Chapter 5) but first needed to change the process of school management and the system whereby funds were allocated to schools.

In the interview in 2010 Kenneth Baker says that he saw the need to reform education by moving the power in education away from the vested interests of the LEAs (the hub) to the rim (parents and schools). Central to these processes of reform were the delegation of funding from LEAs to schools and colleges, and of giving the institutions the opportunity to manage their own finances – the local management of schools (LMS).

Kenneth Baker had been impressed by experimental schemes of delegated budgets which had run over a couple of years in Cambridgeshire and Surrey and he wanted to give a large number of schools the chance to control their own budgets.

A consequence of reform would be that school governors would take more and wider responsibility. He felt that governors should come from a wider range of backgrounds than was the case up until that time. Governing bodies had a majority of members from the teaching force, the LEAs and the teachers' unions – all of whom he suspected would be against his proposals for change. He wanted more business leaders and parents on governing bodies and had no doubt this could be achieved.

The decision to change the processes by which schools received money meant lessening the power LEAs held over the money passed from central government to schools. Making significant changes in this system fitted perfectly with the predominant political philosophy of curbing the power of the LEAs.

To begin the process Keith Joseph had enthusiastically supported the TVEI introduced in 1982, financed through the Manpower Services Commission rather than through LEAs. This was followed two years later by the Education (Grants and Awards) Act 1984 which gave central government control over grants given to LEAs. The money had to be spent on specific government backed projects. In 1987 additional grants were introduced which the government dictated had to be spent on the in-service training of teachers.

The 1986 Education Act which implemented the proposals of *Better Schools* considerably lessened the importance of the LEA as it indicated that, although LEAs retained the responsibility for 'effective management of the money made available' (DES, 1985: para. 246), schools were better placed than LEAs to know how they should spend the money delegated to them. A per capita funding scheme was introduced that would allow money to follow the pupil, with popular schools receiving more resources than unpopular schools as parents exercised choice and sent their children to the former. Whereas Kenneth Baker saw this as being a method of motivating unpopular schools to improve, critics saw it as a way of creating 'sink' schools to which some poorer parents had to send their children because they lacked the resources to give their children the chance to travel to a more distant school (Ball, 2008).

Baker had discussed the notion of changing the funding arrangements for schools with Margaret Thatcher in 1986, pointing out that funds could be targeted at schools in 'hostile' LEAs, thus weakening the power of the LEA. By this he meant subsidising schools that wanted to select pupils and remain grammar schools in areas where such a move would be opposed by the LEA. What he felt was needed was a mechanism for enabling parents help the schools 'escape' from the LEA and become in some sense independent and self-governing (Baker, 1993).

The Education Secretary needed to give schools and parents a democratic process so that the school could 'opt out' of LEA control (see below). Parental ballots seemed to be the answer (Baker, 1993).

Opting out

In order to opt out of LEA control a grouping of one-fifth of parents could ask the governors to organise a ballot of all parents which, if resulting in a vote in favour of opting out, had to be confirmed later by the governors. This was a system that Keith Joseph, reflecting upon it later, said that he would have opposed because of the local political consequences (Ribbins and Sherrat, 1997). Kenneth Baker found that this was indeed the case, with some LEAs 'campaigning unscrupulously . . . and issuing misleading leaflets' (Baker, 1993: 216) in order to subvert his intentions. The Catholic Church in particular reacted against the idea of schools 'opting out' but the Church of England also opposed the practice, although with 'arguments that were not so classy' (Baker, 1993: 218).

When the Education Reform Act became law in 1988 the possibility of schools opting out became a reality – with results which will be discussed in Chapters 5 and 6.

Further reading

DES (1985) *Better Schools*. London: HMSO.
Joseph, K. (1975) *Reversing the Trend*. London: Centre for Policy Studies.
McNay, I. and Ozga. J. (eds) (1985) *Policy Making in Education – The Breakdown of Consensus*. Oxford: Pergamon Press.

CHAPTER FIVE

1988–1992: EDUCATION REFORM: A PERIOD OF TURBULENCE

- Increasing 'competition' in education
- Education reform:
  - a National Curriculum
  - testing and assessment

Introduction

Throughout its period in office from 1979 the Conservative government had been determined to make significant changes to what was seen as a failing education system. This chapter is concerned with the final two years of Margaret Thatcher's term as Prime Minister (1988– 90) and the first two years in office of John Major (1990–2).

The political background and the school and college context is reviewed, followed by a discussion of the Education Secretaries, Kenneth Baker (1986–9), John MacGregor (1989–90) and Kenneth Clarke (1990–2) and the policies they developed.

The Education Reform Act (ERA) of 1988 is considered in some detail. It was the culmination of a great deal of political and educational activity throughout the first nine years of Conservative Party government after the election victory of 1979. The background and subsequent issues related to the Act were elaborated in interviews in 2010 for this book with its originator Kenneth Baker and with John MacGregor who followed him as Education Secretary.

The main themes of the chapter demonstrate how the government pursued its goal of improving the economic standing of the country by raising standards in education using policies articulated in the ERA which enabled competition and privatisation to develop in state education and extended parental choice of schools and colleges (Ball, 2008). The main elements of the Act are still evident in 2012 though they have been adapted according to what has happened in schools and colleges since 1988 and to the particular beliefs of successive governments.

As Kenneth Baker said when interviewed in 2010:

'We changed everything'

Context

Political

Political commentators and politicians, among them McSmith (1994), have argued that the reforms encompassed in the ERA of 1988 were made possible because of the collapse of the two-party system in British politics. In 1987 the third election in succession had produced a Conservative government with a majority of over a hundred seats. 'There was no political force big enough to stop them', wrote McSmith (1994: 183).

Kenneth Baker himself underlined this during an interview in 2010 when he remarked about the power which he had been able to command in pushing legislation through Parliament.

When the election of 1987 was won Kenneth Baker was kept in post to steer the ERA through Parliament in 1988 but in a Cabinet reshuffle in 1989 he was moved to become Party Chairman and John MacGregor, from the Ministry of Agriculture, took over in Education. The move was caused to some degree by the fact that by 1990 the mood nationally was turning against the Conservatives. The Community Charge and the amount of public spending in the form of the size of grants for local authorities were divisive issues within the Party as well as among the general public. The possibility of a poll tax led to riots in the streets. There was unhappiness among Tory MPs with regard to the government's position on Europe and in addition Margaret Thatcher was beginning to position those whom she felt would be worthy successors to her as Prime Minister. Kenneth Baker was one 'who ought to be tested in high office' (Thatcher, 1993: 755) and was hence moved to become Party Chairman.

As a result of this internal Party discontent in the face of an upcoming election the leadership of the government itself changed. In 1990 John Major became Prime Minister after the acrimonious departure of Margaret Thatcher, brought down, according to John Major, by the poll tax and European issues (Major, 1999).

John Major had been Chancellor of the Exchequer and as such supported the policies of Thatcher's government. He inherited a difficult situation, with two years to make an impression before the next election. The economy was in recession, unemployment rising and inflation high. He records that he needed to change the policies on the poll tax and Europe and shake up the culture of the public services. He said that he was certain that 'privatisation' was the way to change that culture and improve performance in the public sector (Major, 1999).

Once the ERA came into force there was a real opportunity for privatisation to occur in education.

The idea that private companies might run schools had been suggested at the DES before the ERA – though it was not developed in any substantial way (Ball, 2008). Kenneth Baker, as he emphasised when interviewed in 2010, was enthusiastic about bringing private sponsorship to schools, whereas his successors as Education Secretary, John MacGregor and Kenneth Clarke, although supporting most aspects of the Reform Act, had mixed views about privatising education.

John Major writing in 1999 considered that selective privatisation had brought great improvement to public services in the 1980s but that some of his colleagues at the time would not acknowledge, as he had, the top quality work done by some teachers. He felt that an extreme right-wing ideology lacked vision and ambition and hindered his attempt to use privatisation for the constructive improvement of the service. He simply wanted to use some aspects of privatisation to help the recipients and the deliverers to make the service better (Major, 1999).

John Major had strong views on education because in his own words 'he had not had much himself' (Major, 1999: 212). He called the DES 'a complacent and bureaucratic department' and for that reason he was happy to have Kenneth Clarke as his Education Secretary, a man who was 'always happy to pick a fight' (Major, 1999: 249). This belligerent attitude, when applied to the DES, also made Clarke a favourite with the right wing of the Conservative Party, so much so that as John Major's government became more unpopular in 1991 and 1992 he was seen as a future Party leader (Balen, 1994). Against the odds, however, in 1992 the government won another election although with a comparatively small majority.

Ball (2008) points out that education reform during the Conservative governments prior to 1997 was linked to the requirements of a knowledge economy in which the public sector had to be businesslike, with the private sector having input into the management and delivery of education. Aspects of the market, including competition and choice, were seen by Margaret Thatcher, Kenneth Baker and John Major as essential (Ball, 2008). Kenneth Baker said when interviewed in 2010 that 'where there is a competitive element, things will always get better'.

As will be seen later, educational institutions were encouraged to become entrepreneurial and competitive and the inspection system of schools was also privatised.

Schools and colleges

Unrest in schools and colleges had been evident throughout the period leading up to the ERA in 1988. As one of the main architects of the government's financial strategies Keith Joseph had always supported the spending restraints associated with them. This had tainted the atmosphere of the whole education scene (Halcrow, 1989) and meant that Kenneth Baker inherited a teaching force in which morale was very low. In 1987 the Teachers Pay and Conditions Bill had become law, removing from teachers the right to be involved in negotiating their own pay and conditions of service thus exacerbating the rift between the Education Secretary and the teachers and leading to a series of strikes (Baker, 1993). Kenneth Baker did, however, introduce the idea of teachers having time allocated to in-service training so that head teachers could bring their staff members together for training. These training days became known as 'Baker Days'.

At a later date one teaching union leader noted that the power of the unions had been used indiscriminately against the Tory government during this period (Davies, 2000) though David Hart, leader of the National Association of Head Teachers (NAHT), remarked in 2005 that Kenneth Baker was a fine Secretary of Education and that the decision to take over the teachers' pay negotiations had been a 'great victory' (Smithers, 2005).

Kenneth Baker also had a desire to bring back selection because, as he expressed strongly in an interview for this book in 2010, he considered that 'comprehensivisation' had been a terrible error. Indeed, when interviewed in 2010, he talked about grammar schools as 'having been destroyed by Shirley Williams in an act of vindictive, doctrinaire socialism'.

His object as Education Secretary, he said, was 'to set up an education system that would provide a ladder for all children and enable them to achieve their potential'.

The ERA as it passed through Parliament was based to some extent on the wish of Margaret Thatcher and Kenneth Baker to curtail the power of local authorities by taking the schools out of LEA control. As will be seen later Kenneth Baker wanted to do this by redirecting central government money for education from the LEAs and paying it directly to the schools.

The sections in the Reform Act that enabled local management of schools and per capita funding were specifically included to allow schools to 'go it alone' and achieve 'grant-maintained' status. This status gave such schools enhanced funding, self-management and control of their own admissions procedures, factors which were expected to be strong motivating factors in the decision to move away from LEA control. When the Reform Act came into force some schools immediately began to think of 'opting out' of LEA control although, in Kenneth Baker's own words in 2010, 'a large part of the educational establishment were bitterly hostile'.

Consequently the development was rather slow moving – by 1997 when the period of Conservative government ended there were still only around a thousand grant-maintained schools, the majority of them secondary, out of a total of over twenty thousand. The arguments about the benefits or otherwise of such 'opted out' schools raged more or less continually throughout the whole period (see, for example, Hughes, 1993). There was even a suggestion that the government might attempt to make all schools grant-maintained and abolish LEAs altogether (Davies, 2000).

As has been noted in Chapter 4, however, the government wanted to keep control of what was taught to children and what the outcomes were of schooling. The result, as set out later in this chapter, was a National Curriculum containing a mass of detail and paperwork plus a system of 'testing' which provoked enormous hostility in schools (Balen, 1994) and meant as John MacGregor said in interview in 2010, that the skills, ability and innovation of teachers were pushed out. Kenneth Baker, speaking in 2010, was adamant that he wanted to ensure that the schools never went back to the situation where children might repeat sections of the curriculum and miss out other sections simply because there was no real coordination of the curriculum across the country or even in a single LEA. Kenneth Clarke was also suspicious of the use of informal teaching methods in primary schools. His personal preference was for formal teaching and streaming in ability groups. In 1992 he set up a group of distinguished academics to report on curriculum organisation in the primary sector – a report which became known as the 'Three Wise Men' report (Alexander et al., 1992) and which stressed the need for an emphasis on literacy and numeracy, an evaluation of teaching techniques and more specialist teaching in the final years of primary education.

In further education colleges the government saw reason for optimism throughout the period 1988–92 and for this reason the colleges were in a constant state of change. Kenneth Baker remembered during interview in 2010 that he had wanted to expand the sector by increasing the funding and raising its status after he had freed the colleges from LEA control. Kenneth Clarke shared with other Conservatives the 'political prejudice' against local authorities and saw in further education an opportunity to 'liberalise and equalise educational opportunity' while at the same time removing some of the power of local government (Balen, 1994: 226).

Thus it was announced that colleges would become 'incorporated' and independent, a move which came about as a result of the 1992 Further and Higher Education Act which was taken through Parliament by John

Patten, Kenneth Clarke's successor in 1992. As a consequence there was an emphasis on local autonomy and colleges grew rapidly and modernised, acting like the businesses they had been asked to become (see Chapter 6).

Thus as education in its entirety became part of the marketised approach to public services further education colleges faced competition not only from each other but from higher education and private training companies. They seized the opportunity to develop a variety of programmes and began to deliver academic courses as well as a wider range of vocational programmes (Lumby, 2001). Kenneth Clarke, when appointed as Education Secretary in 1990, assisted this process by encouraging the development of a new system of national vocational qualifications for those not seeking entirely academic qualifications (Balen, 1994).

When John Major became Prime Minister in 1990 he backed all these initiatives, including the notion of independence for colleges. The delegation of funding and opportunities for self-management which were shaping the schools were thus equally applied in further education. Within five years almost 500 further education institutions had become independent (Baker, 1993).

The Education Secretaries and policy development

Between 1988 and 1992 there were three Education Secretaries, Kenneth Baker (1986–9), John MacGregor (1989–90) and Kenneth Clarke (1990–2). Baker and MacGregor were interviewed for this book in 2010.

Kenneth Baker (1986–9)

Kenneth Baker, as has been seen in Chapter 4, was the principal architect of the ERA. Appointed by Margaret Thatcher in 1986 he remained at the DES until after the Act had passed through Parliament in 1988. When he became Party Chairman in 1989 it was said by his supporters that his presentation skills were required to improve the party image (Thatcher, 1993) and by his detractors that he 'was moved on before having to face the consequences of his own legislation' (Baker, 1993). He himself, when interviewed in 2010, seemed to suggest that some in the Party thought that the implementation of reform was too slow. 'The trouble with the right wing', he said, 'is that they want everything done immediately.'

John MacGregor (1989–90)

His successor John MacGregor emphasised in 2010 that he strongly supported the education policies advocated by Margaret Thatcher. He had been Minister for Agriculture for two years before moving to the Department for Education and Science. Most of his early education had been in the private sector in Scotland. He attended the University of St Andrews and eventually studied law and economics in London. He had been a journalist and businessman before being elected to Parliament in 1974. He felt that all pupils ought to 'get the best out of their education and the best out of themselves' (Ribbins and Sherratt, 1997: 175). He saw educational improvement as fundamental to the development of the economy in a world where competition was fierce and technological change happened quickly – points which he re-emphasised in 2010. When appointed by Margaret Thatcher several colleagues, including Kenneth Baker, were sure that he was the right person to implement the ERA. To do this, however, he felt the need to regain the confidence of the teaching profession and, according to McSmith (1994), was never completely convinced about the reforms. The former trait did not endear him to the right wing of the Conservative Party, including the Prime Minister. She felt that although he had made some progress in reforming the teaching of Science and English he was not forcing through her ideas on the History curriculum (Thatcher, 1993). In 2010 he noted that this was the only thing about which they disagreed. John MacGregor was enthusiastic about his appointment and sorry to be moved on in 1989 after only one year in office, remarking when interviewed in 2010 that his departure was 'unexpected'. The image that he gave to the DES was not of a sufficiently high profile – rather the reverse of Kenneth Clarke who replaced him in 1990. John MacGregor left the House of Commons in 2001 on becoming a life peer.

Kenneth Clarke (1990–2)

Kenneth Clarke was from Nottinghamshire and at the time of writing is still a member of the government, presently serving as Lord Chancellor – to which post he was appointed in 2010. He was educated predominantly in the private sector, although he did attend a state primary school for a brief period. He won a scholarship to an independent school in Nottingham and then went to Cambridge to study law. Here he joined the Cambridge University Conservative Association and met fellow students who would later become colleagues in government. He has always been known as a career politician and was first elected to Parliament for Rushcliffe in 1970. He was appointed to Margaret Thatcher's Cabinet in 1985 and served as Health Secretary, Education Secretary and Home Secretary.

He was not keen to take over Education from John MacGregor in 1990. He had little enthusiasm for the idea of imposing a 'free market' ideology in either 'education' or 'health' (McSmith, 1994) and for this reason was regarded with some suspicion by Margaret Thatcher. However, she felt that someone with his presentational skills and pugilistic attitude was needed to push through the reforms in education and have them presented in an acceptable form to the country. Having agreed with Thatcher that he would not be required to bring in vouchers for education (Balen, 1994) he took charge of the Education Department in November 1990.

Within weeks Thatcher had been replaced by John Major, who felt that he could rely upon Kenneth Clarke's experience to make the DES more effective. In a speech prior to the 1992 election John Major said that 'education was the service most seriously in need of change' (Major, 1999: 249) and that Kenneth Clarke was the right man to make it happen.

John Major's ideas for improving education were set out in the Conservative manifesto for the 1992 election. They included the setting up of an inspectorate independent of the education establishment and the publication of school results, measures with which Kenneth Clarke broadly agreed (Balen, 1994).

However, after the election victory of 1992 Kenneth Clarke was appointed to the Home Office and his position at the DES was taken by John Patten whose period in office will be dealt with at the start of Chapter 6.

Policy development

The basis of most aspects of policy development during the period 1988–92 was the ERA of 1988 which facilitated the inclusion in education policy of those elements of competition and privatisation which were central to a 'free market' philosophy. The major concern of this book is an analysis of education policy, which, by the time it emanates from the DES, has normally been considered in detail by the Education Secretary, ministers in Cabinet and Parliament. Putting that policy into practice is the job of the schools and colleges and/or LEAs. Consequently, although there is some discussion below of the impact of the Act on practice in schools and colleges the fine detail of, for example, the National Curriculum is not set out here in its entirety.

The Education Reform Act 1988

The main sections of the ERA were concerned with

- local management of schools (LMS);
- the constitution of the governing bodies of schools;
- city technology colleges (CTCs);
- grant-maintained schools (GMSs);
- a National Curriculum;
- religious education and worship in schools;

- the testing of pupils and the publication of results;
- inspection of schools.

As discussed earlier the Act had been formulated over a considerable period of time. It has been seen how the policy of allowing schools to manage their own budgets (LMS) along with per capita funding and the reduction of the power of LEAs was seen by government as giving parents increased choice of types of school to which they could send their children. When John MacGregor became Education Secretary in 1989 he had already experienced LMS in his South Norfolk constituency and fully supported the idea. He said in interview in 2010 that it was the aspect of the ERA that he found easiest to take forward because of this positive experience. He had also worked with competent school governors who were business oriented so he was determined to push forward initiatives to encourage governors from industry and commerce to become involved in education. The government consequently encouraged increasing numbers of parents and business people onto school governing bodies to actually take a significant part in running schools – something Kenneth Baker underlined when interviewed in 2010. Governors were given the power to ballot parents about opting out of LEA control so that schools could become grant-maintained and compete for pupils.

Kenneth Baker was concerned that some of his fellow Conservatives, as well as civil servants at the DES, LEAs and the teaching unions would be sceptical about whether it was possible to bring about the revolutionary changes advocated in the ERA. He felt at the time and reiterated in an interview in 2010 that he needed to gain the support of ministerial colleagues by getting something up and running which incorporated the essence of reforms. People would then see the reforms in operation, understand their significance and realise that he meant business (Baker, 1993). John MacGregor noted when interviewed in 2010 that he was one of those who had supported Kenneth Baker's legislation before it became his job to put it into practice. He felt that some of the unions were hindering educational progress and that there was a good deal of misinformation in the media. His own education had led him to respect good teachers and he had wanted to reassure them of his support while they were trying to implement the policy.

Kenneth Baker put forward CTCs as the first element of his reform programme because they incorporated the notion of parental choice, per capita funding, LMS and the separation of schools from LEAs. Starting from a small number he felt that the project would demonstrate the advantages of his policies.

City technology colleges

During an interview in 2010 Kenneth Baker continued to be enthusiastic about a technologically orientated curriculum which attracts the interest of employers and industrialists and enables them to 'enter the secret garden' of education (Baker, 1993: 177). To this end he introduced what came to be known as CTCs, which he insisted must be outside the control of LEAs. He wanted industrialists and employers to partly fund the schools and be involved as governors in their management. He hoped that the first examples would be sited in redundant school buildings in or near the deprived areas of Conservative LEAs. Once the concept had been seen to work he expected it to be embraced across the whole country. He records that he looked forward to a return to the Victorian ideal of endowments by wealthy industrialists which would enhance life in the great cities. He wanted the CTCs to provide adult education, leisure and recreation facilities and training for the local population after school hours – thus helping local communities to deal with the problems created by youngsters in inner cities (Baker, 1993).

The plan initially was for between 12 and 20 such institutions where the school would be free to negotiate the salaries of the staff and select pupils of mixed ability based on parental commitment to education and the child's suitability to cope with a technologically based curriculum. It was Kenneth Baker's intention that these inner-city schools should not be for the children of middle-class parents and not be 'fee paying'. Some of his colleagues, however, insisted that some of the CTCs be sited in the more affluent suburbs and Margaret Thatcher insisted that the possibility of them becoming 'fee paying' must not be excluded (Baker, 1993).

The idea of CTCs first appeared in the Conservative manifesto for the 1987 election and the first to come into being was sited in the northern region of Solihull, an area of 'deprivation' in an otherwise prosperous LEA. The new college was able to take children from nearby areas of Birmingham.

For each CTC local business people were approached for an initial fund of one million pounds. They were expected to maintain their involvement for at least seven years. By 1993 15 such schools had been set up.

John MacGregor and Kenneth Clarke were enthusiastic supporters of the theory behind CTCs, although the latter felt that some in the government were sceptical (Ribbins and Sherratt, 1997). Interestingly Michael Gove, Education Secretary in 2011, referred to CTCs in an interview conducted for this book in 2011 (see Chapter 10).

John MacGregor observed in 2010 that he had wanted to keep the CTC initiative going although it was becoming more difficult to get new sponsors after the initial flush. In addition he noted how keen he was to support GMS but it was important to reassure teachers and gain their confidence if this and other initiatives were to succeed.

Grant-maintained schools

When Kenneth Baker took over at the DES in 1986 he found that there were too many school places for the number of children. Schools had been built to cope with the 'baby boom' of the 1960s and 1970s but the decline in the birth rate had led to a surplus of school places causing a flood of applications from LEAs to close schools. Many were small village schools which offered a good education but which were very uneconomic to staff and maintain. In 1987 Kenneth Baker usually recommended closure but soon came to think that he had been mistaken and withdrew the advice (Baker, 1993). Apart from his political views with regard to LEAs (discussed in Chapter 4) the issue of how to preserve 'good' schools was another reason for trying to give schools the opportunity to opt out of LEA control. He was pleased to find the first application for GMS status was received shortly after the ERA passed through Parliament in 1988 and notes in *The Turbulent Years* (Baker, 1993) that the target for 1994 was for 1,500 GMSs.

Margaret Thatcher was enthusiastic about having a wide range of schools available to parents. She envisaged 'opting out' as a means of establishing GMSs and CTCs alongside the private sector. This would provide a means by which 'pupils like me would be able to gain a good education whilst remaining within the public sector' (Thatcher, 1993: 578). She felt that some process of selection would lead to competition and specialisation in schools. Children from poorer backgrounds would have as much chance to develop their talents as did children in the private sector. She initiated a Grant-Maintained Schools Trust to offer advice to schools on the opportunities the new status provided. A Grant-Maintained Schools Foundation and a Grant-Maintained Schools Advisory Committee also came into being at a later stage to give assistance to GMSs, partly at least because successive ministers felt that initially the DES was against the project (Baker, 1993). John MacGregor recalled when interviewed in 2010 that his own support for GMS was strengthened by his attendance at a conference of grant-maintained school heads and chairs of governors in Leicester at which their experiences were shared with other interested parties. He was encouraged by Margaret Thatcher to extend GMS provision to primary schools at the Conservative Party Conference in 1990. Later John Major supported attempts to increase the numbers of GMSs and was pleased that the number reached a thousand by 1997 (Major, 1999). Perhaps not surprisingly the majority were schools in the Home Counties and rural England and were mainly in Conservative LEAs (McSmith, 1994).

When the Labour Party were in government after 1997 grant-maintained schools became either 'foundation' or 'community schools' as will be discussed in Section 3 of this book.

One of the outcomes of the initiative to set up GMSs which managed themselves was the need for more focused training for head teachers, aspiring head teachers and other teaching staff in leadership roles. Management issues now included responsibility to handle school budgets and manage large and small organisations without being able to rely on the experience of LEA personnel. Consequently, since the late 1980s professional qualifications for head teachers have been developed. In an interview in 1996 Gillian Shephard, who was Education Secretary at that time, considered the introduction of the qualification as one of her most important achievements (Ribbins and Sherratt, 1997).

There now exists a National College for Leadership of Schools, national standards for head teachers and a mandatory qualification for first-time head teachers.

A National Curriculum

A core curriculum to be followed by all pupils in UK maintained schools was probably the element of the ERA which had been most frequently considered by previous Education Secretaries. Suggestions of a core curriculum had been made in Jim Callaghan's Labour government in the 1960s. Shirley Williams in an interview in 2010 remarked that she had been in favour of a core curriculum with perhaps 50 per cent dictated by central government. Aspects of the curriculum in schools had been one of Margaret Thatcher and Keith Joseph's concerns (Thatcher, 1993 and Halcrow, 1989). Indeed Thatcher came to see the National Curriculum as the 'most important centralising measure' (Thatcher, 1993: 593). Kenneth Baker agreed and set out five objectives for the curriculum (Baker, 1993):

- to set a standard of knowledge;
- to give teachers precise objectives;
- to provide parents with precise information;
- to ensure continuity;
- to improve results.

Prior to the involvement of politicians in deciding curriculum content teachers and aspiring teachers were expected as part of their professional duty to be familiar with the philosophical and practical issues surrounding curriculum content. The writings of philosophers such as Hirst and Peters (1970) dealing with curriculum development were a standard part of teacher training in the 1970s. *Better Schools* gave an indication that the government was to take the lead in 'pursuing broad agreement on the objectives of the curriculum' (DES, 1985: para. 302). It conceded, however, that success depended on the cooperation and support of all partners in education and of the *customers* of the schools (my italics).

Interestingly, when politicians embarked upon determining what ought to be in the curriculum they became immersed in the same kind of philosophical arguments with which the teaching profession had always grappled.

Kenneth Baker considered that a National Curriculum was the key to raising standards in schools, but whereas Keith Joseph had argued for a National Curriculum by consent, Kenneth Baker imposed a curriculum. However, he had to have the approval of both Houses of Parliament and the National Curriculum Council (NCC), an organisation set up within the ERA to oversee the curriculum. The NCC was required to consult teachers and make necessary recommendations.

The 1988 National Curriculum for children of compulsory school ages (aged 5 to 16) was divided into Key Stages – 1 (5–7), 2 (8–11), 3 (12–14) and 4 (15–16). It was to consist of:

- **Core subjects** – English, Mathematics, Science and, in Welsh-speaking schools, Welsh.
- **Foundation subjects** – History, Geography, Technology, Music, Art and Physical Education, plus a modern foreign language for older pupils and Welsh in non-Welsh-speaking schools in Wales.
- **Provision for** – Religious Education and worship in schools.

In relation to the Core and Foundation subjects it had to specify:

- knowledge, skills and understanding with regard to pupils of different abilities (attainment targets);
- matters, skills and processes which were required to be taught (programmes of study);
- assessment arrangements (see later).

The inclusion of Welsh as a Core or Foundation subject in the National Curriculum for schools in Wales gave status to a language which had been taught in some Welsh schools since 1947. In 1990 it became a compulsory subject for all children at Key Stages 1, 2 and 3 and similarly at Key Stage 4 in 1999. The teachers were supported nationally in their Welsh language teaching and by the (Qualifications, Curriculum and Assessment Authority for Wales) (ACCAC) set up to oversee statutory testing and assessment and the provision of resources.

The National Curriculum was to be developed with a great deal of detail in order to stop 'inadequate or lazy teachers' missing out sections

(Baker, 1993: 198), although Kenneth Baker remarked during interview in 2010 that he did not feel that politicians ought to tell teachers how to teach. In the 1980s he had assumed that in terms of curriculum content, whereas some subjects would be contentious, others such as maths would be relatively straightforward (Baker, 1993). Special working groups were set up to determine what ought to be in the curriculum of each subject at each Key Stage. The working groups were selected by Kenneth Baker and the officials in the DES but politicians with little experience of schools beyond their own education had strong opinions about such matters and were not slow to make themselves heard.

Baker found that no subject was beyond argument but the debate about the English curriculum became a the most significant area of disagreement. In his view children ought to be able to read by the age of seven and the English curriculum ought to contain a good deal of spelling, grammar and punctuation (Baker, 1993: 191).

He appointed a committee under the guidance of Sir John Kingman, a leading scientist, to review the teaching of English. The resulting Kingman Report (DES, 1988), however, disappointed Baker in that it contained too much 'fashionable nonsense' (Baker, 1993: 191). A further working group was set up under the guidance of Professor Brian Cox to draw up an English curriculum. Brian Cox was an author of 'right-wing Black Papers' (Baker, 1993: 201) but, as he underlined in interview in 2010, Baker was disappointed that the report did not meet his requirements with regard to the rigorous teaching of grammar.

In contrast to her Education Secretary Margaret Thatcher wanted 'a basic syllabus for English and Maths and Science with simple tests "to show what children know"' (Thatcher, 1993: 593). She was annoyed that her 'philosophy' was not followed by those whom her Education Secretary had entrusted to write the National Curriculum. The English and Maths proposals she found unpalatable but the History proposals were her main area of concern. Although she admits to not being a historian she thought that it was uncontroversial that children ought to learn history as a separate subject and learn 'initially tedious' lists of dates and events about British history (Thatcher, 1993: 595). To an extent Baker agreed. A historian himself he said in an interview in 2010 that he had experience of visiting a primary school where aspects such as 'empathy' were being taught. Children were asked to consider how they would feel about the coming of the plague to a thirteenth-century village in France. Since he felt that they knew little about the culture, customs and social structure of such a place it was unlikely, in his view, that they could be expected to gain much learning from the exercise. John MacGregor pointed out during an interview in 2010 that he had studied History with Economics at university. There had been some differences of opinion with Margaret Thatcher about the History Working

Group recommendations in relation to History in the National Curriculum. That apart, he was allowed to get on with introducing the rest of the curriculum. He was concerned that the curriculum was too detailed and proscriptive, and did not sufficiently take into account the 'skills, ability, innovation and inspiration' of teachers but that the stridency of the debate and the Prime Minister's alienation from the National Union of Teachers (NUT) made it difficult to get the support of teachers.

The newly established National Curriculum Council provoked some opposition from teachers for endorsing such a detailed curriculum. The Prime Minister also felt that the whole thing was too detailed (Thatcher, 1993). By 2010 Kenneth Baker himself had come to believe that it ought not to have had a Key Stage 4.

The Prime Minister (Thatcher, 1993) implied that in its construction Kenneth Baker had not been strong enough in resisting the 'vested interests' in education. When John MacGregor was appointed to the DES she expected him to follow her demands more closely, but soon felt that he was not sufficiently strong in following her convictions. MacGregor says (Ribbins and Sherratt, 1997) that he was concerned about the prescriptive nature of the proposals being put forward and wanted to talk to teachers and hear their views about what was required in the curriculum and how to assess progress. When he was moved Kenneth Clarke, his successor, also felt that there was too much detail and prescription in the proposals.

Some commentators, e.g. Ball (2010), have suggested that the underlying themes of the National Curriculum were to firmly establish traditional subjects and to ensure that aspects of British culture were protected against relativism and multiculturalism.

Previously teachers were suspected of using the curriculum for the purpose of waging a 'class war' (Thatcher, 1993). As an example of this, in the interview for this book Kenneth Baker remarked that prior to becoming Education Secretary he had visited a primary school where children were being introduced to the idea of 'conflict' by playing a board game produced by the class teacher. One group was represented by counters with pictures of 'workers' in cloth caps while the other showed 'bosses' in top hats.

When John Major became Prime Minister in 1990 he wanted the National Curriculum to be updated for he believed that in the intervening two years it had been 'hijacked by devotees of progressive learning' (Major, 1999: 394).

Religious Education and worship in schools

The ERA made provision for a broadly Christian-based religious education separate from the Core and Foundation subjects. Kenneth Baker noted that he considered that the teaching of Religious Education (RE) in schools and the act of daily worship had 'fallen by the wayside' (Baker, 1993: 207). He wanted to make it a duty of head teachers, LEAs and governors to provide religious education, a wish that was accepted in principle by most interested parties. The churches, however, wanted to ensure that they were responsible for the syllabi that were to be taught and not have the curriculum content left to a secular body.

Consequently RE became part of a basic curriculum, with each day beginning with a 'hymn and a prayer' (Baker, 1993: 208). Local Standing Advisory Councils for Religious Education (SACREs) were to be established and each LEA was required to set out a new syllabus for its schools. The bodies responsible would consist of members of Christian denominations but not humanists.

Detailed preparation of how exactly RE was to become an element of the legislation was problematic. Conservative colleagues of Kenneth Baker in the House of Lords negotiated with Anglicans, Catholics, Jews, Methodists, Muslims and Sikhs to reach an agreement which was also acceptable to the Prime Minister. In the meantime teachers and teacher unions had misgivings – not least because some schools had virtually no children on roll whose religion was Christianity.

The ERA thus continued the previous practice of every school day beginning with an act of collective worship – an assembly. It had to be broadly Christian in nature and reflect the traditions of Christian belief but could also make allowance for other faiths.

Eventually Kenneth Baker was content that the provision for RE in the National Curriculum had strengthened the subject in schools.

Testing and assessment

The ERA made provision for a Schools Examination and Assessment Council (SEAC) to oversee testing arrangements in schools which would allow for the publication of results and subsequent drawing up of league tables of schools, a factor seen to be essential as a way of giving parents information about schools and hence widening their choice. Kenneth Baker wanted attainment targets at varying ages for children between five and 16, with regular diagnostic 'pencil and paper' testing.

To begin with a Task Group on Assessment and Testing (TGAT) was put in place to provide the initial specifications for testing pupils as they reached the conclusion of each Key Stage.

Recommendations were made to include Standard Assessment Tasks (SATs) and Teacher Assessments (TAs) though eventually the TAs ceased to be used. League tables of schools and LEAs were eventually developed under John Major's government in 1992 using the results of testing to give as much information to parents as possible.

Ball (2010) sees the assessment procedure as an attempt to obtain objective information about the progress of the children, separate from the perceptions of teachers.

Inspection

Prior to the ERA of 1988 the inspection of schools had been carried out by Her Majesty's Inspectorate (HMI) and by local authority advisers employed by the LEA. HMI was an organisation which had two branches, one working with primary schools and the other with secondary and technical schools and in adult education. General inspectors were allocated a group of schools in a region, but from time to time full inspections were carried out by teams of inspectors. They reported to Ministers of State and when required gave professional advice. The main task of local advisers was to advise head teachers and school governors and also to report on the first year of teaching of NQTs (Newly Qualified Teachers) to confirm that they had made enough progress to enter the profession. In the 1970s the DES began to take a more substantive role in planning the school inspection programme of HMI.

HM inspectors were mainly recruited from the 'education establishment' – LEAs, university departments of education, experienced school teachers, etc. LEA advisers tended to be personnel with a similar background. Neither body had authority over schools or teachers but simply gave advice.

The ERA provided for the setting up of a body which would enable a revised inspection system of schools and for the publication of reports on schools. Inspection teams would have to have a 'lay inspector' who was not part of the education establishment.

When John Major advocated the setting up of an independent inspectorate in 1992 he was concerned because the previous system of inspection had been carried out from within the education establishment and there was little accountability. Under his 'Citizen's Charter' he determined to institute a fully independent inspectorate so that eventually organisations would be able to tender for contracts to inspect schools (Major, 1999).

Kenneth Clarke, his Education Secretary, supported these ideals. He initiated the appraisal of teachers and stopped the inspection of schools by HMI and LEAs. HMI was to become a licensing agency but not carry out inspections. He wanted schools to be able to choose and 'buy' in inspections on a regular basis from licensed inspection providers. The Education (Schools) Bill which enabled this system came to Parliament as a result of an internal review of the inspectorate carried out at the behest of Kenneth Clarke, but his plans to allow school governors to choose and then buy in particular inspection teams were thrown out by the House of Lords just prior to the election of 1992 (Balen, 1994). Eventually, however, the Office of Standards in Education (Ofsted) was created in 1992 although it was 1994 before it achieved prominence under the guidance of Chris Woodhead and Professor Stewart Sutherland. The role and impact of Ofsted will be further discussed in Chapter 6.

Conclusion

The years covered in this chapter saw the continuation of policies which were designed to raise standards in schools by the consolidation of measures which allowed competition to take place in schools and colleges. Increased standards would enable the country to compete better economically in an increasingly competitive world. Parliament passed legislation which had a profound effect on education and hence on the lives of a generation of children in schools and of students in colleges, and on their teachers. In particular the formalisation of the National Curriculum and the attempts to enable schools and colleges to operate independently of LEAs were radically different from previous processes in the development of education.

The legislation enabled an education policy to be established which encouraged a 'free market' ideology and brought privatisation and competition to education.

Further reading

Baker, K. (1993) *Those Turbulent Years: My Life in Politics*. London: Faber & Faber.

Crawford, K. (2000) 'The political construction of the "whole curriculum"', *British Educational Research Journal*, 26 (5): 615–30.

DES (1987) *The National Curriculum 5–16: A Consultation Document*. London: HMSO.

Woods, R.G. (ed.) (1972) *Education and Its Disciplines*. London: London University Press.

CHAPTER SIX

1992–1997: EDUCATION PRACTICE UNDER THE MICROSCOPE

- Restructuring the National Curriculum
- Inspection of schools
- Incorporation of FE colleges
- Publication of results

Introduction

The period of government between 1992 and 1997 was the final stage of a Conservative-led government which had lasted since the first election victory of Margaret Thatcher in 1979. After the election of 1992, however, the government majority was only 21 seats.

In the field of education these final five years saw further development of the principles of the Education Reform Act and their implementation and extension. During the period the government became increasingly unpopular and in 1997 there was a 'landslide' victory for the Labour Party, although as will be seen in Section 3 many of the changes in education which had been enacted by the Conservative government were continued or extended, a point underlined in an interview with Michael Gove, Education Secretary, in 2011.

The main themes of this chapter centre around a consolidation of parts of the Education Reform Act such as grant-maintained schools and a simplification of other parts such as the National Curriculum. There was government backing for moves which enabled further 'privatisation' of schools and further education (FE) colleges and increasing recognition of the importance of aspects of vocational education in supporting the economy of the country. Accountability through inspection and the publication of results was emphasised by the government as a means of trying to raise standards in schools and colleges.

Context

Political

Prior to the election of 1992 John Major had already been in power for two years having taken over the reins of government from Margaret Thatcher in 1990. At that time he had inherited a large majority and significant problems – problems which had led to the demise of Thatcher at the hands of her own Cabinet colleagues. The economy was in a parlous state and the Conservative Party in particular had been riven by disputes about Britain's position in Europe. In addition there had been an outcry over the poll tax – a policy dear to Thatcher's heart.

Although most commentators considered that the poll tax issue had receded and John Major himself felt that the European issue was largely settled, later events demonstrated that none of these had really been resolved by the time of the election (Major, 1999). It is interesting in the context of this book to note that although in his autobiography John Major deals at length with preparations for that election, including the preparation of the manifesto, education hardly featured in his thoughts at the time (Major, 1999). When the election was won in 1992 Kenneth Clarke, who had been Secretary for Education, was moved to take over the Home Office and replaced by John Patten. The Prime Minister recorded that 'Kenneth Clarke was a bruiser' who could be 'totally bloody minded' and as such was ideal for the reforms in the justice system which were felt to be necessary (Major, 1999: 308).

Other commentators, for example Malcolm Balen, editor of *The Daily Telegraph*, felt variously that he was put there by John Major either because he was seen as a threat to the leader (historically the Home Office had been a 'graveyard' for politicians who had aspirations to become Party leaders) or because as 'local difficulties' mounted the government was going to need someone of his political and legal skills in a high position (Balen, 1994).

These 'local difficulties' were manifold – and were exacerbated by the fact that the government had only a small majority in the House of Commons. As Gillian Shephard, who became Education Secretary after John Patten, remarked, 'a strong Parliamentary position is what matters in the exercise of power' (Shephard, 2000: 28).

After the election of 1992 the government had to continue to cope with difficult situations. Far from improving, things seemed to go from bad to worse over the next few years. For example:

- John Major called for improved standards of conduct from those in public life just as various allegations of government 'sleaze' dogged the Party.
- There were well substantiated 'leaks' in the press suggesting that the government had made contact with 'terrorist factions' in Ireland, although John Major publicly denied any such contacts.
- Revelations about miscarriages of justice were rife and police morale plummeted just as 'value for money' measures were introduced to the police force.
- The economy went into a further downward spiral with an increase in the rate of VAT on gas and electricity. There was an increase in unemployment.
- On 18 September 1992 (Black Wednesday) the Chancellor Norman Lamont led a humiliating exit from the European Exchange Rate Mechanism in order to assist economic recovery.
- The anti-European wing of the Tory Party was heartened by internal divisions within Europe but dismayed as John Major continued European negotiations.
- In education John Patten was removed from his position as Education Secretary having been worn down by struggles with the education establishment (Major, 1999). In 1994 he was replaced by Gillian Shephard (who was interviewed in 2011 for this book).

Each of these events meant that effective government became more difficult, a situation made more extreme by the deaths of eight Tory MPs, the withdrawal of the 'whip' from eight more and the defection of others to opposition parties.

With the loss of his majority, confidence in John Major waned within his own Party to such a degree that he called a Tory Party leadership election in 1995. The leadership campaign within the Party and the discussion across the country inevitably led to disruption of the process of government and a loss of focus on other issues. For example, it was during this period that Gillian Shephard was able to announce that trouble with the National Union of Teachers had been averted, a fact which was hardly noticed except in educational circles (Shephard, 2000).

Although John Major won the Party leadership election there was a continuing feeling across the country that the government was weakening.

As the unpopular government continued throughout 1995 and 1996 Gillian Shephard, who had replaced John Patten as Education Secretary, considered that education would be an important factor in the approaching election. She noted that John Major was enthusiastic about the Conservative reforms of education and supported a proposal to increase the education budget which enabled them to be put into practice (Ribbins and Sherratt, 1997). The Cabinet, however, voted against continuing to give extra money to education because of straitened economic circumstances (Shephard, 2000).

Subsequent cuts in education spending led to protests and demonstrations across the country as the election loomed. Although John Major later regretted this decision to cut the education budget it was just another factor which contributed to the massive election defeat of 1997.

Schools and colleges

When John Major was elected in 1992 the education service was still in the throes of dealing with the implementation of the Education Reform Act (ERA), including the National Curriculum. Continuity of reform had not been helped by a succession of Secretaries of Education, all of whom supported the ideas behind reform but each of whom had their own ideas about how the Act could be added to or improved. This led to a constant stream of additional Parliamentary legislation, White Papers and reports which for schools, teachers, parents and children meant disturbance and uncertainty in education. This uncertainty was exacerbated during John Major's government by the publication of results and league tables of schools and LEAs and the increase in their use by, for example, estate agents when encouraging middle-class parents to move house in order to place their children in the 'best' schools.

John Patten, who became Education Secretary in 1992 in succession to the rumbustious Kenneth Clarke, came into the post apparently unaware of the potential problems awaiting him in the schools. 'There were no problems', he said in 1994 (Ribbins and Sherratt, 1997: 182) – a view that proved to be over-optimistic. Problems did arise, some of which seem to have been exacerbated by Patten himself.

He did not gain the confidence of the teaching profession, particularly since he refused to talk to the teaching unions (Shephard, 2000) and made derogatory remarks about the professional work of Tim Brighouse, the well respected Chief Education Officer of Birmingham LEA. Everyone who knew Tim Brighouse or who had worked with him in schools or LEAs had the highest regard for his professionalism, his care for children and his keen insight into schools. After much damaging publicity and a court case Patten had to pay damages as a result of his ill-judged comments. David Hart, president of the National Association of Head Teachers, later remarked that John Patten had been an 'appalling' Secretary for Education (Smithers, 2005).

Furthermore, during John Patten's period in office there was a furore among teachers about the excessive amount of paperwork associated with the National Curriculum and in particular about testing (Ribbins and Sherratt, 1997). The fuss included a teacher boycott of the testing process in 1993 which led to the appointment by John Patten of Ron Dearing, a senior civil servant, to lead the School Curriculum and Assessment Authority (SCAA). The SCAA replaced the National Curriculum Council and the Schools Examinations and Assessment Council in the Education Act of 1993.

The SCAA reported on the National Curriculum and associated issues in 1993. As a result of the report many aspects of the National Curriculum were restructured and simplified in a way which pleased the Prime Minister (Major, 1999) and mollified the teaching profession. For a time further trouble in the schools was avoided.

The 1993 Act was a significant piece of legislation which followed on from the ERA of 1988. It consisted of over three hundred sections plus large numbers of amendments. Simon Jenkins (2010) reflected that with hindsight the 1993 Act ought to be seen as the result of an obsession to increase the number of GM Schools even though there was a noticeable lack of interest amongst the 24,000 state schools in the UK.

This enormous piece of legislation:

* created a framework to enable support to be given to schools designated as 'failing' by the Office for Standards in Education (Ofsted);
* set up the Schools Curriculum and Assessment Authority (SCAA);
* helped clarify legal issues with regard to Special Educational Needs;
* ruled on the exclusion of pupils from schools;
* set out a framework within which school places could be planned;
* set up a Funding Agency to assist GM schools.

Although the number of GM schools had increased only slowly it had become obvious, as Gillian Shephard reiterated in an interview in 2011, that as the 'safety blanket' of LEA support was withdrawn, some other organisation was needed to help such schools with administrative and financial issues where required. In 1993 the Funding Agency for Schools was set up to carry out just such a function. Shephard, however, was clear that this was not to be seen as a substitute LEA (Shephard, 2000) and John Patten saw it as a 'light touch' body for carrying out the administrative functions of GM schools and giving advice when required (Ribbins and Sherratt, 1997).

By 1993 evidence was accumulating that as a result of allowing schools to opt out and exercise a form of selective intake some schools were avoiding any involvement in the local community and leaving other schools to cater for the least able and the least well off. Nevertheless the Education Secretary announced in 1994 that he would allow GM schools to move towards selecting pupils by ability – a move that pre-dated a later Conservative pledge to extend selection if they were re-elected in 1997.

The Office for Standards in Education (Ofsted) was formed in 1992 within the Education (Schools) Act. Before then individual schools would be inspected very rarely, but now all schools were inspected in a four-year cycle and the results were put on public display. The Ofsted inspection teams were put together by private companies and had to include one person who had no experience in education. This was a contributory factor to the opposition the inspection teams received in many schools and in the world of education in general. When inspection reports were used to lambast schools which were perceived as 'failing' this opposition intensified, particularly when in 1994 the Education Secretary proposed the formation of new mechanisms to 'turn around' schools that had 'failed' an Ofsted inspection (Ribbins and Sherratt, 1997). John Major, however, was pleased with the idea of 'hit squads' (Major, 1999: 398) to take over 'failing schools'.

Ofsted became very controversial in 1994 when Sir Chris Woodhead (knighted in 2011) was appointed HM Chief Inspector of Schools. He held the post under both Labour and Conservative governments but in later years was accused of using inaccurate and misleading information to exaggerate problems within the education sector and denigrate the competence of large numbers of teachers (Davies, 2000).

Further Education colleges were 'freed' from the influence of LEAs by the Further and Higher Education Act 1992 which allowed them to become 'businesses', compete for students and become involved in commercial activities. Those working in and alongside further education colleges at this time (for example the authors of this book) can readily recall how the colleges developed a culture which became entrepreneurial in responding to local business needs and expanded their areas of activity. Many began to explore the possibility of attracting foreign students and used 'franchising' procedures to teach degree-level work in conjunction with local universities. For example, in 1992 in Birmingham the University of Central England (UCE), later called Birmingham City University (BCU), set up what was termed the 'Ninth Faculty' under the direction of the Faculty of Education. Local further education colleges and sixth-form colleges were invited to join the project. The intention was to enable colleges to expand quickly by providing pathways for under-represented groups in the city to access higher education. The status of the relationship was defined by a memo of cooperation in which the university had responsibility for quality assurance and the colleges were accredited to provide most of the teaching and teaching facilities. The scheme proved to be extremely popular, not just with under-represented groups who had not previously had access to HE but also with businesses and public services which took advantage of the opportunities for staff training. Consequently, in the example above, there were programmes for employees from Land Rover, Rover, the local health service and local charities.

In the national context changes in the funding mechanism also allowed some rather questionable practices to occur in the 'education marketplace'. In general, however, commercial freedom for colleges brought great benefits to many people who had previously not been able to enter further or higher education.

Gillian Shephard replaced John Patten in 1994. Speaking in an interview in 2011 she emphasised the importance of the quality of teachers and her conviction that teachers and head teachers deserved support. She was keen to become involved with teachers and to be seen to be supporting their work in schools. She is on record as saying that she believed, along with John Major, that education was quite properly the responsibility of the state. She felt that John Major was attempting to move the Party back to towards 'compassionate Conservatism' but was hamstrung by the strident rhetoric of previous administrations which had passed on a belief that everything in the public domain had to be 'cut' (Shephard, 2000: 49). A policy of privatisation did not mean that the government or the Education Secretary did not see some value in the work of public servants in general and teachers in particular.

To make some attempt to demonstrate this Gillian Shephard reversed John Patten's position and made contact with the teachers' unions as soon as she took office. Thus she did what John Patten had been afraid of and risked the ire of the right wing of the Party. In her view it was simply 'good managerial sense' (Shephard, 2000: 109). The relationship between the department and the teaching force was improved and constructive discussions proceeded. The National Union of Teachers (NUT) called off a threatened boycott of testing in schools and Shephard resolved to attend the annual Easter conferences held by the teachers' unions. As a result she was castigated in the right-wing press as being too close to the teachers (Shephard, 2000).

Similar problems of public perception were experienced in 1996 when a Review of Qualifications for 16–19 year olds was carried out for the department by a committee led by Sir Ron Dearing. He had been asked by the Education Secretary to advise on how academic and vocational routes of study might be brought together in order to increase student participation in further education as a preparation for work. The intention was to increase the competitive position of the country and ensure that value for money was achieved within the qualifications structure. Furthermore, Sir Ron Dearing was asked to develop a National Vocational Qualification (NVQ) and a General National Vocational Qualification (GNVQ). His task was helped by the 1995 merger of the Department for Education and the Department for Employment into the DfEE but complicated by a directive from Gillian

Shephard that the Advanced General Certificate of Education (GCE at A level) must not be discarded and that the standard of the traditional A level must not be 'watered down'.

The report produced a series of recommendations which were criticised in schools and colleges as not being sufficiently wide-ranging (Cummings, 2000) and by the right-wing press as interfering with the status of A levels and being too radical.

Recommendations (largely ignored) included the notion of bringing NVQ, GNVQ, GCSE and A level into a common framework, of having 'applied' A levels, Advanced Certificates and Diplomas, and giving students the opportunity to begin degree-level studies while still at school.

One recommendation that was accepted led to the merging of the roles of the Schools Curriculum and Assessment Authority (SCAA) and the National Council for Vocational Qualifications (NCVQ) but academic and vocational education remained separate and A level examinations were not altered.

The following section will consider the roles of the Education Secretaries who were in post between 1992 and 1997. It includes reference to their own thoughts about specific policies which they had tried to develop, the problems they encountered and what they felt were their achievements while in office.

The Education Secretaries and the development of policy

Two education secretaries were in post during the government of John Major between 1992 and 1997 – John Patten in the first two years and Gillian Shephard from 1994 until the election was lost in 1997.

John Patten (1992–4)

In 1992 Kenneth Clarke was replaced at the Department for Education by John Patten who was enthusiastic to become Education Secretary. He had experienced a predominantly private education in the rigorous environment of a Jesuit grammar school before taking a degree in geography at Cambridge and later teaching at Oxford. In an interview in 1994 (Ribbins and Sherratt, 1997) he proudly noted that while teaching he had seen the intake of students per year studying geography at his Oxford college double in size to ten. Several of these were from comprehensive schools. He saw himself as a strong Roman Catholic with 'old-fashioned' views about education. He thought that pupils had to be taught 'to work hard, to care and to be competitive' (Ribbins and Sherratt, 1997: 175).

He had entered Parliament with John Major in 1979 and was enthusiastic about the ideas of Keith Joseph whom he regarded as the man who had analysed the problems inherent in the education system and seen the way to solve them (Ribbins and Sherratt, 1997). John Patten strongly supported the notion that the economic future of the country depended upon having high education standards in schools and thus backed the ERA. He liked, in particular, the idea of GM schools, local management of schools and per capita funding (see Chapter 5) which enabled parents to have an increased choice of schools. He felt that there had been too little opportunity for businessmen, parents and employers to influence education. Rather than worrying about the total budget for education, the need was to ensure that money was spent wisely and that attention was paid to the disparity between education results in the UK and those of the country's economic competitors (Ribbins and Sherratt, 1997). Patten admired Kenneth Baker for the way in which he had driven through the National Curriculum and set high standards to which pupils and teachers could aspire.

However, although he was enthusiastic about the ERA, he was prepared to accept that there had been problems with the speed and implementation of educational reform and the amount of paperwork which had burdened the teaching profession. In his view, haste was exactly what had been required to push through reform in 1988, a comment that underlines those of McSmith (1994) and Kenneth Baker (interview 2010) who suggested that with a large Parliamentary majority contentious legislation could and should be driven through Parliament.

John Patten regarded the notion of introducing reform slowly or by means of 'pilots' with 'loathing' (Ribbins and Sherratt, 1997: 179). He was particularly proud to have initiated the publication of information about what was happening in schools. This was part of the Prime Minister's Citizen's Charter to enable scrutiny of what was happening in schools and elsewhere in the public sector. The Prime Minister believed that the publication of league tables ranking the results of schools and local authorities had the effect of making organisations work harder and thus improve standards (Major, 1999). Critics, however, felt that because of the publication of league tables, some schools began to refuse access to pupils with learning difficulties because such pupils would depress school results and lower their standing with parents (Gillard, 2011).

Patten was always concerned about the lack of achievement of the bottom 40 per cent of pupils, with illiteracy being as high in 1994 as it had been in 1982. He thought that what was needed was more students in higher education, better exam results and more students following vocational qualifications. There had been a preoccupation with 'low achievers, indifferent schools and disaffected pupils' which had resulted at least in part from the pre-1986 'laissez-faire' attitude of the DES and LEAs and even earlier from when Shirley Williams had been Education Secretary. She had 'watered down' the concern about standards expressed by Jim Callaghan the Labour Prime Minister in the 'Ruskin speech' of 1976 (Ribbins and Sherratt, 1997: 175).

Speaking with hindsight about the period of Conservative government from 1992 Patten emphasised the significance of two factors, first the move from an 'inputs' to an 'outputs' model and second the removal from LEAs of the obligation to submit plans to develop comprehensive schools (Ribbins and Sherratt, 1997). In spite of his experience with comprehensive school pupils at Oxford he did not feel that comprehensive schools were the way forward in the secondary sector. In the White Paper *Choice and Diversity: A New Framework for Schools* (DES, 1992) he supported the idea of increasing the range of types of schools in order to counter what he saw as a 'depressing drift towards uniformity' in schools (Ball, 2010: 122). Specialisation in schools, which had been part of Margaret Thatcher's vision (Thatcher, 1993), was very much on his agenda (Gillard, 2011). He saw a future in which schools would be specialists in technology, science, language, business and maths – and where vocational education was taken seriously. He wanted a range of qualifications to include GNVQ and NVQ to match the differing needs and aptitudes of different children. In his opinion the comprehensive system had put 'organisation before results' (Ribbins and Sherratt, 1997: 170) – whereas he wanted to drive up education standards.

Towards the end of his period in office Patten reflected on the significance of Ofsted which had pointed out the importance of teacher expectation in the achievement of pupils, and the role of schools in giving pupils the opportunity to achieve high standards (Ribbins and Sherratt, 1997). Ofsted had begun its work during Patten's period in office as part of his drive to improve standards. Wide use was made of the organisation's power to inspect schools and, later, LEAs.

The Prime Minister said that his contemporary John Patten had not been allowed to thrive in the Education Department because of 'a constant battle' with the old establishment within the Department and with teachers' unions (Major, 1999: 398). Certainly David Hart, president of the National Association of Head Teachers praised Kenneth Baker as having been a very competent Education Secretary but he was very derogatory about John Patten's time in office (Smithers, 2005). As has been seen John Patten refused to have any contact whatsoever with teachers' unions.

When summing up his feelings about the period in which he had been Secretary of Education John Patten said that he saw himself as having tried to restore power to the centre, wresting it back from LEAs and redistributing it to schools. He expected all schools to have grant-maintained status by 1997, a view which turned out to be wildly optimistic even though GM schools were allowed to borrow commercially and hence have even more control over their own destiny (Ribbins and Sherratt, 1997). He suggested that LEAs and even the office of Education Secretary could eventually disappear with

LEAs becoming part of 'all singing, all dancing' Social Services or Housing Departments (Ribbins and Sherratt, 1997: 192) as power moved entirely to the schools. He was pleased, he said, to have increased the education budget, the level of teachers pay and standards in schools (Ribbins and Sherratt, 1997).

Gillian Shephard (1994–7)

Gillian Shephard was appointed Education Secretary in 1994 by John Major. She was MP for her home locality of South West Norfolk and had a degree in modern languages. She worked briefly as a schoolteacher before serving as an Education Inspector in the Education Office of her local authority and also as Chair of the Education Committee. As she underlined in an interview in 2011, in this regard she was one of the few Education Secretaries with real experience in the 'front line' of education. Fascinated by local politics she had been a local councillor before being elected to Parliament in 1987. In her early days as a Conservative MP she was a strong supporter of Margaret Thatcher and served as a junior minister in her government. When Thatcher left office Shephard allied herself with John Major and was greatly respected by him for her firm and businesslike manner (Major, 1999). The respect was not entirely mutual for she said in interview in 2011 that it was Michael Heseltine, the Deputy Prime Minister, who had given her most support in Education. However, in her view John Major's period as Prime Minister saw the consolidation of Thatcherism, an increase in privatisation, a reduction in the welfare state and the development of a 'Citizen's Charter', all of which she saw as highly desirable. She saw these factors as driving forward the policy of enhancing the country's economic standing as a result of increased educational standards (Ribbins and Sherratt, 1997).

She held various offices in the Department of Social Security and the Treasury before being appointed as Secretary of State for Employment, Minister of Agriculture and then Education Secretary in 1994. She was pleased to take on the Education Department because of her background in education and because she saw the importance of education in improving standards, making the economy competitive and helping children and schools raise their expectations (Ribbins and Sherratt, 1997). She said in an interview in 2011 that she saw education as a way of transforming society. In this context she regarded nursery education and the rationalisation of vocational education as priorities, so that all children could have a good start to their school lives and that all could have an education suited to their capabilities.

Although not personally enthusiastic, under pressure from colleagues she tried to revive the idea of education vouchers for nursery education, a policy which was advocated by many Conservatives in spite of the fact that Keith Joseph, in Margaret Thatcher's era, had decided that vouchers were politically unacceptable (see Chapter 4). Gillian Shephard noted in the interview in 2011 that in spite of her reservations the scheme had created a 'market' but that in 1996 when she had wanted to introduce pilot schemes for the introduction of vouchers she was irritated that the department was not properly geared up to enable such a new initiative to happen. When the policy failed to gain momentum, it was perhaps somewhat ironic that the Prime Minister laid the blame for its demise at the door of the private sector which he thought had failed to see the opportunities it offered (Major, 1999).

As Education Secretary and when interviewed in 2011 Shephard was very enthusiastic about GM schools which she thought provided a 'marvellously good education', allowing significant interaction with their communities and enabling a freedom within which the entrepreneurial spirit in schools could emerge 'untrammelled by the pettiness of an LEA'. In 1996 she still felt that a majority of parents wanted selection and considered allowing GM schools to select a proportion of their intake (Ribbins and Sherratt, 1997). While serving in local government she had been horrified by the moves away from selection and towards comprehensive schools as supported by the Labour government. In an attempt to encourage them to become grant maintained such schools were given the facility to borrow money commercially as new financial rules were introduced in the Nursery Education and Grant Maintained Schools Act of 1996. This brought the 'privatisation' of schools a step closer.

According to Shephard (2000) John Patten's resignation in 1994 was triggered by his frustration that the department was not equipped to run 'education' from the centre. In spite of the rhetoric of Kenneth Baker and more latterly of Kenneth Clarke, she agreed with Patten and the Prime Minister that the power in education still resided with the civil servants and local education authorities who were keen to exercise it. In an interview in 2011 she said that except in relation to GM schools she had not been able to reduce that power significantly. As if to confirm this, although there was strong government enthusiasm for GM schools and continued attempts to get schools to opt out of LEA control, there was still surprise in government when Conservative councils opposed 'opting out'. 'Deplorable' said Major (1999: 398).

The Education Secretary's experience and respect for the efforts of local government officers and councillors meant that she had a much less antagonistic view of their work and value than some of her colleagues and predecessors as Education Secretary. She felt that although some LEAs had abused their power the attitude of people like Kenneth Clarke towards local authorities hindered sensible discussion about their role in local government. She had a job to understand (Shephard, 2000) how Clarke's antipathy for LEAs could be reconciled with his equally strong feeling against 'big government' and in this respect she was one of the few Conservatives of the period who perceived that moving power to the consumers was difficult to square with the government taking so much power to the centre.

In 1995 while Shephard was Education Secretary, the Department for Education merged with the Department for Employment to form one large department (DfEE), a measure which brought education, training, careers advice and the qualifications structure together into one department. This change was strongly advocated by Michael Heseltine the Deputy Prime Minister and was in accord with the Shephard's thinking since throughout her time in government she saw a need to bring business and education closer together. In this context she saw that it was necessary to change attitudes towards vocational education and hence supported the development of vocational qualifications. Under her guidance there were significant moves to link together the business community, schools, the careers service and vocational training.

When interviewed in 2011 she reckoned that one of her major achievements when in office was to bring 'peace and understanding' to education and to restore support to teachers. She had taken the Conservative agenda forward in education and considered that measures such as the reform of funding and the provision for local management of schools enabled schools to opt out of LEA control and helped GM schools to become a spur to other schools to improve themselves.

She saw the introduction of the qualification for head teachers as one of her most important achievements (Ribbins and Sherratt, 1997) since schools 'freed' from LEA control needed trained and qualified leaders. She strongly supported every aspect of the Education Reform Act and admired Kenneth Baker for having forced it through Parliament in 1988. She thought that the National Curriculum ought to have been in existence many years previously. In the course of the interview in 2011 she remarked that during her time in office she had taken the opportunity to bring attention back to teachers from the previous fixation with systems and structures.

After the election defeat of 1997 Shephard remained in Parliament and was made a life peer in 2005 as Baroness Shephard of Northwold.

Policy development

In his autobiography John Major sums up what he saw as his government's achievements in education during his period in office from 1992 to 1997. These centre around the consolidation of the policy of giving choice to parents and making information about schools readily available for scrutiny (Major, 1999).

Gillian Shephard and John Patten agreed with his sentiments about parental choice. Patten justified the change from earlier minimal state interference in the curriculum to almost total control by reference to the changes in society which meant that a more mobile workforce enabled people to work in different parts of the country and hence move their children from school to school. There needed to be common nationwide standards and common experience across schools. Shephard thought that central control of the curriculum was essential to ensure that all pupils were receiving the education they needed but she never explained why independent schools were not required to teach the National Curriculum while GM schools did not have exemption (Ribbins and Sherratt, 1997). Patten, speaking in 1994, was particularly proud of the fact that on his watch the publication of results had made people 'aware for the first time ever of what went on in our schools' (Ribbins and Sherratt, 1997: 199). Shephard emphasised the importance of her efforts within government to ensure that independent schooling was maintained as an option for those who were able to afford it while increasing the range of choice in the state sector. She underlined the benefits of testing and of performance tables (Ribbins and Sherratt, 1997).

Conclusion

During the period covered by Chapter 6 more emollient language was used by politicians as parts of the National Curriculum and testing and assessment were simplified in order to reduce the amount of time teachers were spending on administration. Privatisation continued apace with colleges being removed from LEA control and becoming more 'businesslike'. The divide between vocational and academic courses of study, however, remained largely untouched. Private companies were encouraged to become involved in the inspection process and school results were published in order to encourage competition between schools.

These developments continued what had been happening since 1979 as the landscape of education in the UK was completely changed to fall in with the Conservative philosophy of introducing the practices of the marketplace to education.

Critics, e.g. Davies (2000), Ball (2007) and Gillard (2011), note that, while being strongly critical of comprehensive schools, the government had realised that many schools and parents were not enthusiastic about 'opting out' and did not support selection. CTCs and GM schools were not as popular as had been expected. During these final years in office this led to a change in emphasis from arguments which had been about bringing back selection to the notion of 'specialism' in which specific schools were seen as having expertise in, for example, modern languages, sport and technology.

Further reading

Lumby, J. (2001) *Managing Further Education*. London: Paul Chapman.
Mansell, W. (2007) *Education by Numbers: The Tyranny of Testing*. London: Methuen.
Shephard, G. (2000) *Shephard's Watch: Illusions of Power in British Politics*. London: Politico's.

Conclusion to Section 2

The period covered by Section 2, from 1979 to 1997, was a time of significant change in education in the UK. A concern to improve standards in schools and colleges was emphasised in order to assist the economic development of the nation. The Education Reform Act of 1988 led to increased assessment and accountability in schools and colleges. An attempt was made to move power from local education authorities to schools and colleges but also to central government as the ethos of a competitive market was applied to education. An increased range of choices was given to parents as aspects of education were privatised.

In her autobiography, *Shephard's Watch: Illusions of Power in British Politics* (Shephard, 2000), the Education Secretary in post at the end of this period provides a thoughtful consideration of the way in which power was wielded both by local government and national politicians. She was clear that politics had been very much 'amateur in its flavour' (Shephard, 2000: 95) with ministers being chosen for their media skills and in order to maintain a political and geographical balance in the government. Business acumen, managerial skills and knowledge of relevant subjects were not seen as having much import in the choice of ministers.

Certainly in the choice of Education Secretaries (with the exception of Gillian Shephard) the lack of experience in education is evident and may have contributed to the general feelings of dissatisfaction which pervaded the teaching profession during the period. Interviews carried out with Education Secretaries have shown, however, that they were unanimous in their support for the changes that were being put in place and confident that they had improved education during the period 1979– 97.

1997–2010: BLAIR AND BEYOND

Preamble

After 18 years of Conservative government the electorate were ready for a change and a new beginning. The voters had become disillusioned with the Major government and 1997 saw the election of the first Labour government since 1979 with a landslide victory. The theme song of Labour's election campaign was 'Things Can Only Get Better', which was an apt summary of the mood of the country at the time of the election. The Labour Party won the 1997 general election with 419 seats and a majority in the House of Commons of 179 seats. This was 33 more than the majority enjoyed by Atlee's 1945 election landslide and it was based on a record 10 per cent swing from the Conservatives.

During the 1980s and early 1990s the Labour Party had endured a series of election defeats, but following the appointment of Neil Kinnock as Party leader they began the process of modernisation. Tony Blair, who became leader of the Labour Party in 1994 following an agreement with Gordon Brown to allow him to become leader at a later date, continued the process of modernisation with a small team of supporters. 'New Labour', as the Party was commonly known, became established as the party of government.

The modernisation of the Labour Party involved moving away from the traditional left of British politics to the centre ground and the adoption of a range of policies aimed at fully developing a market-led system with social justice. It was an attempt to develop social democracy allied to economic freedom and prosperity. In the 1997 Labour Party manifesto Tony Blair argued: 'In each area of policy a new and distinctive approach has been mapped out, one that differs from the solutions of the old left and those of the Conservative right' (Labour Party, 1997: 1). It is difficult to give a precise definition of the approach but it came to be characterised by the term the 'third way' (Blair, 1998; Powell, 2000; Giddens, 1998, 2000; Hargreaves, 2009).

There was a strong emphasis on the new and modernisation, although many of the policies instigated by New Labour can be seen as a continuation of those developed by the previous Conservative government. Strong central control with an increasing use of quangos and greater involvement of the private sector were all features of the modernisation process.

Improving all parts of the public sector was identified by New Labour as a major priority and areas such as health and education experienced significant reform during the period of the Labour government. Blair recognised the importance of education and played a key role in the development of policy. Education came to be at the forefront of domestic policy for the Labour government and the role of Secretary of State grew in importance. The previous strong relationship between the local authorities and the Labour Party was broken. The power and influence of the local authorities in the education system were greatly reduced during this period and schools were given greater autonomy.

Given the importance of education policy during the previous period of office of the Conservative Party it is hardly surprising that education was identified by the Labour Party as a key policy area. Improving educational standards and providing better opportunities for the less well off were cornerstones of New Labour policy. Set against the background of globalisation the need to create a 'world-class education and training system' became a central theme of many education policies. Much emphasis was placed on creating an education system that was fit for the twenty-first century. Wider improvements in the performance of the British economy, largely based around the financial services sector, also provided the scope for a large-scale investment in education.

Blair was succeeded by Gordon Brown as Prime Minister in 2007, but there was real continuity in policy terms. The groundwork for this was established by David Blunkett who was the Secretary of State during the first Labour government from 1997 to 2001. Importance was placed on raising standards and giving schools greater freedom from local authorities, while at the same time putting in place strong central control, often through 'arm's length bodies'. A number of Secretaries of State followed David Blunkett, but the focus on raising standards, especially in literacy and numeracy, and creating a 'world-class' system continued. There was an unprecedented expansion in the numbers of teachers and a huge school building programme partly to offset the relative lack of investment in previous decades. This era saw the largest expansion in the education system since the 1950s.

There were a huge number of individual policy initiatives and an increase in bureaucracy during this period with the use of targeted funding for particular projects. Many schools complained of 'innovation overload' and the problem of developing a coherent policy given the scale of change being implemented. However, underlying the policies was a desire for social justice with a strong focus on tackling exclusion. Education was seen by the Labour government as a means of providing social mobility to groups who had previously been failed by the education system. Underpinning the various policy initiatives was the drive to move from a separate education system to an integrated children's service which would provide a full range of support to children and parents.

In 1997 there was great optimism and a strong desire not to repeat the mistakes of previous Labour governments. Labour wanted to be seen as a political party that could effectively manage the British economy and remove the boom and bust syndrome that had been prevalent in previous decades. For a large part of the Labour government's period of office they succeeded and there was rapid economic growth and prosperity. However, by the end of first decade of the twenty-first century Britain had entered the worst financial and economic crisis since the 1930s.

CHAPTER SEVEN

1997–2001: THE FIRST LABOUR GOVERNMENT SINCE 1979

- Raising standards
- National strategies
- Specialisation and choice
- Poverty and social exclusion
- Reform of post-16 education and training

Introduction

After 18 years of Conservative government 1997 saw the election of a Labour government with a large majority in Parliament who were committed to education. The new Prime Minister Tony Blair had responded when asked about his priorities for his new administration by replying 'education, education, education'. Given the huge parliamentary majority of the Labour government almost any education reform was possible. Among education professionals there was widespread support for the new government and there was a genuine mood of optimism and of a new beginning after many years of Conservative government. This was the start of a new era with New Labour being given a huge mandate by the electorate.

As we pointed out in the previous chapter there was a strong sense of disillusionment with the outgoing Conservative administration and a feeling that 'things could only get better'. The most important issues for teachers were class sizes and the level of education funding which had been constrained for a number of years (Galton and Macbeath, 2008). There was a need for renewed financial investment in education and intellectual investment in terms of new ideas and approaches. The teaching profession was ready to embrace change and in 1997 expectations were high for positive reforms and a significant increase in public expenditure to start to repair the education system.

The Labour Party manifesto for the 1997 general election had stated: 'Education will be our number one priority; and we will increase the share of national income spent on education as we decrease it on the bills of economic and social failure' (Labour Party, 1997: 5). Specific policy promises included:

- cut class sizes to 30 or under for all five, six and seven year olds;
- nursery places for all four year olds;
- attack low standards in schools;
- access to computer technology;
- lifelong learning through a new University for Industry;
- more spending on education as the cost of unemployment falls.

(Labour Party, 1997: 7)

Context

The importance of education in improving Britain's economic performance was at the heart of the new government's policy initiatives and there was a strong belief that raising educational standards would enable Britain to compete with the rest of the world: 'We are talking about investing in human capital in an age of knowledge to compete in the global economy' (DfEE, 1997: 3). In some ways making the link between education and a successful economy was not new and can be seen most clearly in the arguments put forward in the 1976 Ruskin College speech (see Chapter 3). The economic argument for improving school standards can be put forward in a straightforward manner:

- In a global economy Britain must be able to effectively compete with other countries.
- Given Britain is not able to compete on the basis of cost due to the emergence of low-cost economies we have to focus on ideas, innovation and high skill sectors (the so-called knowledge economy).
- To enable Britain to compete, standards in our schools have to be high and rising at least as fast as those in our competitors.
- The government has a responsibility to ensure that standards continue to rise in schools and colleges and to develop strategies and systems that produce skilled and motivated young people.

- This will involve major changes in the education system in order to maintain our level of economic competitiveness.
- A successful education system will produce young people who are able to make a positive contribution to the economic well-being of the country.
- A flexible and skilled workforce will enable Britain to successful compete in a global economy.

At first reading this appears to be a persuasive argument, but in reality the path to economic prosperity is extremely complicated for any country. Education and training does have a part to play in the process, but other issues such as economic policy, global economic conditions and cultural factors all play a part. It is not always clear what business expects education to deliver (Gleeson and Keep, 2004). There are a number of issues surrounding the purpose and type of education that is provided to young people. It is relatively easy to blame the perceived low standards in education for Britain's relatively poor economic performance, but more difficult to provide hard evidence (McCulloch, 1998). However the 'economic argument' for education reform was a significant factor in providing justification for many of the policies that were introduced by the incoming Labour government. In 1996 Tony Blair told the Labour Party conference: 'Give me the education system that's 35th in the world today and I'll give you the economy that's 35th tomorrow.'

Did the change of government actually make any difference to education policy? The emphasis remained on choice, competition and the belief that the market could be used to improve standards. However, as with the previous Conservative administration, the new government was also keen to retain control over a number of strategic areas such as the curriculum, assessment and the training of teachers. An outcome of this dual approach of marketisation through increased competition between schools and greater central government control often exercised through an increasing number of government agencies was the continued marginalisation of the local authorities. Within the government there was a strong belief in the correlation between a successful education system and economic success. The key to economic prosperity was the development of high standards in education and so the incoming government was determined to introduce education policies that would raise standards and provide a more skilled and educated workforce (Abbott, 2004).

Schools and colleges

The first act of the new government was to abolish the Assisted Places Scheme. The government then set about introducing a number of polices, the overall approach being set out in the White Paper *Excellence in Schools*.

The White Paper was produced in a short period of time – 67 days – and established the guiding principles that would influence Labour education policy during their first term of office (Barber and Sebba, 1999). The principles identified in the White Paper were:

1. Education will be at the heart of government.
2. Policies will be designed to benefit the many, not just the few.
3. The focus will be on standards, not structures.
4. Intervention will be in inverse proportion to success.
5. There will be zero tolerance of underperformance.
6. Government will work in partnership with all those committed to raising standards.

(DfEE 1997: 5)

During their first year in office the government introduced seven education bills and policy statements. The Standards and Effectiveness Unit (SEU) was established within the newly named Department for Education and Employment (DfEE). This Unit, under the leadership of Michael Barber, was responsible for making things happen and was part of the process identified by New Labour as 'deliverology'. This process aimed to ensure that policies from central government were implemented quickly and in full (Bangs et al., 2011; Chapman and Gunter, 2009). According to Barber:

> The best way to think about it is to imagine what is implicit when a minister makes a promise. Supposing that a minister promises, as David Blunkett did, to improve standards of reading and writing among eleven year-olds. Implicit in this commitment is that, in one way or another, the minister can influence what happens inside the head of an eleven year-old in, for example, Widnes. The delivery chain makes that connection explicit. (Barber, 2007: 85)

The incoming Secretary of State, David Blunkett, had been the shadow spokesperson for education since 1994. He had been able to develop a detailed understanding of the major issues and so was able to instigate policies quickly:

> We had worked policy through. We'd produced two substantive documents that had to go through our conference procedure . . . We wanted to change standards, we needed leadership in schools, we needed high-quality teaching, we needed to revamp the materials, the equipment, the buildings that children are learning in and teachers teaching in, we needed to recruit first-class teachers. (Blunkett, interview, 2010)

The new government was clear about what they wanted to achieve and the methods it was going to use to make the necessary changes to improve standards. Despite the similarities there were two key differences with the previous government. Firstly, after almost twenty years of reductions in public spending, the new government managed to find additional resources for education. Secondly, the Prime Minister was actively involved in education policy and would provide significant political support for the changes that were going to be implemented. For example, in 1997 the creation of the Social Exclusion Unit was announced and this was linked directly to the Prime Minister's Cabinet Office. This Unit aimed to address the issues of poverty and educational under-achievement by the promotion of joint polices between government departments.

Standards

The 1997 White Paper identified raising standards as 'the Government's top priority' (DfEE, 1997: 9). A number of studies and international league tables claimed to show that English school pupils performed less well than pupils in other countries in reading, science and mathematics (see, for example, Reynolds and Farrell, 1996; Brooks et al., 1996). Barber (2007: 27) claimed: 'A report published in 1996 from the National Foundation for Educational Research showed standards of literacy that year were about the same as they had been in 1948.'

There are a number of dangers in placing too much emphasis on international comparisons and comparing data over time in the way suggested by Barber. There was a great deal of debate about the reliability of the data which claimed to show relative underperformance by English school pupils (Brown, 1998). However the Labour government was determined to implement policies designed to drive up standards of educational achievement. In particular the government appointed a number of specific groups in an attempt to drive up standards, examples of which include:

- Standards and Effectiveness Unit
- Standards Task Force
- Literacy Task Force
- Numeracy Task Force
- Special Needs Advisory Group
- New Deal Advisory Group.

The purpose of the groups was to debate policy and to put forward strategies for implementation and the two best examples of policies introduced were the National Literacy Strategy and the National Numeracy Strategy.

The aim of the literacy strategy was to raise standards of literacy in primary schools and was developed from the Conservative National Literacy Project (see Chapter 6) and work carried out by the Labour Party in opposition (Barber, 2007; DfEE, 1998a). The aptly named literacy hour was a major feature of the strategy and directed primary schools to allocate an hour, broken into four components, to the teaching of literacy. Although the literacy hour was not compulsory there was an expectation that every school would follow the framework unless they could provide a more effective approach. To formalise the strategy the government announced that it would set national targets for literacy of 80 per cent of the cohort reaching level 4 in the National Curriculum Tests by 2002. The figure was then expected to rise to 95 per cent by 2007. These were stiff targets given that only 58 per cent of the cohort achieved level 4 in 1996. Other parts of the literacy strategy included the appointment of a literacy coordinator and a school governor with the responsibility for overseeing literacy strategy in every primary school. Other policies to improve literacy were implemented in secondary and adult education, including pilot strategies for improving literacy at Key Stage 3, adult literacy clinics, a number of promotional schemes to encourage the purchase of books by young people and free books for schools.

The National Numeracy Strategy had a similar approach to the National Literacy Strategy and built on earlier work of the previous government's National Numeracy Project (DfEE, 1999a). However, it was more liberal than the Literacy Strategy and encouraged schools to develop their own approaches to the development of numeracy, but it did emphasise whole-class teaching and regular homework, and there was also the expectation that primary pupils would have a maths lesson every day of between 45 and 60 minutes. Again, the government announced targets for pupils with the aim that 75 per cent of eleven year olds should reach level 4 in the National Curriculum maths tests by 2002. In 1996 the figure reaching this level was 54 per cent of eleven year olds, or as Stephen Byers, the School Standards Minister, told radio listeners when attempting to put the policy in context, that seven times eight equals 54 per cent! (Docking, 2000). The National Numeracy Strategy also provided funding for 300 numeracy advisers and a range of support materials were developed. In addition, in 1999, the government set targets for levels of achievement in maths for each local authority in England. These targets varied from 70 per cent of eleven year olds achieving level 4 to 97 per cent in Richmond upon Thames.

These two strategies illustrate the emphasis the government placed on raising standards and the methods they were prepared to use to ensure that standards did actually improve. There was a clear expectation that standards would rise and these were quantified with specific targets for improvement, with government ministers being held accountable. Particular classroom

Standards:
- Reduction of class sizes in KS1 to a maximum of 30.
- LEAs responsible for the promotion of high standards in primary and secondary education.
- LEAs to produce an Education Development Plan for approval by the Secretary of State.
- Additional powers for the Secretary of State to intervene in poor performing LEAs.
- Extension of LEAs power to intervene in failing schools.
- Secretary of State's powers to intervene if a school is failing clarified and extended with the power to close a school.
- Every school to have a written behaviour policy including measures to tackle bullying.

LEAs and funding arrangements:
- Increased delegation of funding to schools.
- LEAs required to produce a financial scheme subject to external audit.
- Clarification of the funding of Maintained schools including all maintained schools in an LEA being funded on the same basis.

Types of school:
- Classification of maintained schools as community, voluntary (aided or controlled) or foundation schools.
- Clarification of procedures for opening, altering and closing schools.
- Secondary schools allowed to send some pupils to an FE college for part of their education.

School admissions:
- Secretary of State to issue a Code of Practice on admissions.
- Specialist schools able to admit 10 per cent of their intake on the basis of aptitude in the specialism.
- Selection for banding permitted.

Other provisions:
- Establishment of nutritional standards for school meals.
- Clarification of LEA responsibilities relating to nursery education and the development of an Early Years development plan.
- Establishment of Education Action Zones (EAZs).
- Simplification of the roles and responsibilities of governing bodies.

Figure 7.1   Main features of the School Standards and Framework Act 1998

methods were put forward for use in schools and these were supplemented by additional resources to support teachers and teaching.

The major piece of government legislation during this period was the School Standards and Framework Act 1998 which had a significant impact on schools. It was an important piece of legislation, although not on the scale or significance of the 1988 ERA and the 1993 Education Act, and it set out the future direction for schools and LEAs. The emphasis was on standards although the detail of the Act was more concerned with structures and 89 of the 145 sections related to the structure of schools which included finance, admissions and types of schools. Interestingly there was no mention of comprehensive schools anywhere in the Act (Chitty, 2004; Tomlinson, 2005). Later in the chapter we will return in detail to some of the major initiatives arising from the Act, but a summary of the Act is contained in Figure 7.1.

Specialisation and choice

A feature of previous government policy was the establishment of a variety of different types of school to foster the development of a quasi market in education. This policy continued with the Labour government although there was a re-branding of the various types of school. For example, schools with grant-maintained status opted to become foundation schools. The Fair Funding initiative clarified some of the issues surrounding the funding of schools. Increased funds were delegated to schools with a reduction in the amount of funding available to the LEAs.

The number of specialist schools continued to grow and in 1999 Tony Blair and David Blunkett announced a target of 800 specialist schools by 2002. The demand for places at specialist schools had risen during the period, connected in part to the decision to allow these schools to select up to 10 per cent of their intake on the basis of aptitude. In addition it was announced that the number of Beacon Schools would rise to 1,000 by 2002. In urban areas there was a drive to move away from what Tony Blair's communications director, Alastair Campbell, described in February 2001 as 'bog standard comprehensives' to a more diverse range of school provision. In March 2000 the City Academy programme was announced by David Blunkett. The City Academies were designed to replace failing schools and were completely free of any LEA involvement. They were to be controlled by sponsors which could be central government, business, religious or community groups. They were also given much greater autonomy and more flexibility in areas such as curriculum provision and teachers' pay and conditions. The plethora of initiatives in the inner cities created a variety of types of school and the involvement of a wide number of partners, while at the same time there was a further reduction in the involvement of the

LEA. We will return to the impact of the academies initiative in Chapters 8 and 10.

Curriculum

We have already considered two important curriculum reforms with the introduction of the literacy and numeracy strategies. The implementation of the strategies resulted in the narrowing of the primary curriculum to accommodate the extra time that was required to deliver additional literacy and numeracy. During this period the structure of the National Curriculum remained virtually unchanged following the Dearing Review in 1993 (see Chapter 6). However, a number of other developments had a significant impact on the school curriculum.

In the 14–19 sector school pupils were allowed to 'disapply' parts of the National Curriculum and to attend a local further education college for part of the week. This policy was an attempt to provide a more relevant curriculum and to raise the status of vocational education. Curriculum 2000 introduced the first major reform of the A level since its introduction in 1951 in an attempt to broaden the post-16 curriculum and was a further attempt to raise the status of equivalent vocational programmes (QCA, 1999). Curriculum 2000 introduced a six-unit A level qualification broken down into a three-unit A/S qualification at the end of the first year of study. The full A level – or A2 as it has become known – is achieved by successful completion of three further units. These developments were mirrored by similar changes in vocational qualifications with the creation of vocational A levels. In addition post-16 students were able to take an increased number of courses in an attempt to broaden the curriculum. The changes to post-16 education were introduced quickly and would return to cause the government and the Secretary of State problems over the following years.

Significant developments were taking place in the use of ICT and the Labour government was keen to ensure that pupils were able to 'respond as individuals, parents, workers and citizens to the rapid expansion of communication technologies, changing roles of employment, the continual globalisation of the economy and society' (QCA/DfEE, 1999: 3). There was significant investment in ICT provision in schools with funding for a National Grid for Learning and the promise of a £1 billion fund for the development of ICT.

The Advisory Group on Education for Citizenship and the Teaching of Democracy in Schools was established in 1997 under the chairmanship of Sir Bernard Crick and published a report in September 1998 (QCA, 1998). The so called 'Crick Report' outlined the main aims of Citizenship education and the content that should be included. The Report aimed at no less than a change in the political culture of this country both nationally and locally: for people to think of themselves as active citizens, willing, able and equipped to have an influence in public life and with the critical capacity to weigh evidence before speaking and acting; to build on and to extend radically to young people the best in existing traditions of community involvement and public service, and to make them individually confident in finding new forms of involvement and action amongst themselves. (QCA, 1998)

Over the following five years Citizenship was introduced as a discrete part of the National Curriculum mainly delivered through the Personal, Social and Health Education (PSHE) programme. It was intended that Citizenship would account for approximately 5 per cent of National Curriculum time. The first stage of this process was the introduction of Citizenship as part of the non-statutory PSHE framework at Key Stage 1 in September 2001.

Poverty and social exclusion

A fundamental policy objective of the new government was to reduce poverty and social exclusion. A range of policies across a number of government departments were introduced to address a range of social problems. In education two major policy developments were introduced during this period: EAZs and Sure Start.

EAZs were set up in disadvantaged areas following bids from schools which worked in collaboration with a number of other organisations including local businesses, LEAs and other agencies. Twenty-five EAZs were established in 1998/9 with a further 47 in 2000. Initially they were expected to operate for three years, but this was then extended to five years and after that date they were expected to become self-financing. Initially the EAZs were funded from central government with additional support from business. According to Ofsted (2003: 5) they were intended 'to tackle problems of underachievement and social exclusion in disadvantaged areas by devising innovative methods and strategies that would involve disaffected pupils more fully in education and improve their academic performance.' The EAZs can be viewed as part of the wider Excellence in Cities initiative (DfEE, 1999b) which was designed to raise standards in inner-city schools. The Labour government was determined to tackle the low standards found in many inner-city schools and to improve the life chances of young people who lived in these areas in particular by 'an improvement in parental confidence in the capacity of city schools to cater for ambitious and high achieving pupils' (DfEE, 1999b: 1). Little consideration was given to the broader social and economic factors that might contribute to the problems faced by inner-city schools (Tomlinson, 2005). Six broad areas were identified to help to raise standards in the inner-city areas:

- extra Beacon and specialist schools;
- greater opportunities for gifted and talented pupils;
- learning support units for disruptive pupils;
- learning centres with advanced IT provision;
- new smaller EAZs;
- provision of learning mentors.

These initiatives were designed to offer disaffected and vulnerable pupils the academic and pastoral support required to succeed in school. Over 1,000 schools in inner-city areas received targeted funding and resources to raise standards (Abbott, 2004). There was strong emphasis on schools working together with the identification of excellent schools (Beacons) which would work with other schools to raise standards. This would be achieved, for example, by sharing facilities, running training programmes and the exchange of staff. The Beacon schools received additional funding for this development work.

There was a strong emphasis on the Early Years sector and a National Childcare strategy was launched in 1998. The strategy advocated 'free nursery places, and 25 Early Excellence Centres to be set up across the country which would serve as "models" for high quality practice integrating early education with childcare' (Sylva and Pugh, 2005: 11). Another specific policy initiative which aimed to reduce social exclusion and which would ultimately lead to rising standards was the Sure Start programme which was introduced in 1999 (DfEE, 1999c). Sure Start was a £425 million programme for 0–3 year olds in poor areas and it brought together health, childcare, family services, support for special needs and education. Over 500 programmes were established involving between 500 and 900 under-4s and their families. The Sure Start programme actively encouraged the involvement of parents, was responsive to local needs and, unlike the majority of other initiatives, was not subject to competitive bidding. Anning and Hall (2008: 4) have pointed out this approach differed from other initiatives: 'Sure Start exemplified a tension between the rhetoric of local empowerment and the realities of central government control.'

Education Secretaries and development of policy

A great deal of work on the development of education policy had been carried out, following Tony Blair's election as Labour Party leader in 1994, by David Blunkett who had been appointed Shadow Secretary of State for Education. Following the election victory the new government was well prepared to begin the process of policy development. Certainly the pace of reform outlined in the previous chapter continued with the new government, as Ball (1999) commented: 'Whatever else one would want to say about Labour's education policies there is certainly no shortage of them.' The pace and amount of legislation continued with the new government determined to bring about rapid change. David Blunkett recognised the sheer volume of policy and the problems it could cause but given the issues the government had to deal with suggested he could have done more:

> I began to feel I was doing too much. I began to feel that the criticism that there were too many initiatives, and therefore it was like waves coming up the beach, had some truth in. But looking back I'm not sure that I pressed hard enough. (Blunkett, interview, 2010)

The Labour government continued the Conservative approach of encouraging schools to take more control of their own affairs and to develop the idea of a quasi market in education. There were changes in emphasis, for example the decision to move away from grant-maintained schools to increasing the number of specialist schools, but the principle of extending choice for parents and pupils remained in place. Yet there was a paradox at the heart of the system as the government extended central control over a number of key areas of the education system. We have noted earlier the setting of specific targets for schools by the government and direction given to classroom practice by initiatives such as the literacy hour. The Teaching and Higher Education Act 1998 (DfEE, 1998b) established the principle of setting up a General Teaching Council (GTC) which would be responsible for standards of professional practice. The Act also enabled the inspection of teacher training institutions by HMI and the introduction of a leadership qualification for head teachers.

The role of the LEA in the education system continued to develop. With the emphasis being placed on delivery of high standards, the LEAs were expected to step back from the day-to-day control of schools in their areas. The 1997 White Paper *Excellence in Schools* set out what was expected:

> The LEA's task is to challenge schools to raise standards continuously and apply pressure when they do not. The role is not one of control. Those days are gone. An effective LEA will challenge schools to improve themselves. Being ready to intervene when there are problems, but not interfere with schools that are doing well. (DfEE, 1997: 27)

The previous government had introduced the inspection of LEAs by Ofsted with the support of the Audit Commission in the Education Act 1997.

The Labour government used the powers given to the Secretary of State to intervene in failing LEAs to the full. A limited number of LEAs were identified as having serious weaknesses e.g. Hackney and Manchester. In 1999 the private company, Cambridge Education Associates, took over the day-to-day operations of Islington LEA.

David Blunkett was clear about the changing nature of the LEAs:

> The LEAs at their best have been a driving force for improvement and change . . . some Education Authorities were actually condoning inadequacy and underperformance. So we had to do something about it and we tried to do it collaboratively . . . But there were authorities that were so dysfunctional. (Blunkett, interview, 2010)

Specific initiatives continued to undermine the role and purpose of the LEAs as schools and other organisations were given direct control. Examples of this process include an increasing number of schools being given specialist status and the introduction of EAZs. We will return, in detail, to the function and purpose of the EAZs later in this chapter but they were based in areas of social deprivation.

Central control of the education system was exerted by the DfEE and through a whole range of 'arm's length bodies' which had responsibility for particular areas of policy. New organisations were created and existing ones saw their powers increased. Examples include:

- the Adult Learning Inspectorate (ALI);
- the Qualifications and Curriculum Authority (QCA);
- the Teacher Training Agency (TTA);
- the British Educational Communications and Technology Agency (Becta);
- the National College for School Leadership (NCSL);
- the Learning and Skills Council (LSC).

A significant change in post-16 education and training was instigated with the publication of the White Paper *Learning to Succeed: A New Framework for Post-16 Learning* (DfEE, 1999d). An underlying principle behind the reforms for post-16 education and training which we have outlined was the belief that they would lead to a more successful economy: 'Lifelong Learning will . . . ensure the means by which our economy can make a successful transition from the industries and services of the past, to the knowledge and information economy of the future' (DfEE, 1999d: 3).

The White Paper set out major structural changes for the sector and established the Learning and Skills Council (LSC) which replaced the Further Education Funding Council (FEFC) and the Training and Enterprise Councils. The LSC took over responsibility for all post-16 education and training with the exception of higher education, and had control of planning, finance, quality and management of the sector. The appointment of the chair of the LSC and members of the Council was the responsibility of the Secretary of State. It was envisaged that Business would provide the biggest group of representatives on the Council. In addition local LSCs were established to coordinate local provision and to work in conjunction with LEAs to develop more coherent 14–19 provision. Additional funding was made available to FE colleges to widen participation and Individual Learning Accounts were established with individuals being given £150 to spend on training programmes. High achieving FE colleges were going to be identified as Beacons of Excellence. The inspection of post-19 courses and work-based routes would be the responsibility of ALI with Ofsted retaining responsibility for inspection of 16–19 courses in schools and colleges. The proposals contained in the White Paper became law with the passing of the Learning and Skills Act in 2000.

These changes were controversial and the huge amount of power given to the LSC was a course of concern (Batty, 2000). The Secretary of State had also acquired significant control through the ability to appoint the members of the LSC. The establishment of bodies such as the LSC and other connected organisations to take control of specific parts of the education and training system was a significant feature of the Labour government. The government had overall control of these organisations through the appointment of the chair and the board members and by the ability to determine levels of funding, while at the same time appearing to allow them to make their own decisions. During the period 1997–2001 a plethora of policy initiatives were introduced by these organisations and a number of controversial key individuals associated with particular polices were kept in place following the general election. For example, Chris Woodhead remained at Ofsted, Anthea Millet at the Teacher Training Agency (TTA) and Nicholas Tate at the QCA. Probably the most controversial was Chris Woodhead who had been a severe critic of teachers and the teaching profession during his time as chief inspector of schools and whose retention in post by the Labour government was badly received by teachers. His eventual resignation in 2000 led to much rejoicing in staffrooms throughout the country.

Conclusion

The period 1997–2001 started off with high expectations for radical reform of the education system and a desire to move away from the previous 18 years of Conservative rule. There was a large amount of goodwill for the incoming government from the teaching profession. Education professionals welcomed the election of a Labour government and were confident that a more positive approach to education and teachers in particular would follow. As we have seen there was an enormous amount of policy with a wide range of initiatives being introduced by the government. The driving force for this policy deluge was the desire to raise standards across the education system.

The pace and amount of reform was immense but there were strong similarities to what had gone before. There was still a strong emphasis on the importance of markets and continued attempts to increase the involvement of private sector partners. At the same time central government retained close control of the system often through unelected bodies who were responsible for the day-to-day implementation of policy. Many of the key individuals who were closely involved in this process remained in post. The role of the LEAs also continued to evolve with the loss of powers to schools and other organisations and pressure to play a more active part in the raising of standards.

Although there was a strong focus on standards, structural changes continued to be made to the system, not least in the type and funding of schools. There was a strong emphasis given to addressing the issues facing less advantaged members of the community in the inner cities. As a result many policies were directed at raising educational standards in inner-city areas.

Despite the similarities with the previous administration there were also some important differences. Additional resources started to be devoted to education with a recognition that there was a need for significant investment following years of underfunding by successive governments. The Labour government was not afraid to intervene directly in classroom pedagogy and to tell teachers what they expected them to do and how to teach in order to raise standards. There was a strong belief in the importance of education to improve economic performance and to help to alleviate poverty. Education was a major part of government policy and the Prime Minister Tony Blair was deeply interested in and committed to improving the education system. As a consequence education was at the core of government policy and high on the agenda in Downing Street. This certainly made it easier for David Blunkett to get the political support to introduce radical policies. After many different Secretaries of State in a relatively short period of time, David Blunkett provided stability. He had been Shadow Secretary of State since 1994 and continued in the post in government until the 2001 general election. The frequent rotation of ministers in the previous government had made it difficult to establish any degree of continuity. By 2001 the government had established a clear rationale for their policies and had instigated significant reform of the system.

Further reading

Blunkett, D. (2006) *The Blunkett Tapes: My life in the Bear Pit*. London: Bloomsbury.

Docking, J. (ed.) (2000) *New Labour's Policies for Schools: Raising the Standard*. London: David Fulton.

Tomlinson, S. (2005) *Education in a Post-Welfare Society* (2nd edn). Buckingham: Open University Press.

CHAPTER EIGHT

2001–2007: THE SECOND PHASE OF THE LABOUR GOVERNMENT

- The introduction of Academy schools
- Building Schools for the Future
- Every Child Matters
- The Tomlinson Report

Introduction

In this chapter we will consider the second phase of the Labour government from 2001 to 2007. This will include their second term of office and part of the third term following the general election victory in 2005 up to the resignation of Tony Blair and the appointment of Gordon Brown as Prime Minister in 2007.

Following the re-election of the Labour government in 2001 the emphasis on raising educational standards and developing diversity of provision continued. In the second term the emphasis shifted slightly from the primary to the secondary sector, although there was a desire to build on the gains that had been made in primary education. Underpinning the drive to raise standards was a belief in the power of education to transform the life chances of individuals and to bring about improved economic performance. However, this period saw a number of controversies surrounding a range of key policies and individuals. A 26-month period saw three Secretaries of State for Education and questions being raised about a number of key policies that had been introduced between 1997 and 2001. Despite this, the rapid pace and amount of reform continued with the introduction of a range of landmark policies, including the creation of Academies, the setting up of a major building programme for schools, Building Schools for the Future, and a Green Paper, *Every Child Matters* (DfES, 2003), that would have a profound impact on the organisation and structure of the education system as a whole.

Context

Political

During their first term in office the Labour government had placed a strong emphasis across the administration on domestic policies. During the second and third terms of the administration international events began to dominate the government agenda. The invasion of Iraq in 2003 was to prove a turning point for the government and to distract the attention of the Prime Minister away from domestic matters to the international stage. This process began well before the invasion of Iraq and continued until and beyond the resignation of Tony Blair in 2007. However, the mechanisms that had been established to develop and deliver domestic policy were firmly in place, and in 2001 education was still a major priority following the general election. Following the 2001 Election the Labour government retained a huge majority in parliament with the loss of only six seats and Tony Blair was in place to lead the government for a second consecutive term.

If the Iraq war dominated the political agenda during the early and middle period of the administration the replacement of Tony Blair by Gordon Brown came to dominate events leading up to 2007. The transition from Tony Blair to Gordon Brown was not smooth and there was a sustained period of hostility and infighting between supporters of the two men leading up to the eventual resignation of Tony Blair.

For the 2001 election the Labour Party manifesto again identified education as 'Labour's number one priority' (Labour Party, 2001: 18). A large number of the proposals set out in the manifesto had been contained in the Green Paper, *Schools: Building on Success: Raising Standards, Promoting Diversity, Achieving Results* (DfEE, 2001). The Green Paper set out Labour's achievements especially in primary education and started to shift the focus of policy to the secondary and post-16 sector. According to data presented in the Green Paper standards of literacy and numeracy had significantly improved with the greatest gains being made in the most disadvantaged areas (DfEE, 2001). For example, by 2001 the LEA with the lowest score in Key Stage 2 English was now doing better than the 1996 national average (DfEE, 2001: 13). The manifesto contained promises to increase spending on education and to employ more teachers. Emphasis in the manifesto was again placed on encouraging greater diversity among state schools with continuing reform of post-14 education seen as a priority. After raising standards in primary education, although the pressure was not removed from the primary sector to continue to improve, the government wanted to achieve similar results in the secondary sector. An integral part of the process to raise standards in the secondary sector was to ensure an increase in the participation rate of young people going into higher education to 50 per cent of the cohort. Again this aim was seen as an essential part of ensuring economic prosperity and creating a highly skilled workforce to enable the UK to compete in a global economy.

The 2005 general election victory saw Tony Blair being returned to power for a historic third term as Prime Minister. The overall government majority was reduced in an election dominated by the aftermath of the Iraq war, but the government still had a large working majority in Parliament. The 2005 Labour manifesto set out the government's achievements and, for example, claimed that while in 1997 Britain was 42nd in the world league for education, by 2005 was the third best in the world for literacy at age 10 and the fastest improving for maths (Labour Party, 2005: 30). Education was once again identified by the Labour Party as 'our number one priority' and there was a commitment to additional funding, continuing emphasis on specialisation by schools and a focus on post-14 education and training with a commitment to prevent students dropping out of the system at 16. In the manifesto there was an emphasis on bringing new providers into the state system where they 'can help boost standards and opportunities in a locality' (Labour Party, 2005: 37).

Schools and colleges

Following the 2001 election victory the government renamed the department as the Department for Education and Skills (DfES). The new Secretary of State, replacing David Blunkett who moved to the Home Office, was Estelle Morris who had previously been the Schools Minister. The first policy document introduced by the new Secretary of State was the White Paper *Schools: Achieving Success* (DfES, 2001). The White Paper built on the 2001 Green Paper and outlined plans to extend choice and diversity. A key element of this policy was the determination to increase the number of specialist schools and to develop other forms of schooling including the establishment of City Academies and the expansion of 'faith-based' schools. New qualifications were introduced with the development of vocational GCSE programmes. In addition the White Paper set targets for secondary schools with the intention that at least 20 per cent of pupils should achieve five or more A* to C grades at GCSE by 2004, rising to 25 per cent by 2006 (DfES, 2001).

The main proposals in the White Paper were included in the Education Act 2002 and this Act contained a great deal of material on the legal status of school organisation and the curriculum. In particular, the Act clarified some of the proposals contained in the 1998 Schools Standards and Framework Act (see Chapter 7). The Act further strengthened choice and diversity by requiring LEAs to advertise in order to enable interested groups or individuals to bid to run a new school. The situation relating to the establishment of academies was clarified. Schools were to be allowed to work together in federations. It was also made easier to change the Key Stage 4 curriculum and to move away from the National Curriculum model which had been established in 1988 (Chitty, 2004).

The new Academies were located in areas of socio-economic disadvantage and were intended to replace failing schools which had low levels of achievement. Often the existing schools were in serious decline as parents opted for other more popular schools. The Academies were seen as a fresh start with new leadership, significant investment from sponsors and government, and new buildings. They were removed from LEA control and were able to set different employment terms and conditions for teachers and select up to 10 per cent of their intake. In effect an Academy was a new school, although in most cases it developed from the ruins of a previous institution and was seen by the government as a means of raising educational achievement in some of the most deprived areas of the country (Gorard, 2009). The Academies programme received strong political and practical support from the Prime Minister who believed they would play a significant part in combating social disadvantage. Tomlinson (2005: 127) claims Academies were 'in effect private schools publicly funded'. The creation of yet another type of school created significant controversy which we will return to in Chapters 9 and 10.

The other significant policy initiative to encourage greater diversity in the school system was the expansion of the specialist schools. Again this initiative had the strong support of the Prime Minister and was seen as a means of raising standards through the development of a particular approach, whereby promotion of a particular ethos and excellence in the subject specialism which would bring about school improvement. The specialist schools bandwagon was not based on the research evidence on school effectiveness, but large numbers of schools opted for specialist status (Levacic and Jenkins, 2006). Certainly the extra resources available to a specialist school were attractive to head teachers and governors. Schools were required to raise £50,000 and this was then matched by the government, although schools which did not achieve certain standards were not eligible to bid for specialist status. The number of schools opting for this status was significant and by 2007/8 88 per cent of all secondary schools in England had achieved at least one of the specialisms and in some local authorities every school was specialist (DCSF, 2008a). In Chapter 9 we will return to the impact of specialist schools when we consider the overall record of the Labour government.

The Specialist Schools Trust, which was renamed the Specialist Schools and Academies Trust (SSAT) in 2005, had originally been established in 1987 to promote the City Technology Colleges (see Chapter 4). The SSAT is a non-governmental organisation and a registered charity which provides support for specialist schools and academies and acts as a lobbying group. With strong support from the government expenditure by the SSAT increased from under £3 million in 2001 to almost £50 million in 2007 (Mongon and Chapman, 2009).

The SSAT is another example of a non-elected organisation playing a significant part in the development and implementation of education policy during this period. This can be contrasted with the continuing decline in the influence and powers of the local authority. The most significant change in the status of the LEAs came about as a result of the 2005 Education Act. This piece of legislation moved the funding of maintained schools from the local authorities to central government. The system of funding schools through local government financial settlements had been in operation since the Balfour Education Act in 1902. The 2005 Act also strengthened the role of the Teaching and Development Agency for Schools (TDA) in developing the school workforce, and again provided opportunities for organisations and groups to open new schools.

Following the general election victory in 2005 the government published the White Paper *Higher Standards, Better Schools for All: More Choice for Parents and Pupils* (DfES, 2005b). Tony Blair outlined in the Foreword to the White Paper his view of how education had been transformed by his government and the next policy steps required to achieve a 'world-class' system (DfES, 2005b: 1). The White Paper set out proposals to give schools greater freedom and to establish 'independent non-fee paying state schools' (DfES, 2005b: 4). These so-called Trust schools would have wide-ranging powers, including the ability to set their own admissions criteria, employ their own staff and appoint the board of governors. The proposals generated a great deal of controversy and opposition across the education spectrum, especially in some parts of the Labour Party. By the time the White Paper became the Education and Inspections Bill in 2006 the government had faced its biggest revolt in Parliament with 46 Labour MPs voting against the third reading. The Bill became law only with the support of the Conservative opposition and the Secretary of State for Education Ruth Kelly (December 2004–May 2006) had a difficult task in steering the bill through Parliament (Chitty, 2009).

The period between 2001 and 2007 saw a large amount of additional resources being devoted to education. Overall there was increased spending on education, despite funding difficulties in particular years. For example in 2002, Gordon Brown, the Chancellor of the Exchequer, directed an extra £15 billion of funding to education over a three-year period. Expenditure per pupil increased and more resources were made available to schools to support the drive for higher standards (Levacic, 2008). Methods of funding schools continued to develop and there was a movement away from universal funding to continued emphasis on the development of a 'bidding culture'. Schools were encouraged to bid to receive funding for particular initiatives. Many schools became proficient at acquiring additional funding through this process while others were less successful. From the government's perspective this method of funding enabled resources to be directly channelled to particular areas that they wanted to impact on, rather than the risk the possibility of the resource being lost in more general funding streams.

Another significant resource initiative during this period was the Building Schools for the Future scheme (BSF) which was a programme to rebuild every secondary school in England. It was the most ambitious school building programme for over one hundred years and aimed to provide flexible and well-designed buildings that would provide opportunities for new ways of teaching and learning. BSF was first announced in 2003 with a significant amount of funding coming from the Private Finance Initiative (PFI). A second round of funding was announced in 2004. While generating considerable controversy about the involvement of the private sector, the overall cost and the levels of bureaucracy associated with BSF, many schools benefitted from this investment with new buildings appropriate for the twenty-first century, many of which were in areas of socio-economic deprivation. Schools which had lacked any form of significant capital investment over successive governments were being rebuilt. BSF was cancelled, amid great controversy, in 2010 by the incoming Coalition government which will be considered in more detail in Chapter 10.

The terrible murder of eight year old Victoria Climbie in 2000 by relatives who were looking after her led to a major review of childcare policies. What made this tragedy particularly disturbing was the range of agencies and organisations that were aware of Victoria's circumstances yet she was still murdered. An independent statutory inquiry led by Lord Laming concluded that a failure of communication between the various agencies was a major factor in Victoria's death which was 'a gross failure of the system' (Laming, 2003: para. 1.18). A Green Paper, *Every Child Matters*, set out wide ranging proposals for the reform of the childcare system in England:

> We want to put children at the heart of our policies, and to organise services around their needs. Radical reform is needed to break down organisational boundaries. The Government's aim is that there should

be one person in charge locally and nationally with the responsibility for improving children's lives. Key services for children should be integrated within a single organisational focus at both levels. (DfES, 2003: 9)

The Green Paper also identified five outcomes for children that all children's services were expected to achieve:

• Being healthy: enjoying good physical and mental health and living a healthy lifestyle.
• Staying safe: being protected from harm and neglect.
• Enjoying and achieving: getting the most out of life and developing skills for adulthood.
• Making a positive contribution: being involved with the community and society and not engaging in anti-social or offending behaviour.
• Economic well-being: not being prevented by economic disadvantage from achieving their full potential in life.

(DfES, 2003: 6–7)

These outcomes will be familiar to anyone working in education during this period because schools were expected to play a major part in ensuring these were achieved by all young people. While it is hard to disagree with any of the outcomes it is much more difficult to see in practice how they can be achieved or which agency has responsibility. There are a number of contradictions inherent in the policy and a number of professional groups may be involved in each area (Dyson et al., 2009).

Subsequently in 2004 the government passed the Children Act which:

• established integrated children's services departments in local authorities by bringing together education and child and family social care;
• set up children's trusts which brought together health and childhood services with the other functions;
• developed shared and agreed working practices between people working with children;
• instigated common skills and greater cooperation among staff working with children.

A practical outcome for schools following the move to an integrated approach was the continued development of the extended schools movement by encouraging schools to provide a range of services on their premises. Extended schools 'provide a range of services and activities, often beyond the school day, to help meet the needs of children, their families and the wider community' (DfES, 2005a: 7). Examples include the integration of health services into school, the provision of childcare and running parenting classes (DCSF, 2007a). By 2005 the government had already spent £160 million on this initiative and were promising to provide a further £680 million by 2008.

In 2007 the DfES was reorganised and renamed the Department for Children, Schools and Families to reflect the movement to integrated provision and multi-agency collaboration. Tomlinson (2005) comments on the irony of the government promoting greater collaboration between organisations while at the same time giving schools greater freedom, an issue we will return to in the next chapter.

The desire to reduce social exclusion and improve participation of young people in education and training continued throughout this period and the announcement in 2002 of the extension of the Education Maintenance Allowance (EMA) was a significant part of this policy. The EMA was a payment made to 16–19 year olds from low income families who remained in full-time education. The EMA had been successfully piloted in a number of LEAs since 1999 and was extended nationwide in 2004 with a maximum of £30 per week being paid to young people who stayed in education post-16 where the annual income does not exceed £19,630 (Maguire and Thompson, 2006). Another aspect of this policy was the creation of Connexions in 2001, a multi-agency body made up of a number of agencies involved in working with young people such as the careers service, social services, and youth and probation service. Connexions provided learning mentors who gave support to young people to encourage and facilitate participation in education and training. These measures were designed partly to deal with a group of young people who were referred to as 'not in education, employment or training' (NEET). The problems associated with the NEET group of young people who had dropped out of the system was a recurring issue during this period and the government introduced a range of polices designed to encourage and enable them to become economically active.

Education Secretaries and the development of policy

In the previous chapter we identified that David Blunkett had provided continuity by remaining as Secretary of State for Education during the government's first full term of office. David Blunkett had been the longest serving Secretary of State for a significant period of time. However, the years 2001–7 were markedly different with four Secretaries of State during this period.

Estelle Morris (2001–2)

Initially, after the 2001 election, continuity was provided by Estelle Morris who had previously been Schools Minister in the first Labour administration. Morris was a former teacher having worked in an inner-city comprehensive school for a number of years prior to becoming a Member of Parliament in 1992. This is a rare example of the Secretary of State having first-hand experience of working as a teacher in a state school. As we noted earlier, Morris continued with the policy of encouraging greater diversity in the schools system, but she began to run into a number of difficulties associated with the implementation and outcome of various polices.

Despite being a former teacher Morris alienated many members of the teaching profession with her criticism of comprehensive schools and the claim that they did not respond to individual needs (Morris, 2002). Worse was to follow when she was reported as saying that some schools 'I simply wouldn't touch with a bargepole.' At the same time the Secretary of State was attempting to push through major reform of the teaching profession with a substantial increase in funding tied to changes in working practices, especially a greater role for teaching assistants in the classroom. Failure to meet literacy and numeracy targets inherited from the previous Secretary of State also contributed to her difficulties as did other problems relating to the performance of the Criminal Records Bureau (CRB) in checking the background of new teachers and her intervention in the case of two students expelled from a school in Surrey. However, the most significant problem was the crisis over the marking and grading of A level scripts in the summer of 2002. In the previous chapter we described the changes introduced by Curriculum 2000 to the structure and curriculum of A level examinations, and the first results of the new-style A level examination were published in August 2002. The pass rate had risen by a record rate and there were allegations of marking discrepancies at the examination boards. It seemed that the changes to the A levels had not been handled properly and that teachers were underprepared, especially for the new coursework arrangements. In September 2002 the Chair of the QCA resigned amid recriminations and buck passing between a number of senior figures. In late October Morris resigned as Secretary of State. Despite the difficulties of the previous few months her departure was unexpected and in her resignation letter she explained that she had found it difficult to exert strategic leadership. Morris explained the difference between being a Junior Minister and being Secretary of State:

> The job is completely different. I remember in my first few weeks as Secretary of State, when you received your weekend box or boxes, there weren't quite as many papers as when I was Minister of State.

Yet the nature of the work was different, far more strategic, requiring more thought and probably with wider consequences. In children's language it was 'harder stuff'. That's a very good way of summing up the difference between the two. When I was Minister of State a lot of the papers I got at weekends would have been operational decisions about policies or follow-up papers, following discussions we'd been having during the week. The stuff I got at weekends as Secretary of State were often big decisions about the future direction of the Government that needed a much finer judgment and more thought. Of course, when it was time to implement or develop these policies, Secretaries of State, and their Ministers of State worked together. (Morris, interview, 2010)

Charles Clarke (2002–4)

Following the resignation of Estelle Morris, Charles Clarke became the new Education Secretary. Clarke was an experienced and combative politician who was keen to continue with the choice and diversity agenda. The policy direction was set out in *A Five-Year Strategy for Children and Learners* which argued that the system had to 'be both freer and more diverse' and designed around the needs of the individual through a process of 'personalisation'. This would be achieved through greater choice for students and parents and different types of school (DfES, 2004a: 4).

Clarke was the Secretary of State when Mike Tomlinson finally produced his report on 14–19 qualifications. Tomlinson, a former Chief Inspector of Schools, chaired a working group that carried out a review of 14–19 qualifications (DfES, 2004b). The so-called Tomlinson Report recommended major changes to the existing system with the introduction of a new Diploma for all school-leavers. There were also changes to assessment, coursework and the introduction of core skills in literacy, numeracy and ICT. An extended project would be introduced and the Diploma would recognise work experience and extra-curricular activities. The recommendations of the report were intended to close the academic–vocational divide and promote a post-14 curriculum that would meet the needs of the twenty-first century. The report was extremely well received by educationalists and promised the opportunity for the most significant reform of the 14–19 sector for many years. However, between the publication of the report and the subsequent White Paper Clarke moved to the Home Office and was replaced as Education Secretary by Ruth Kelly. The move of Clarke to the Home Office was caused by David Blunkett's surprise resignation as Home Secretary and is an example of how unplanned political events can impact on policy. It is impossible to prove whether the outcome might have been different if Clarke had remained as Secretary of State for Education, especially given the Prime Minister's scepticism of some of the proposals in the Tomlinson Report. The subsequent White Paper, *14–19 Education and Skills* contained proposals to simplify the vocational qualifications system and introduce specialised diplomas (DfES, 2005c). However, the White Paper did not contain any proposals for the replacement of GCSEs and A levels with an overarching Diploma or incorporate the main findings of the Tomlinson Report.

Ruth Kelly (2004–6)

The rejection of the main recommendations of the Tomlinson Report was clearly a political act because the government did not want to enter the 2005 general election faced with the claim by the opposition that they were going to abolish GCSE examinations and A levels (Mansell, 2005: 13). Ruth Kelly had the difficult job of inheriting a number of issues from her predecessor in the knowledge that the 2005 general election was fast approaching (Barber, 2007). It is no surprise that political expediency had to play an even more significant part in government decision-making during late 2004 and early 2005, but a landmark opportunity for structural reform of the 14–19 sector had been missed despite the rhetoric employed to justify the changes that were introduced. Ruth Kelly argued that her decision not to implement Tomlinson was based on educational factors:

> I disagreed with Tomlinson on that point. I still do. I think if you are going to introduce a new examination system which is supposed to be broad-ranging and all-encompassing then the only way of inspiring confidence in that system is to have a strong and easily understood thread of continuity with the past. I was of the view that over time whether the new qualifications embedded A levels or not would become immaterial, people would choose the learning that suited them. I think if you go back through what I said at the time and in speeches and so forth, you'll see I used very, very similar words to words that Ed Balls subsequently used, which is that I thought over time the Diploma would become the 'qualification of choice'. But in order to get them off the ground and for employers and universities to give them the credibility that we needed, they had to be able to recognise and relate to the new qualifications. Hence the decision to keep A levels within the system. A levels could be taken outside the Diploma or inside the Diploma. The key for pupils was that you weren't taking such a gamble with your future educational career if you went down the Diploma route if you knew at least at the end of it not only would you have the Diploma but you'd also have an A level qualification. (Kelly, interview, 2011)

When asked about the involvement of the Prime Minister in the decision Ruth Kelly replied:

> I think he possibly would have had more input had I not fundamentally agreed with retaining A levels within the Diploma. That would have been a very different conversation. But I was very, very comfortable with that. (Kelly, interview, 2011)

Following the general election victory Ruth Kelly remained in post until May 2006 when she was replaced by Alan Johnson who was Secretary of State until the resignation of Tony Blair as Prime Minister in 2007.

Alan Johnson (2006–7)

Alan Johnson had a relatively short period of time as Secretary of State and was an interesting choice for the job having left school at 15. During his time as a school pupil he was in receipt of free school milk and his main education was provided through correspondence courses while working as a postman. He maintained the existing drive for greater choice and diversity, but he placed a strong emphasis on social mobility, remarking:

> You know there are probably not many Secretaries of State who were free school milk kids. I was a free school milk kid so that bit of it and the social mobility thing was very important to me. (Johnson, interview, 2010)

The lasting legacy of Alan Johnson's time as Secretary of State was the raising of the school-leaving or participation age to 18 by 2013. Under this proposal, announced in January 2007, all young people would stay in education, training or an apprenticeship until the age of 18. This was the first major change in the school-leaving age since ROSLA in 1972.

Conclusion

A recurring feature of this period is the drive to fragment the comprehensive system and to develop greater choice and diversity. This was achieved through the continued expansion of specialist schools and the development of Academies. The number of individuals and organisations involved in education continued to grow as the opportunities for sponsorship and the private provision of services increased. While keen to build on past achievements the focus of the government during this period, switched from the primary to the secondary sector. As the overall economy prospered the level of resources devoted to education continued to grow with increases in the levels of expenditure per pupil and substantial capital expenditure directed to school rebuilding. This was an unprecedented period of expansion in the education sector with an increase in teaching and support staff in schools.

The range of initiatives coming from central government to schools continued at a fast pace across a vast range of policy issues. There was a fundamental shift in the way in which education was organised with the movement to an integrated approach involving the full range of children's services. The role of the local authority changed and declined as central government control increased, allied with greater freedom for individual schools. The local authorities continued to move from being providers to commissioners of education. The paradox of increased competition through the development of marketisation while at the same time greater central government control remained at the heart of Labour policy. Education was seen as a crucial element in improving economic performance and providing opportunities for social mobility.

Political factors continued to have an impact with frequent changes of Secretary of State. This contributed to some uncertainty during the period although the Labour reform project remained on track despite changes in personnel. A unique opportunity to reform the 14–19 sector was missed with the refusal of the government to implement the recommendations contained in the Tomlinson Report. Broader political issues diverted the Prime Minister Tony Blair from the domestic agenda, although his interest in education and commitment to changing the system remained in place. However, an era was about to draw to a close with a new Prime Minister about to take over as Tony Blair resigned, after years of controversy and speculation, from office in June 2007.

Further reading

Barber, M. (2007) *Instruction to Deliver*. London: Politico's.

Chapman, C. and Gunter, H. (eds) *Radical Reforms. Perspectives on an Era of Educational Change*. London: Routledge.

DfES (2003) *Every Child Matters*, Cmnd 6272. London: TSO.

CHAPTER NINE

2007–2010: THE FINAL PART OF THE NEW LABOUR PROJECT

- Development of a Children's Plan
- Introduction of an integrated system
- Raising standards
- Post-14 reform

Introduction

In this chapter we will focus on the final part of the New Labour project as Tony Blair is replaced by Gordon Brown as Prime Minister in June 2007. The handover of power brought to an end one of the longest running sagas in recent British political history. Prior to 2007 there had been intense speculation about the date when Blair would stand down as Prime Minister. For a number of years there had been an ongoing dispute between Tony Blair and Gordon Brown who had been Chancellor of the Exchequer since the election of the Labour government in 1997. The dispute was centred around the alleged agreement made between Blair and Brown about the leadership of the Labour Party and when Blair would actually hand over power to Brown. This disagreement had a destabilising effect on the government and there was a split between the Blair and Brown camps in the Labour Party and in the Cabinet which was made public by several leaks and 'off-the-record' briefings to the press.

Education policy during this period built on earlier policy initiatives and consolidated the new structures that had been developed between 2001 and 2007. There was continued emphasis on the implementation of Every Child Matters, further development of the Academies movement, ongoing centralisation around the Department of Children, Schools and Families and the familiar mantra about standards. The choice of a key Brown loyalist, Ed Balls, as Secretary of State for Children, Schools and Families reinforced the importance of education in the new administration. This period was not without controversy in education and, for example, questions continued to be raised about the involvement of private companies in education provision and there were major issues associated with pupil assessment.

Context

Political

Despite the power struggle between Tony Blair and Gordon Brown the new Prime Minister wanted to continue the reform agenda that had been instigated by the previous Labour administration and there was to be no significant change of direction in education policy between 2007 and 2010. The new Brown government was keen to develop its own particular focus while continuing with the process of reform that had been set in motion. In particular greater emphasis was placed on cooperation between schools rather than continued competition (Bangs et al., 2011). However, as the political context between 2001 and 2007 came to be dominated by the Iraq war, the final period of the Labour government was overshadowed by the global economic crisis that started to engulf the world economy.

Between 1997 and 2007 the Labour government had achieved relative economic stability and there had been a period of sustained economic growth largely driven by an expansion in credit alongside high levels of debt. A significant proportion of the economic growth during this period had been based on the financial services sector. Domestically the problems created by the failure and subsequent nationalisation of the Northern Rock Bank in 2007 and 2008, and internationally by the failure of Lehman Brothers Investment Bank in 2008, were the result of the worst financial crisis since the Great Depression of the 1930s.

Positive economic performance had been reflected in the continued growth in the level of resourcing devoted to education. The proportion of national income spent on education had increased from 4.7 per cent in 1997 to 5.6 per cent in 2007–8 (DfES, 2006). Average expenditure in real-terms per secondary school pupil in England had increased from £3,300 to £4,530 in 2005–6. In the previous chapter we described the huge school building programme that the government had instigated. There had also been a significant increase in the size of the education workforce:

Teacher numbers have grown by 36,200 since 1997. There are now 435,400 full-time equivalent (FTE) teachers in the maintained schools sector in England, the highest level since 1981. Support staff numbers have also risen with 287,100 FTE support staff in schools including 152,800 teaching assistants, an increase of 162,800 since 1997. (DfES, 2006: 11)

From 2007 the worsening economic conditions forced the government to scale back on the rate of increase in the level of education funding, although the significant cuts in education expenditure did not occur until after the election of the Coalition government in 2010 (see Chapter 10).

Despite initial enthusiasm and widespread support for the new Prime Minister, especially his role in coordinating the initial international response to the global financial crisis, the Brown premiership quickly ran into a series of political difficulties. Brown's period of office came to be categorised by a failure to act decisively which was graphically illustrated by the postponement of the general election until the latest possible date in 2010, when it had been widely expected there would be a general election in autumn 2007 or early 2008 to provide a mandate for the new Prime Minister. Political infighting between cabinet members, leadership challenges and weak government became the norm as the Labour government came to the end of 13 years in power.

Schools and colleges

The Children's Plan provided the foundation for government policy during 2007 and 2010 (DCSF, 2007b). It built on the policies introduced in the Children Act 2004 and provided continuity with previous government policy aiming 'to make England the best place in the world for children and young people to grow up' (DCSF, 2007b: 3). According to Ed Balls, the Children's Plan offered the opportunity for a fundamental shift in emphasis:

> But the truth is that the Children's Plan was an attempt at cultural change. It was an attempt to say that every school should succeed, not just some. That every child should succeed whether it was a child in an affluent area in a school that was relatively affluent as much as in a school which has got concentrated disadvantage and that can only happen if schools get the support they need and schools are open to the idea that actually every child in their school matters and therefore they may sometimes need to have a bit of support pushed at them. And that is why the ethos of the Children's Plan, focused on the child not the institution, was a big change. (Balls, interview, 2010)

In particular the move towards an integrated approach to children's services was the driving force behind ongoing reform, with the Children's Plan being underpinned by five principles:

- Government does not bring up children – parents do – so government needs to do more to back parents and families.
- All children have the potential to succeed and should go as far as their talents can take them.
- Children and young people need to enjoy their childhood as well as grow up prepared for adult life.
- Services need to be shaped by and responsive to children, young peoples and families, not designed around professional boundaries.
- It is always better to prevent failure than tackle a crisis later.

(DCSF, 2007b: 4)

The Children's Plan set ambitious goals for 2020 with targets to improve child health, to enhance success in school with at least 90 per cent achieving at or above the expected level in English and maths by age 11, to enable at least 90 per cent of young people to achieve five higher-level GCSEs and to halve child poverty by 2010 with eradication by 2020. Specific proposals included a 'root-and-branch' review of the primary curriculum to be carried out by Sir Jim Rose, the former director of inspection at Ofsted who had been one of the 'three wise men' (see Chapter 5). In addition there was to be further investment in continuing professional development (CPD) for teachers by making teaching a Masters-level profession. Legislation was to be introduced to raise the participation age to 17 from 2013 and 18 from 2015 the first change since ROSLA in 1972 (see Chapter 3). The control of funding for 16–19 learning was moved from the Learning and Skills Council back to the local authorities and further support was provided for NEETs to encourage them to stay in education and training. Emphasis was also placed on raising standards in 'coasting' schools which were defined as schools where students achieve in excess of the 30 per cent five A*–C grades at GCSE including English and Maths, but where pupil progression from Key Stage 2 to Key Stage 4 was below average. 'Coasting schools' would be encouraged to work cooperatively with other schools and would receive additional support, especially to improve Assessment for Learning. The emphasis on encouraging schools to work together was a significant departure from previous policy, but in other respects the direction of education policy continued as before.

During the three years of the Brown administration an overriding emphasis on bringing children's services together, prioritising the needs of children and parents and moving away from a separate education service were at the core of government policy:

Delivering the vision set out in the Children's Plan will require a series of system-wide reforms to the way services for children and young people work together. By putting the needs of children and families first, we will provide a service that makes more sense to the parents, children and young people using them, for whom professional boundaries can appear arbitrary and frustrating. By locating services under one roof in the places people visit frequently, they are more likely to find the help they need. And by investing in all those who work with children, and by building capacity to work across professional boundaries we can ensure that joining up services is not just about providing a safety net for the vulnerable – it is about unlocking the potential of every child. (DCSF, 2007b: 18)

The White Paper *Your Child, Your Schools, Our Future* continued the emphasis placed on developing an integrated approach in schools by, for example, supporting 'the creation of multi-agency teams in schools, bringing together a wide range of children's services professionals' (DCSF, 2009a: 9). There was also ongoing support for greater partnerships and cooperation between schools, continued recognition of the importance of excellent teaching with effective leadership and further development of the commissioning role of local authorities to ensure effective provision of children's services. However, fundamental aspects of the New Labour agenda continued to be clearly identified as the process of reform continued:

Taken together, these proposals will build on the foundations of the progress made over the last 12 years, to create a world-leading system of schooling which reflects the needs of the 21st century: responding to the challenges of a changing global economy, a changing society, rapid technological innovation and a changing planet. They will ensure that every school develops and extends the potential and talents of every child and young person to give them the skills they need for the future, so that every child can enjoy growing up and achieve high standards. And fundamentally, they will create a system which progressively breaks the link between disadvantage and low educational attainment. (DCSF, 2009a: 13)

The drive to create a world-class system, to ensure young people are equipped with the right set of skills to be successful in a global economy and to embrace technological change can be traced back to the early days of the Labour government in 1997 and are constant themes during the 13 years the Labour Party were in office (see Chapter 7). There was a clear determination to create a school system that was suitable for the twenty-first century by meeting the needs of individual children through:

- maintaining high aspirations for all children and young people and providing excellent personalised education and development to ensure that all are able to progress and reach high standards;
- enabling schools to play a key role in identifying and helping to address additional needs, working at the centre of a system of early intervention and targeted support;
- providing a range of activities and opportunities to enrich the lives of children, families and the wider community, and contributing to community objectives such as local cohesion, sustainability and regeneration.

(DCSF, 2008b: 6)

The planned introduction of a School Report Card from 2011 was intended to improve accountability and to provide further information about the performance of individual schools. The intention was to replace the existing achievement and attainment tables with the School Report Card. The Card would provide:

> Our key statement on the outcomes we expect from schools, and the balance of priorities between them, ensuring more intelligent accountability across schools' full range of responsibilities. It will report on outcomes across the breadth of school performance: pupil attainment, progress, and well-being; a school's success in reducing the impact of disadvantage; and parents' and pupils' views of the school and the support they are receiving. (DCSF, 2009c: 3)

This provides a good summary of the direction of Labour policy during this period. There was a continued emphasis on raising academic standards while having a strong concern for the welfare of individual children. In addition there was a recognition that education had a key role to play in dealing with a number of social problems. The role of parents and pupils in education was acknowledged as a key issue, with high expectations being placed on individual schools to perform to a high standard. There was also an acceptance that the broader context in which the school operated was a significant factor in determining outcomes so that 'fair comparisons could be made between schools' (DCSF, 2009c: 3).

The so-called Rose Review of the primary National Curriculum was set up in 2008 by the Secretary of State to raise standards in primary schools, especially to promote reading, writing and numeracy, to introduce modern foreign languages and to reduce prescription (DCSF, 2009b). At the same time the Cambridge Review of English Primary Education was being undertaken by a group 'commissioned and funded by an independent foundation, it was directed by an academic with no public or professional political allegiances and none of its authors works for the government or one of its quangos' (Richards, 2010: 390). The Cambridge Review (Alexander, 2010) offered a very different set of outcomes to those contained in the Rose Review. The outcome and implementation of the two reports is worth considering because they illustrate the importance of the government in directing policy and the difficulty faced by any outside organisation hoping to influence policy. Despite gathering extensive coverage in the media the Cambridge Review proposals were ignored by the government while the recommendations contained in the Rose Review were accepted as government policy. The Cambridge Review did create controversy and it did not escape criticism (see, for example, Campbell, 2011). However, it was a significant piece of work conducted by a highly respected team which carried out a major review of primary education. Nevertheless it was sidelined by the government, although as we shall see in Chapter 10 the Coalition government, which replaced Labour after the 2010 election, set aside the reform of the primary curriculum put forward by Rose.

An earlier review of the secondary National Curriculum had been set up in 2007 with the aim of 'freeing up' the Key Stage 3 curriculum. A set of statutory aims were put forward that the secondary curriculum should enable young people to become:

- successful learners who enjoy learning, make progress and achieve;
- confident individuals who are able to live safe, healthy and fulfilling lives;
- responsible citizens who make a positive contribution to society.

(QCA, 2007)

In addition, two skills frameworks were introduced:

- functional skills of English, maths and ICT which aim to develop the application of numeracy, literacy and ICT skills.
- personal, learning and thinking skills (PLTS) which include creative skills, independent enquiry, self-management and team working.

A number of non-statutory cross-curricular dimensions were also developed:

- identity and cultural diversity;
- healthy lifestyles;
- community participation;
- enterprise;
- global dimension and sustainable development;
- technology and the media;
- creativity and critical thinking.

The development of cross-curricular dimensions reflected the direction of policy towards an education system that aimed to address a whole range of social, cultural and lifestyle issues in addition to high academic standards. However, raising standards remained at the forefront of government policy. In June 2008 Ed Balls announced a national challenge plan to get the worst performing secondary schools to improve or face closure. A total of 638 secondary schools which had less than 30 per cent of pupils achieving five A*–C GCSE grades were targeted to show improvement. Additional resources of £400 million were provided with approximately £200 million being used to convert 70 schools into academies. The government was still committed to applying additional pressure on schools that were considered to be underperforming. Part of the package of measures designed to support the 638 schools identified included individual support from 'superheads' who had a successful track record in improving under-performing schools and the establishment of National Challenge Schools where the existing school would be replaced with a new school linked through a trust to a school considered to be strong and high-performing. Although cooperation between schools was being promoted as a response to perceived low standards this was another example of the government encouraging schools to work together in partnership.

The first Diplomas in construction and the built environment, creative and media, engineering, society, health and development, and information technology were introduced in 2008. The Diplomas offered a mixture of practical, including work experience, and classroom-based learning in 14 different vocational areas and could be combined with GCSEs and A levels. The Diploma initiative built on the proposals contained in the 2005 White Paper *Education and Skills* (see Chapter 8) and provided the opportunity for significant change in the 14–19 curriculum. Allied to a proposed review of A levels in 2013 the announcement by the Secretary of State of the introduction of three new academic Diplomas in languages, science and humanities from 2011 was viewed as major challenge to the existing A level system. The Diplomas were the latest in a series of initiatives to reform and restructure the 14–19 curriculum to address issues around specialisation, lack of relevance, parity of esteem between academic and vocational qualifications, and the level of participation in education and training post-16. The Diplomas can be viewed as a continuation of the drive, highlighted by the proposals to raise the school-leaving age, by the Labour government to create a distinct 14–19 phase. Staff and students in schools and colleges began to accept the idea that continuing education beyond GCSE was the norm rather than the end of compulsory school at the age of 16 (Hodgson and Spours, 2008; Higham and Yeomans, 2011).

The organisation of Diplomas required schools, further education colleges, higher education institutions, and the local authority within a local area to work more closely together to ensure adequate provision for students. The move to greater cooperation in this aspect of work was another example of the government's desire to foster cooperation and was a reversal of the long-established policies that had promoted competition between schools and colleges and which had resulted in a number of tensions. Despite initial problems regarding issues such as organisation, mistrust between previously competing institutions, assessment and status, the Diplomas were starting to become established in schools and colleges by 2010.

Education Secretaries and the development of policy

Ed Balls (2007–10)

The appointment of Ed Balls as Secretary of State for Children, Schools and Families in 2007 was a surprise given his previous experience had been in the Treasury. Ed Balls had only been a Member of Parliament since 2005, but prior to that he had worked for Gordon Brown as an economic advisor during his time as Chancellor of the Exchequer. Following his election to Parliament in 2005 Ed Balls became Economic Secretary to the Treasury and when Brown became Prime Minister he appointed Ed Balls as Secretary of State, a post he held until the election defeat in 2010. He became the second longest serving Education Secretary in the Labour government. The appointment of Ed Balls, a Brown loyalist, was taken as an indication that the Prime Minister considered education as a policy priority. The new department that Ed Balls took charge of was given additional areas of responsibility. These included youth justice with the Justice Ministry, youth sport with the Culture Department and children's health with the Department of Health. While retaining control of 14–19 education within the DCSF, adult education along with higher education transferred to a new Department of Innovation, Universities and Skills. The new department was significantly larger in scope, but smaller in terms of resources:

> On one level it's a smaller department because by losing Higher Education – measured in billions – the amount of money controlled by the Department came down but we took on joint responsibility for children's health, youth justice, schools' sports, drugs and alcohol. And I certainly saw this as being not just about those parts of public service where we control the money but using our influence more widely. (Balls, interview, 2010)

According to Ed Balls the new broader remit of the Department was not a new development and reflected the general thrust of policy prior to 2007:

. . . the truth is that it was much more of an evolution. Obviously having a Children's Secretary and a Children's Plan was a wider remit and a focus on the national level – that was new but at the same time Alan Johnson as Education Secretary had been very focused on many of those issues before and so there was continuity there and Sure Start, free nursery care, ECM, the 2004 Children's Act – all these things came before me which I was building upon so there was an evolution there. I think for Bev Hughes, who was Children's Minister, this was a liberation to get on and do more of what she'd been trying to do for years. It was not an abrupt change. (Balls, interview, 2010)

During his period of office Ed Balls built on the earlier work of the Labour government a point he was quick to reinforce:

> I think the important thing for me to say is that I didn't think I had enough time, of course, but I also know that if it hadn't been for literacy and numeracy hours, the Partnership, Building Schools for the Future, Every Child Matters, I couldn't have done what I've done so in that sense there is continuity and you try to accelerate and push it forward . . . (Balls interview, 2010)

One of the features of the Labour government had been the growth of private organisations providing services to education. Organisations such as Capita had secured large contracts to manage literacy and numeracy projects (Ball, 2007; Beckett, 2007). One of the largest contracts, £156 million, had been awarded to an American company, Educational Testing Services (ETS), to administer the SATs tests for Key Stage 2 and 3 students. In 2008 ETS failed to meet the deadline to return the test results to schools. According to Chitty (2009: 109) there had been problems with marker recruitment and retention, large numbers of markers were given the wrong information about the location and time of training; there was a delay in getting papers to markers, unmarked scripts were being returned to schools and there was inadequate call-centre capacity. At the time this total breakdown in the assessment system caused huge distress and annoyance. The publication of school league tables was severely delayed and in October 2008 Ed Balls announced the abolition of the national tests at Key Stage 3. This was a major reversal of policy given that testing at the end of each Key Stage and the publication of results had been a fundamental part of successive government policy. The surprise announcement to scrap the Key Stage 3 tests without consultation also caused further controversy.

The government body responsible for the testing regime was the Qualifications and Curriculum Authority (QCA). In Chapter 8 we described the role played by non-elected organisations in running and directing education policy. Organisations such as the QCA were established because 'government have felt the need for arm's length agencies to do their work, to sometimes save their bacon and occasionally to carry the blame' (Bangs et al., 2011: 156). The QCA was accountable to the Secretary of State but had responsibility for curriculum and assessment, and it certainly carried the blame for the fiasco of the SATs results at Key Stages 2 and 3. The head of the QCA, Ken Boston, eventually resigned but the Secretary of State remained in post. Interestingly, Boston had been appointed as head of the QCA following the crisis over the marking and grading of A level scripts in 2002, when the then Secretary of State Estelle Morris resigned. Boston was highly critical of the government's role in the collapse of the SATs system, but he bore the responsibility and despite his criticism of ministers and civil servants he was forced to step down as head of the QCA (Curtis and Shepherd, 2009).

Following the general election defeat of 2010, Ed Balls was defeated for the leadership of the Labour Party by Ed Milliband. Balls subsequently returned to his economic roots and became Shadow Chancellor of the Exchequer.

Conclusion

During the period 2007–10 the pace of change continued at a rapid rate and there were a succession of policy initiatives aimed at raising standards and creating a world-class education system. Ed Balls claimed:

> . . . and in some ways my frustration of myself is that I tried through the Children's Plan to do too much. Hands up. The reason was because I sort of knew I didn't have that much time and there was so much to be done. If I had a ten-year project we'd have – but you know that's life. (Balls, interview, 2010)

The pace of change did not slacken despite the political difficulties and the worsening economic conditions faced by the government. By the time of the general election in 2010 there was no evidence to suggest that the government had run out of ideas.

There was clear continuity between the Blair and Brown governments, but this period was marked by a shift to greater cooperation between schools and a developing role for local Authorities. There was continued reform to the curriculum with significant emphasis being placed on the 14–19 sector. The move away from an isolated education system continued with a strong emphasis being placed on the development of an integrated system built around the child. The renaming and branding alongside the additional responsibilities assumed by the DCSF serves as a practical reminder of how strong this policy drive became to the government. Continuity was provided by the second longest-serving Labour Secretary of State who, despite being considered as a career politician, relished his time as Secretary of State. Ed Balls explained how he was offered the post by Gordon Brown and his willingness to serve as Secretary of State:

> We ended up in the six months before Gordon Brown becoming Prime Minister designing a new Department for Children, Schools and Families which would be the Whitehall equivalent of Every Child Matters on the national stage, and then the day before the reshuffle the Prime Minister (or Chancellor as he was) said to me: 'Of all the Departments you could choose which one would you go to?' So in a sense I chose it rather than the other way round. I thought that would be the one. He had been thinking: 'Shall I make him Chancellor?' I'd actually been thinking probably I might be offered Health. He then said to me the day before: 'If you could choose which Department would you choose?' And I said: 'Children, Schools and Families'. It is sort of the opposite of the normal thing. So when I got my call the next day I didn't get told: 'I'll be offering you Children, Schools and Families.' He said: 'Fine, that's where we are.' And I said: 'Great' the day before I got the job I spent the whole day negotiating with Jack Straw about how we would have joint responsibility for Youth justice between DCSF (as it was to become) and the Justice Ministry. So I was in an unusual position. I didn't know I was going to have the job at that point but that's what I was doing and I had spent a lot of time as a Treasury Minister dealing with issues around disabled children, special schools, mainstream schools, what you had to do to give every child a chance. And so I was quite up for this job.' (Balls, interview, 2010)

Further reading

Bangs, J., Macbeath, J. and Galton, M. (2011) *Reinventing Schools, Reforming Teaching*. Abingdon: Routledge.

Chapman, C. and Gunter, H. (eds) (2009) *Radical Reforms: Perspectives on an Era of Educational Change*. London: Routledge.

Conclusion to Section 3

The Labour government was elected in 1997 on a wave of optimism and a strong desire for change. When the Labour Party was in opposition there had been a great deal of planning and preparation and after the general election policies were quickly put into place. The first Secretary of State, David Blunkett, was able to implement significant reform with a strong degree of continuity with the previous government's policies. The move towards greater competition and the development of a market system, continued involvement of the private sector, the importance of education in determining economic prosperity and the unrelenting drive to raise standards would all have been familiar to the previous government. However, Labour policies continued to evolve and the emphasis on an integrated children's service and the reforms to the 14–19 curriculum, for example, signified a major departure from Conservative policies.

The first and final phases of the period saw two periods of continuity from long-serving Secretaries of State. The period between the terms of office of David Blunkett and Ed Balls was characterised by frequent ministerial changes, but this did not deflect from the general direction of policy. During the Blair premiership there was strong direction from Downing Street and successive Secretaries of State were very aware of the key importance of education to the Prime Minister. Politically education was seen as a major factor in securing electoral success and it continued to grow in importance in terms of media coverage and public involvement.

Raising standards was the starting point for the Blair government in 1997 and the initial pace of reform was intense with a fierce drive to do so. It is important to remember the role played by the Prime Minister and his enthusiasm for change in education. Over a long time period, it is difficult to maintain this drive because eventually there has to reach a point were low standards cannot be blamed on a previous government. If David Blunkett had known the Labour Party was going to remain in power for 13 years there is a possibility that a more measured approach might have been adopted, although there was a strong sense that urgent action was required when the Labour Party won the 1997 general election:

> . . . we had to then re-set the agenda with excellence for everyone which was saying it's standards not structures. We want to change standards, we need leadership in schools, we need high-quality teaching, we need to revamp the materials, the equipment, the buildings that children are learning in and teachers are teaching in, we need to recruit first-class teachers. Before we got in we were down to a four-day week in some schools. There was a massive recruitment crisis and a major problem in maths and science. It's hard to remember; there were hundreds – not one or two – hundreds of schools reliant on outside toilets. There were roofs leaking, windows were falling out, parents were marching in market towns in 1995 after Ken Clarke's 1995 budget. So the whole thing was in a kind of meltdown . . . (Blunkett, interview, 2010)

Inevitably education polices can take a long time to reach fruition, a point acknowledged by David Blunkett when interviewed in 2010:

> I knew it would take a long time. I didn't know it would take quite this long. I used to joke that when I was in my dotage drinking a nice glass of red wine sat in the garden I would think of the things I'd done. But it does take much, much longer for all of this to feed through . . . (Blunkett, interview, 2010)

So what was the legacy of the Labour government? There was a significant increase in the number of teachers and support staff and more effective training and development with a strong emphasis on leadership. The school building stock had been transformed with unprecedented levels of investment through Building Schools for the Future. Schools were better equipped and extensive use had been made of new technologies to support teaching and learning. There was significant curriculum reform with a focus on numeracy and literacy and there had been constant pressure to drive up standards. Different types of school had been established with schools being given greater autonomy and increased involvement from outside organisations. The number and influence of 'at arm's length bodies' continued to grow as the government shifted responsibility to organisations such as the TDA and QCA. There was a fundamental shift from a narrow education provision to an integrated children's service. After 13 years a great deal of change had been implemented, although many issues remained to be dealt with. The 2010 general election result would herald further change again.

CHAPTER TEN

2010 AND BEYOND: INTERESTING TIMES

- Academies and new types of school
- Curriculum reform
- Markets and marketisation
- Deficit reduction

Introduction

In this chapter we will look at the establishment of the Coalition government and the range of education policies that have been introduced since 2010. After the longest period of continuous government by the Labour Party between 1997 and 2010 the general election produced a historic and surprising outcome. After 13 years of Labour government the May 2010 general election failed to produce a conclusive result and the outcome, following a period of negotiation between the main political parties, was the first coalition government since the Second World War. At the beginning of this book we considered the legacy of the last coalition government, the 1944 Education Act. In this final chapter we return again to look at the policy initiatives of a coalition government, although one operating in very different circumstances.

Despite difficult economic conditions and the most severe financial crisis since the 1930s, the main opposition Party was unable to secure a working majority in Parliament. It was only by entering into a Coalition Agreement with the Liberal Democrat Party that the Conservative Party was able to establish a government with David Cameron as Prime Minister.

During the later part of the Labour government significant differences began to appear between the policies being implemented and the views of the Conservative opposition. In particular, the move towards an integrated children's service that had been a cornerstone of the Brown administration was viewed with concern by the Conservative Party (Bangs et al., 2011). In opposition the Conservative Party placed much more emphasis on the importance of individual schools rather than the system in promoting educational improvement. It is against this political background that we start to consider the nature and impact of Coalition government policies.

Context

Political

Despite the seeming unpopularity of the Labour government with the electorate, the outcome of the 2010 general election proved inconclusive and no single political party was able to form a government with a working majority in Parliament. The Labour Party gained 258 seats in the election but were unable to continue in government. The Conservative Party did not gain enough seats for an outright parliamentary majority and for the first time since the Second World War a coalition government was established in the United Kingdom between the Conservative and the Liberal Democrat parties. The dominant party in the Coalition was the Conservatives with 306 seats in Parliament compared to 57 seats for the Liberal Democrats. The new Prime Minister was David Cameron with the leader of the Liberal Democrats, Nick Clegg, being appointed Deputy Prime Minister. The majority of the Cabinet was comprised of Conservatives while the Liberal Democrats were given a minority of Cabinet posts, e.g. Business and Energy. In addition a number of Liberal Democrats MPs were given Junior Ministerial posts. Michael Gove, a Conservative, was appointed as Secretary of State for Education with one of his team of five Junior Ministers being from the Liberal Democrat Party.

A five-page document set out the operational terms in government and Parliament of the Coalition (Cabinet Office, 2010a). A more detailed programme document developed the specific policy areas that the Coalition would work on during their term of office (Cabinet Office, 2010b). There was a particular focus on the 'need to reform our school system to tackle educational inequality which has widened in recent years and to give greater powers to parents and pupils to choose a good school' (Cabinet Office, 2010b: 28). The programme document was relatively short on detail but contained a number of general statements that the Coalition would seek to implement. A new political reality developed after the general election with the need for unity between the members of the Coalition and potentially the opportunity for greater consensus.

As we noted in the previous chapter there was an ongoing economic recession which continued to dominate the policy agenda. There was a drive by many governments around the world to reduce their financial deficit and in some countries, such as Greece and Ireland, to prevent total economic collapse. The Coalition government operated against a background of severe economic and financial problems and the drive by the Chancellor, George Osborne, to reduce the deficit by cutting public expenditure has become a defining feature of the Coalition government. Slow or non-existent economic growth with rising unemployment, especially among young people, has been a feature of the first part of the Coalition government's period of office.

The significant growth in the amount of resources devoted to education that had taken place since 1999 came to an end as austerity measures began to be introduced. According to the Institute of Fiscal Studies (IFS) there will be a 13 per cent cut in real terms in expenditure on education between 2010–11 and 2015 (Chowdry and Sibieta, 2011). If these estimates prove correct it 'would represent the largest cut in education spending over any four-year period since at least the 1950s' (Chowdry and Sibieta, 2011: 1). This is a significant change, especially given the scale of the increase in expenditure on education that had occurred during the first decade of the twenty-first century.

The reduction in expenditure on education is likely to fall on all areas, but the major impact will be on Early Years provision, 16–19 education and capital expenditure. Compared to other areas of public expenditure education has, to some extent, been protected from the worst of the cuts. Spending on schools has received some protection and the introduction of the pupil premium has diverted funds to disadvantaged pupils. However, the general level of per pupil funding will not increase during the lifetime of the Coalition government. There can be no doubt that education, alongside other areas of the public sector, faces difficult financial times with a reduction in real terms in the overall level of resource that is allocated to schools and colleges.

Schools and colleges

The first piece of legislation introduced by the Coalition government was the Academies Act which was rushed through Parliament and received Royal Assent at the end of July 2010. The Act allowed all schools to become Academies and removed the right of local authorities to take part in the consultation process required to establish an Academy. The focus on Academies during the Labour government had been on failing schools but the new legislation granted Ofsted-rated 'outstanding' schools the right to become Academies. The Coalition government intend to give every school the opportunity to become an Academy as they seek to promote greater autonomy in schools.

This Act was followed by the publication of the White Paper in November 2010 *The Importance of Teaching* (DfE, 2010). Many of the proposals of the White Paper were included in the Education Act 2011. The title of the White Paper is intriguing and suggests that the teaching profession is seen as central to the government's aim to improve the education system. Fundamental to the reforms being introduced by the Coalition government is the drive to develop a radical new school system which is supported by improved choice and access for all. David Cameron and Nick Clegg identify three key aspects of the education system that require particular attention:

> The first and most important lesson is that no education system can be better than the quality of its teachers . . . The second lesson of world-class education systems is that they devolve as much power as possible to the front line, while retaining high levels of accountability . . . The third lesson of the best education systems is that no country that wishes to be considered world class can afford to allow children from poorer families to fail as a matter of course. (Cameron and Clegg, 2010: 3–4)

To achieve these aims Cameron and Clegg use language that would have been familiar to the previous government:

> The White Paper signals a radical reform of our schools. We have no choice but to be radical if our ambition is to be world-class. The most successful countries already combine a high-status teaching profession, high levels of autonomy for schools, a comprehensive and effective accountability system and a strong sense of aspiration for all children, whatever their background. Tweaking things at the margins is not an option. Reforms on this scale are absolutely essential if our children are to get the education they deserve. (Cameron and Clegg, 2010: 4–5)

It appears that the rhetoric does not change despite the election of a new government, and after 13 years of continuous change further significant reform of the education system was identified in the White Paper. In a sense this is inevitable especially when the previous government has spent a considerable period of time in office. This was the case in 1997 with the election of the Blair government and the same applied to the new Coalition government. After a lengthy period of time in opposition there is a strong desire to start to get things done quickly. The White Paper outlined a number of areas where significant reform would take place, as discussed below.

Curriculum, assessment and qualifications

A review of the National Curriculum has been instigated with the establishment of an expert panel. The focus of the review is on core subject knowledge and the review is expected to introduce new curricula for English, Mathematics, Science and PE in 2013 and for other subjects in 2014. In addition systematic synthetic phonics has been identified as the best method for teaching reading with £7.7 million being made available to primary schools in a matched funding scheme for the purchase of phonics products.

The introduction of an English Baccalaureate (E-Bacc) which would include English, Maths, Science, a humanities subject and an ancient or modern foreign language was designed to encourage students to study academic subjects up to the age of 16. The E-Bacc was part of the Coalition government's response to the criticism that some secondary schools had manipulated the curriculum through the introduction of vocational programmes to improve their results in performance tables.

School funding

Against a background of cuts in public expenditure £2.5 billion per year has been allocated to the pupil premium to focus resources on the most deprived pupils. The pupil premium is designed to raise educational standards among the poorest sections of society and to reduce the attainment gap between rich and poor pupils. The maximum amount of funding will be devolved to individual schools and the Coalition government is seeking to create a system that is a 'clear, transparent and fairer national funding formula based on the needs of pupils' (DfE, 2010: 15).

Behaviour policies

Proposals to improve behaviour in schools include giving greater powers to head teachers and teachers and requiring Ofsted, as part of the inspection process, to focus more strongly on behaviour. In particular, teachers will be given greater powers to search pupils, to use reasonable force where necessary and change and improve the exclusion process.

Accountability

A crucial part of giving more autonomy to schools is the need to ensure that they are accountable. More information will be made available to parents and performance tables will focus on achievement and aim to raise aspirations. The Ofsted inspection system will be reformed and the reforms to the curriculum will set high expectations by ensuring pupils have a 'broad education (the English Baccalaureate), a firm grip of the basics and are making progress' (DfE, 2010: 13).

School improvement policies

The Coalition government is determined to shift the focus for school improvement away from a centralised approach to an increased emphasis on the individual school. Head teachers, teachers and governors will have a key role to play in this process and it is expected that head teachers of excellent schools will support other schools through the extension of National and Local Leaders of Education. Teaching schools will be established to disseminate good practice and to take greater responsibility for the initial training and continuing professional development of teachers.

Teaching and school leadership

The quality of teaching and teachers has been identified by the Coalition government as a major factor in determining the effectiveness of the education system. There has been a continued drive to attract the best graduates into teaching and to move training into schools through the reform of initial teacher training. The Coalition plans to cut the amount of bureaucracy to enable schools to focus on 'doing what is right for the children and the young people in their care' (DfE, 2010: 9).

School system

New types of school will be established including Free Schools and the expansion of the Academies programme. Schools will be freed from excessive bureaucracy and given greater freedom and autonomy to develop their own ethos and approach. Local authorities will be expected to act as 'champions for parents, families and vulnerable pupils' and to ensure a 'good supply of high quality school places' (DfE, 2010:12). A central part of the reform process is the fundamental belief that giving greater freedom to schools will result in higher standards:

> Across the world, the case for the benefits of school autonomy has been established beyond doubt. In a school system with good

quality teachers, flexibility in the curriculum and clearly established accountability measures, it makes sense to devolve as much day-to-day decision making as possible to the front line.

In this country, the ability of schools to decide their own ethos and chart their own destiny has been severely constrained by government guidance, Ministerial interference and too much bureaucracy. While Academies and City Technology Colleges (CTCs) have taken advantage of greater freedoms to innovate and raise standards, these freedoms too have been curtailed in recent years. Meanwhile, it has been virtually impossible to establish a new state-funded school without local authority support, despite convincing international evidence of the galvanising effect on the whole schools system of allowing new entrants in areas where parents are dissatisfied with what is available. (DfE, 2010: 11)

Given this belief that increased school autonomy will lead to an improvement in standards the Coalition government has promoted a new schools system based around different types of schools. A fundamental part of this process is the extension of the Academies programme, but the establishment of other types of school have been encouraged by the Secretary of State. The University Technical Colleges (UTCs) and Free Schools are examples of new and different types of school being established by a range of groups. The UTCs policy is being led by the former Education Secretary Kenneth Baker through his Baker Dearing Education Trust and its origins can be traced back to the CTCs initiative (see Chapter 4). The UTCs are aimed at the 14–19 age group and will focus on vocational education with a strong business involvement.

A more controversial policy has been the introduction of Free Schools which are funded by the state and can be established by local people in response to local demand. In September 2011, 24 Free Schools opened despite a range of criticism which argued that the evidence on the benefits of these type of schools was mixed and there was potential negative impact on established schools (see, for example, Allen, 2010; Benn, 2011b). Drawing on the Charter Schools in the USA and the Free Schools that have been developed in Sweden the government 'invited teacher groups, parent groups, charities and others to apply to set up their own schools' (Gove, 2011). The debate about the effectiveness of these schools will continue but what is remarkable is the speed with which they were established. Previously opening a new school had been a lengthy process, but the first Free Schools opened their doors to new pupils 15 months after the election of the Coalition government. Opening up the education sector to new schools which could bring about change, without any involvement from local authorities, has become a reality. At this stage it is too early to judge the outcome of these initiatives but historically the pace of development is extremely fast.

Under the Coalition government a number of external organisations have continued to extend their influence in the education sector. For example, organisations such as Teach First and Teaching Leaders have increased their involvement in initial teacher training and the continuing professional development of teachers. This is part of the Coalition government's drive to encourage the involvement of a wide range of organisations to develop different provision models. At the same time the number of 'arm's length bodies' was being slashed as the Coalition embarked on a massive cost-cutting exercise designed to reduce the level of public expenditure and as part of the drive to give greater autonomy to schools. The General Teaching Council and the Qualifications and Curriculum Development Agency were two notable examples of major bodies that were closed.

Cost-cutting has been a significant feature of Coalition government education policy as a number of flagship projects introduced by the previous Labour government were scrapped. Examples include the EMA (see Chapter 8) and the Building Schools for the Future programme. The announcement of the end of the Building Schools for the Future programme brought forward legal challenges from local authorities as schools which were expecting building work to commence in the near future suddenly discovered that the plans had been scrapped. The abolition of the EMA created a great deal of controversy and opposition from some members of the Coalition. Despite these setbacks the direction and pace of change continued.

Vocational education

In 2010 the Coalition government instigated a review of vocational education directed by Professor Alison Wolf. Writing in the foreword to the Wolf Report Michael Gove traced the issues back to the nineteenth century:

> Since Prince Albert established the Royal Commission in 1851 policy-makers have struggled with our failure to provide young people with a proper technical and practical education of a kind that other nations can boast. 160 years later the same problems remain. Our international competitors boast more robust manufacturing industries. Our technical education remains weaker than most other developed nations. And, in simple terms, our capacity to generate growth by making things remains weaker. (DfE, 2011: 4)

Professor Wolf was asked 'to consider how we can improve vocational educational for 14–19 year olds and thereby promote successful progression into the labour market and into higher level education and training routes' (DfE, 2011: 19). The Wolf Report recognises that there is a great deal of good work taking place in schools and colleges but a number of problems remain:

- the lack of high-quality vocational opportunities for 16–17 year olds, which results in young people moving in and out of short-term programmes and employment – described as 'churn' – and being unable to either progress or to find suitable employment;
- the large number of low-level vocational qualifications available which do not allow progression and which hold little value in the labour market;
- the low levels of achievement in English and mathematics (the benchmark considered as GCSE A*–C) among this cohort. Wolfe cites over 50 per cent of young people failing to achieve both these qualifications by the end of Key Stage 4; at 18 the percentage is still below 50 per cent.

The Wolf Report contains 27 recommendations that have been accepted by the Coalition government which can be summarised under three 'organising principles':

- Vocational qualifications should lead to progression and enable young people to go on to further education and training or into the labour market.
- Providing good information and guidance to young people and their parents/carers is important.
- The vocational education system needs to be simplified with a reduction in the number of qualifications.

The Wolf Report can be viewed as part of the Coalition government's drive to raise standards by moving towards a curriculum that places more emphasis on academic subjects. There is a recognition of the differences between academic and vocational qualifications:

> In recent years, both academic and vocational education in England have been bedevilled by well-meaning attempts to pretend that everything is worth the same as everything else. Students and families all know this is nonsense. (DfE, 2011: 8)

There is a strong drive by the Coalition government to get the basics right which will then give young people the widest range of options to go on to further education or training. According to the Coalition Government, refocusing the school system on academic standards rather than the perceived lower aspirations of vocational qualifications will provide more opportunities for more young people. At the end of January 2012 the DfE announced a significant reduction in the number of vocational qualifications that will be counted in school performance tables. This was designed to stop schools using student's success in vocational qualifications as a means of boosting their performance table positions. When interviewed in 2011 Michael Gove argued strongly:

> I believe that one of the big problems that English state education has had for generations is the assumption that an academic education can only ever be accessible by a minority. That was institutionalised through the grammar school/secondary modern split in the past but even in those areas where the 11 plus no longer reigns, the shadow of it still has an effect in that when, for example, we had a debate about the English baccalaureate people including Andy Burnham say: 'Well this is an elite measure for a minority.' I emphatically don't believe that. I think you can have schools, in fact I think the best schools are those which are socially comprehensive, which reflect the community in which they sit, that draw from a wide range of backgrounds and abilities but which are determined to have the highest possible ambitions for their students and to have (this is a bit of cliché) a no excuses culture. To say: 'You can succeed.' Ninety-eight per cent of parents in the millennium cohort study when they are asked: 'What would you like your child to do? Would you like them to go to university?' say 'yes'. You and I naturally assume and hope that our children will go to university. If they choose not to we will love them just as much. But we hope that it will be their choice rather than something that will be denied them because education hasn't equipped them for it. I think that there are many more children who are capable of making that choice. They may decide that actually it is not for them but being able to access it and to allow for it at the moment and that is why I think that the Academies programme has been so inspirational.

Education Secretaries and the development of policy

Michael Gove (2010–present)

Michael Gove had been appointed Shadow Secretary of State for Children, Schools and Families in 2007. He had been elected as an MP in 2005 after a career as a journalist. He had been educated at an independent school after winning a scholarship and then went on to Oxford University. During his time in opposition he developed a thorough understanding of the education system and recognised the advantage this gave him when he became Secretary of State:

> I think it is always helpful – there is never any hard and fast rule for this – but I think it's always helpful if you've had the chance in opposition to think about any job that you might do in Government. (Gove, interview, 2011)

Following the general election legislation was quickly introduced and there have been significant policy announcements in a relatively short period of time. This process has been helped by the close working relationship Gove had established with the Prime Minister:

> However well or badly I've done the job at least I've had the comfort of knowing that my instincts are aligned with, and the policy I want to pursue, is the same policy as the PM wants us to pursue and I think that has been helpful. (Gove, interview, 2011)

How much of the policy initiatives are new? The emphasis on creating some form of market in education through the establishment of different types of schools can be traced back to the Thatcher government, but Gove also sees a continuation of policy from the Blair government:

> I would argue that it's continuity with what happened or what was intended to happen when Tony Blair was Prime Minister rather than with the 2007–2010 Gordon Brown/Ed Balls period because I would argue that there was actually a fisura in reform between 2007–2010 and that we've picked up the reform momentum. That momentum was already being checked, I think, even immediately after the 2005 election. Funnily enough it's one of things in the Paper today can be seen through that prism but when David Cameron became firstly Shadow Education Spokesman and then leader of the Conservative Party he was determined to ensure that the Conservatives supported the aims of Tony Blair's White Paper and the Bill that Ruth Kelly was bringing into the House of Commons in 2005/6. Now that White Paper and that Bill generated a significant battle in the Labour Party. Tony Blair and Andrew Adonis had recognised that you needed both structural and standards-based reform. That you needed to have a progressively greater degree of autonomy at individual school level and the 2005 White Paper discusses not just the Academy programme and how it might be expanded but also the idea of parent or citizen promoted schools for the man in the street. (Gove, interview, 2011)

Policy development

The flagship policy of the Coalition government has been the drive to increase the number of Academies with the aim of creating autonomous schools. This policy has generated controversy and opposition (see, for example, http://www.antiacademies.org.uk) but Gove claims:

> It is an extension but there are two things I would say: the first is that there is also a link with what happened in the 1980s as well because there are parallels between the Academies programme for converter schools and grant-maintained schools but there are several things I would say: the first is that John Major was explicit that schools were being bribed to become grant-maintained schools (perfectly legitimately actually) but we are not doing that. There is no cash advantage to being an Academy. The second thing is that all schools that convert have to show that they are using their additional freedoms to help at least one other underperforming school so collaboration is embedded in the process. And then the third thing is that we've allowed schools to convert on the basis of how high performing they are and of course there are some high-performing schools, indeed a significant number in better-off areas, but my argument is (a) well that's a reflection of how far Labour still had to go because it was the case that excellence was concentrated in particular areas but (b) isn't it a good idea rather than simply leaving these schools to cultivate a good education for the children who are fortunate enough to be within their catchment area to secure a place there, isn't it better to mobilise and liberate these schools to support, collaborate with, or take over underperforming schools in more difficult areas so that we can all see the benefit of improvement. So that you can have people like the United Learning Trust or the Harris Academy chain moving out from areas of success and taking on new challenges but you can also have highly effective head teachers like Barry Day of Greenwood Dale taking over other less well performing schools and helping to turn them around. (Gove, interview, 2011)

A major criticism of the Academies programme has been that it is politically driven but Gove, in a speech in January 2012, argued that it was concerned with pupils:

> It's ironic, if you think about it. The popular critique of our reform programme has most often been of its underpinning motives. The talk was of an 'ideologically driven Academies programme' and 'ideologically

motivated school reforms'. We're supposed to be the ideologues. And yet . . . The Academies programme is not about ideology. It's an evidence-based, practical solution built on by successive governments – both Labour and Conservative. The new ideologues are the enemies of reform, the ones who put doctrine ahead of pupils' interests. Every step of the way, they have sought to discredit our policies, calling them divisive, destructive, ineffective, unpopular, unworkable – even 'a crime against humanity'.

During his short time in office Michael Gove has attracted criticism and there have been a number of legal challenges to his policies. However, he has remained committed to raising the performance of the poorest group of school pupils and to provide increased opportunities for all pupils to achieve academic success. Despite the challenges there has not been any discernable slowing down of the amount of policy initiatives or any change in the direction of travel of the Coalition government.

Conclusion

It is too early to reach conclusions on the effectiveness of the educational reforms being introduced by the Coalition government. However, the amount of change has been rapid with a number of significant initiatives being introduced. The election of a Coalition government has done little to lessen the pace of change and education policy has remained at the forefront of government policy.

While many of the policies can be traced back to previous Conservative and Labour governments it is clear that a revolution is taking place in England's schools. A major review of the content of the curriculum and assessment is taking place. Fundamental changes are being implemented in the way in which teachers are trained. Schools are being given much greater autonomy with a continuing reduction in the power and influence of local authorities. New and different types of school are being established under the overall control of central government. The Ofsted inspection system is being reviewed with a new Chief Inspector who previously had been the head teacher of an Academy school. These changes are being carried out against a background of difficult economic conditions and reductions in public expenditure. However, it seems that nothing can stop the momentum of education reform. The reforms being introduced will fundamentally change the nature and form of education in England. Interesting times lie ahead.

Further reading

Benn, M. (2011) *School Wars: The Battle for Britain's Education*. London: Verso.

DfE (2010) *The Importance of Teaching*. London: TSO.

APPENDIX:
Table of Ministers/Secretaries of State 1945–Present

Date	Name	Party	Title
May 1945 – February 1947	Ellen Wilkinson	Lab	Minister of Education
February 1947 – November 1951	George Tomlinson	Lab	Minister of Education
November 1951 – October 1954	Florence Horsbrugh	Lab	Minister of Education
October 1954 – January 1957	Sir David Eccles	Con	Minister of Education
January 1957 – September 1957	Viscount Hailsham	Con	Minister of Education
September 1957 – October 1959	Geoffrey Lloyd	Con	Minister of Education
October 1959 – July 1962	Sir David Eccles	Con	Minister of Education
July 1962 – March 1964	Sir Edward Boyle	Con	Minister of Education
April 1964 – October 1964	Quintin Hogg	Con	Secretary of State for Education and Science
October 1964 – January 1965	Michael Stewart	Lab	Secretary of State for Education and Science
January 1965 – August 1967	Anthony Crosland	Lab	Secretary of State for Education and Science
August 1967 – April 1968	Patrick Gordon Walker	Lab	Secretary of State for Education and Science
April 1968 – June 1970	Edward Short	Con	Secretary of State for Education and Science
June 1970 – March 1974	Margaret Thatcher	Con	Secretary of State for Education and Science
March 1974 – June 1975	Reginald Prentice	Lab	Secretary of State for Education and Science
June 1975 – September 1976	Fred Mulley	Lab	Secretary of State for Education and Science
September 1976 – May 1979	Shirley Williams	Lab	Secretary of State for Education and Science
May 1979 – September 1981	Mark Carlisle	Con	Secretary of State for Education and Science
September 1981 – May 1986	Sir Keith Joseph	Con	Secretary of State for Education and Science
May 1986 – July 1989	Kenneth Baker	Con	Secretary of State for Education and Science
July 1989 – November 1990	John MacGregor	Con	Secretary of State for Education and Science
November 1990 – April 1992	Kenneth Clarke	Con	Secretary of State for Education and Science
April 1992 – July 1994	John Patten	Con	Secretary of State for Education
July 1994 – May 1997	Gillian Shephard	Con	Secretary of State for Education and Employment
May 1997 – June 2001	David Blunkett	Lab	Secretary of State for Education and Employment
June 2001 – October 2002	Estelle Morris	Lab	Secretary of State for Education and Skills
October 2002 – December 2004	Charles Clarke	Lab	Secretary of State for Education and Skills
December 2004 – May 2006	Ruth Kelly	Lab	Secretary of State for Education and Skills
May 2006 – June 2007	Alan Johnson	Lab	Secretary of State for Education and Skills
June 2007 – May 2010	Ed Balls	Lab	Secretary of State for Children, Schools and Families
May 2010 – present	Michael Gove	Con	Secretary of State for Education

REFERENCES

Abbott, I. (2004) 'Government initiatives: excellence in cities and gifted and talented', in V. Brooks, I. Abbott and L. Bills (eds), *Preparing to Teach in Secondary Schools*. Maidenhead: Open University Press.

Aldrich, R. (ed.) (2002) *A Century of Education*. London: RoutledgeFalmer.

Alexander, R. J. (ed.) (2010) *Children, Their World, Their Education. Final Report and Recommendations of the Cambridge Primary Review*. London: Routledge.

Alexander, R., Rose, J. and Woodhead, C. (1992) *Curriculum Organisation and Classroom Practice in Primary Schools*. London: DES.

Allen, R. (2010) 'Replicating Swedish "free school" reforms in England', *Research in Public Policy*, Summer: 4–7.

Anning, A. and Hall, D. (2008) 'What was Sure Start and why did it matter?', in A. Anning and M. Ball (eds), *Improving Services for Young Children: From Sure Start to Children's Centres*. London: Sage.

Auld Report (1976) *Report of the Public Enquiry: The William Tyndale Junior and Infants Schools*. London: Inner London Education Authority.

Bailey, B. (2002) 'Further education', in R. Aldrich (ed.), *A Century of Education*. London: RoutledgeFalmer.

Baker, K. (1993) *The Turbulent Years: My Life in Politics*. London: Faber & Faber.

Balen, M. (1994) *Kenneth Clarke: A Biography*. London: Fourth Estate.

Ball, S. J. (1986) *Sociology in Focus: Education*. London: Longman.

Ball, S. J. (1999) 'Labour, learning and the economy: a political sociology perspective', *Cambridge Journal of Education*, 29 (2): 195–206.

Ball, S. J. (2007) *Education plc: Understanding Private Sector Participation in Public Sector Education*. London: Routledge.

Ball, S. J. (2008) *The Education Debate*. Bristol: Policy Press.

Ball, S. J. (2010) *The Education Debate* (2nd edn). Bristol: Policy Press.

Bangs, J., Macbeath, J. and Galton, M. (2011) *Reinventing Schools, Reforming Teaching*. Abingdon: Routledge.

Barber, M. (1992) *Education and the Teacher Unions*. London: Cassell.

Barber, M. (1994) *The Making of the 1944 Education Act*. London: Cassell.

Barber, M. (1996) 'New Labour, 20 years on', *TES Magazine*, 11 October.

Barber, M. (2007) *Instruction to Deliver*. London: Methuen.

Barber, M. and Sebba, J. (1999) 'Reflections on progress towards a world-class education system', *Cambridge Journal of Education*, 29 (2): 183–93.

Bash, L. (1989) 'Education goes to market', in L. Bash and D. Coulby, *The Education Reform Act: Competition and Control*. London: Cassell Education.

Bastiani, J. (1978) *Written Communication Between Home and School*. University of Nottingham, School of Education.

Batty, P. (2000) 'Post-16 Bill muddies waters', *Times Higher Education Supplement*, 21 January.

Beckett, F. (2007) *The Great City Academy Fraud*. London: Continuum.

Bell, R., Fowler, G. and Little, K. (1973) *Education in Great Britain and Ireland*. London: Open University Press.

Benn, C. and Chitty, C. (1996) *Thirty Years On: Is Comprehensive Education Alive and Well or Struggling to Survive?* London: David Fulton.

Benn, M. (2011a) *School Wars: The Battle for Britain's Education*. London: Verso.

Benn, M. (2011b) 'Why are we following the US into a schools policy distaster. Available online at: http://www.guardian.co.uk/education/2011/nov/28/us-charter-academies-free-schools (accessed 25 January 2012).

Bernstein, B. (1970) 'Education cannot compensate for society', *New Society*, 15 (387): 344–7.

Bernstein, B. (1973) *Class, Codes and Control*, Vol. 1. London: Paladin.

Beveridge, W. (1942) *Social Insurance and Allied Services*. London: HMSO.

Blackburn, F. (1954) *George Tomlinson*. London: Heinemann.

Blair, T. (1998) *The Third Way*. London: Fabian Society.

Blunkett, D. (2006) *The Blunkett Tapes: My Life in the Bear Pit*. London: Bloomsbury.

Board of Education (1933) *Infant and Nursery Schools* (The Hadow Report). London: HMSO.

Board of Education (1938) *Report of the Consultative Committee on Secondary Education* (The Spens Report). London: HMSO.

Board of Education (1943) *Educational Reconstruction* (White Paper). London: HMSO.

Board of Education, Committee on Public Schools (1944) *The Public Schools and the General Education System* (The Fleming Report). London: HMSO.

Brooks, G., Pugh, A. K. and Schagen, I. (1996) *Reading Performance at Nine*. Slough: NFER.

Brown, M. (1998) 'The tyranny of the international horse race', in R. Slee, G. Weiner and S. Tomlinson (eds), *School Effectiveness for Whom?* London: Falmer.

Brown, P. (1977) 'The Third Wave: education and the ideology of parentocracy', in A. H. Halsey, H. Lauder, P. Brown and A. Wells (eds), *Education: Culture, Economy and Society*. Oxford: Oxford University Press.

Butler, R. A. (1971) *The Art of the Possible*. London: Hamish Hamilton.

Cabinet Office (2010a) *The Coalition Agreement for Stability and Reform*. London: Cabinet Office.

Cabinet Office (2010b) *The Coalition: Our Programme for Government*. London: Cabinet Office.

Callaghan, J. (1976) *Towards a National Debate*. Oxford, Ruskin College.

Cameron, D. and Clegg, N. (2010) 'Foreword' by the Prime Minister and Deputy Prime Minister, in *The Importance of Teaching: Schools White Paper*.

Campbell, R. J. (2011) 'State control, religious deference and cultural reproduction, some problems with theorising curriculum and pedagogy in the Cambridge Primary Review', *Education 3–13*, 29 (4): 343–55.

Carlisle, M. (1997) Cited in P. Ribbins and B. Sherratt, *Radical Educational Policies and Conservative Secretaries of State*. London: Cassell.

Carr, W. and Hartnett, A. (1996) *Education and the Struggle for Democracy*. Buckingham: Open University Press.

Central Advisory Council for Education (England) (CACE) (1954) *Early Leaving* (The Gurney-Dixon Report). London: HMSO.

Central Advisory Council for Education (England) (CACE) (1959) *Fifteen to Eighteen* (The Crowther Report). London: HMSO.

Chapman, C. and Gunter, H. (eds) (2009) *Radical Reforms: Perspectives on an Era of Educational Change*. London: Routledge.

Chataway, C. (1991) 'At the Education Ministry: his Junior Minister's view', in A. Gold (ed.), *Edward Boyle: His Life by His Friends*. London: Macmillan.

Chitty, C. (1989) *Towards a New Education System: The Victory of the New Right?* Lewes: Falmer Press.

Chitty, C. (1996) 'The role of the state in education', in J. Ahier, B. Cosin and M. Hales (eds), *Diversity and Change: Education, Policy and Selection*. London: Routledge.

Chitty, C. (2002a) 'The role and status of LEAs: post-war pride and *fin de siècle* uncertainty', *Oxford Review of Education*, 28 (2&3): 261–73.

Chitty, C. (2002b) *The Right to a Comprehensive Education*, Second Caroline Benn Memorial Lecture. Available online at: http://www.socialisteducation.org.uk/article/caroline-benn-memorial-lecture-2002 (accessed 10 January 2012).

Chitty, C. (2004) *Education Policy in Britain*. Basingstoke: Palgrave Macmillan.

Chitty, C. (2009) *Education Policy in Britain* (2nd edn). Basingstoke: Palgrave Macmillan.

Chowdry, H. and Sibieta, L. (2011) *Trends in Education and Schools Spending*. London: IFS.

Cox, C. B. and Dyson, A. E. (eds) (1969a) *Fight for Education: A Black Paper*. London: Critical Quarterly Society.

Cox, C. B. and Dyson, A. E. (eds) (1969b) *Black Paper Two: The Crisis in Education*. London: Critical Quarterly Review.

Cox, C. B. and Dyson, A. E. (eds) (1970) *Black Paper Three*. London: Critical Quarterly Review.

Crawford, K. (2000) 'The political construction of the "whole curriculum"', *British Educational Research Journal*, 26 (5): 615–30.

Cretney, S. M. (2005) 'Hogg, Quintin McGarel, second Viscount Hailsham and Baron Hailsham of St Marylebone (1907–2001)', *Oxford Dictionary of National Biography*, Oxford University Press; online edn, January 2011, http://www.oxforddnb.com/view/article/76372 (accessed 24 April 2012).

Crook, D. (2002) 'Local authorities and comprehensivisation in England and Wales 1944–1974', *Oxford Review of Education*, 28 (2&3): 247–60.

Crook, D., Power, S. and Whitty, G. (1999) *The Grammar School Question: A Review of Research on Comprehensive and Selective Education*. London Institute of Education.

Cummings, A. (2000) 'The Dearing Review of qualifications 16–19: attempting to reconcile the irreconcilable', *Curriculum Journal*, 11 (3): 365–83.

Cunningham, P. (2002) 'Primary education', in R. Aldrich (ed.), *A Century of Education*. London: RoutledgeFalmer.

Curtis, P. and Shepherd, J. (2009) 'Ed Balls accused over Sats tests fiasco by ex-QCA head', *Guardian*, 23 April.

Dale, R. (1989) *The State and Education Policy*. Buckingham: Open University Press.

Davies, N. (2000) *The School Report*. London: Vintage.

DCSF (2007a) *Extended Schools: Building on Experience*. Nottingham: DCSF.

DCSF (2007b) *The Children's Plan. Building Brighter Futures*. London: Stationery Office.

DCSF (2008a) *Eighty-Nine New Specialist Schools Announced*, Press Notice 2008/0023. London: DCSF.

DCSF (2008b) *21ˢᵗ Century Schools: A World-Class Education for Every Child*. London: DCSF.

DCSF (2009a) *Your Child, Your Schools, Our Future: Building a 21ˢᵗ Century Schools System*. London: Stationery Office.

DCSF (2009b) *The Rose Review. Independent Review of the Primary Curriculum: Final Report*. London: DCSF.

DCSF (2009c) *A School Report Card: Prospectus*. London: DCSF.

Dean, D. W. (1986) 'Planning for a post-war generation: Ellen Wilkinson and George Tomlinson at the Ministry of Education, 1945–51', *History of Education*, 15 (2): 95–117.

Dean, D. W. (2006) 'Consensus or conflict? The Churchill government and educational policy 1951–55', *History of Education*, 21 (1): 15–35.

Dell, E. (n.d.) 'Frederick William Mulley'. Available online at: http://www.oxforddnb.com/view/article/58032?docPos=1.

Dennison, W. F. (1985) 'Education and the economy: changing circumstances', in I. McNay and J. Ozga (eds), *Policy-Making in Education: The Breakdown of Consensus*. Oxford: Pergamon Press.

DES (1961) *Better Opportunities in Technical Education*. London: HMSO.

DES (1965) *The Organisation of Secondary Education*, Circular 10/65. London: HMSO.

DES (1967) *Children and Their Primary Schools: A Report of the Central Advisory Council for Education* (The Plowden Report). London: HMSO.

DES (1968) *Public Schools Commission: First Report*. London: HMSO.

DES (1977a) *Local Arrangements for the School Curriculum*, Circular 14/77. London: HMSO.

DES (1977b) *A New Partnership for Our Schools* (The Taylor Report). London: HMSO.

DES (1977c) *Education in Schools: A Consultative Document*, (Green Paper). London: HMSO.

DES (1978) *Special Educational Needs* (The Warnock Report). London: HMSO.

DES (1985) *Better Schools*, Cmnd 9469. London: HMSO.

DES (1987) *The National Curriculum 5–16: A Consultation Document*. London: HMSO.

DES (1988) *Report of the Committee of Inquiry into the Teaching of English Language* (The Kingman Report). London: HMSO.

DES (1992) *Choice and Diversity: A New Framework for Schools*. London: HMSO.

DfE (2010) *The Importance of Teaching: Schools White Paper*. London: Stationery Office.

DfE (2011) *Review of Vocational Education* (The Wolf Report). London: Stationery Office.

DfEE (1997) *Excellence in Schools*, Cmnd 2681. London: Stationery Office.

DfEE (1998a) *The National Literacy Strategy: Framework for Teaching*. London: DfEE.

DfEE (1998b) *Teaching and Higher Education Act*.

DfEE (1999a) *The National Numeracy Strategy: Framework for Teaching Mathematics from Reception to Year 6*. London: DfEE.

DfEE (1999b) *Excellence in Cities*. London: DfEE.

DfEE (1999c) *Sure Start: A Guide for Trailblazers*. London: Stationery Office.

DfEE (1999d) *Learning to Succeed: A New Framework for Post-16 Learning*, Cmnd 4392. London: Stationery Office.

DfEE (2001) *Schools: Building on Success: Raising Standards, Promoting Diversity, Achieving Results*, Cmnd 5050. London: Stationery Office.

DfES (2001) *Schools: Achieving Success*, Cmnd 5230. London: Stationery Office.

DfES (2003) *Every Child Matters*, Cmnd 586. London: HMSO.

DfES (2004a) *A Five-Year Strategy for Children and Learners: Putting People at the Heart of Public Services*, Cmnd 6272. London: Stationery Office.

DfES (2004b) *Curriculum and Qualifications Reform: Final Report of the Working Group on 14–19 Reform* (The Tomlinson Report). Nottingham: DfES Publications.

DfES (2005a) *Extended Schools: Access to Opportunities and Services for All*. Nottingham: DfES.

DfES (2005b) *Higher Standards, Better Schools for All: More Choice for Parents and Pupils*, Cmnd 6677. London: Stationery Office.

DfES (2005c) *14–19 Education and Skills*, Cmnd 6746. London: Stationery Office.

DfES (2006) *The Five Year Strategy for Children and Learners: Maintaining the Excellent Progress*. London: DfES.

Docking, J. (2000) *New Labour's Policies for Schools: Raising the Standard*. London: David Fulton.

Douglas, J. W. B. (1964) *The Home and the School*. London: MacGibbon & Kee.

Dyson, A. et al. (2009) 'Swing, swing together', in C. Chapman and H. Gunter (eds), *Radical Reforms: Perspectives on an Era of Educational Change*. Abingdon: Routledge.

Eccleshare, R., Geoghegan, V. and Kenny, M. (2003) *Political Ideologies*. London: Routledge.

Evans, R. (2012) *The History of Technical Education: A Short Introduction*. Available online at: http://www.tmag.co.uk/extras/history_of_Technical_Education_v2.pdf (accessed 30 January 2012).

Eysenck, H. (1964) *Crime and Personality*. London: Routledge.

Fieldhouse, R. (1994) 'Labour's FE policy 1945–51', *History of Education*, 23 (3): 287–99.

Fitz, J., Edwards, T. and Whitty, G. (1989) 'The Assisted Places Scheme: an ambiguous case of privatisation', *British Journal of Educational Studies*, 37 (3): 222–34.

Francis, M. (1995) 'A socialist policy for education: Labour and the secondary school, 1945–51', *History of Education*, 24 (4): 319–35.

Galton, M. and Macbeath, J. (2008) *Teachers Under Pressure*. London: Sage in association with the National Union of Teachers.

Galvani, R. (2010) 'The changing experience of English secondary education', *Reflecting Education*, 6 (1): 75–89.

Giddens, A. (1998) *The Third Way: The Renewal of Social Democracy*. Cambridge: Polity.

Giddens, A. (2000) *The Third Way and Its Critics*. Cambridge: Polity.

Gillard, D. (2011) 'Education in England: A Brief History'. Available online at: http://www.educationengland.org.uk/history (accessed 5 January 2012).

Gleeson, D. and Keep, E. (2004) 'Voice without accountability: the changing relationship between employers, the state and education in England', *Oxford Review of Education*, 30 (1): 37–64.

Godwin, C. D. (2002) 'Government policy and the provision of teachers', *British Journal of Educational Studies*, 50 (1): 76–99.

Gold, A. (ed.) (1991) *Edward Boyle: His Life by His Friends*. Basingstoke: Macmillan.

Gorard, S. (2009) 'What are Academies the answer to?', *Journal of Education Policy*, 24 (1): 101–13.

Gordon, P. (2002) 'Curriculum', in R. Aldrich (ed.), *A Century of Education*. Abingdon: RoutledgeFalmer.

Gove, M. (2011) Speech to the Policy Exchange on Free Schools. DfE website (accessed 21 January 2012).

Gove, M. (2012) Speech on Academies. DfE website (accessed 23 January 2012).

Halcrow, M. (1989) *A Single Mind*. London: Macmillan.

Halsey, A. H. (1972) *Educational Priority Volume 1: EPA Problems and Policies*. London: HMSO.

Hargreaves, A. (1985) 'The politics of administrative convenience: the case of the middle schools', in I. McNay and J. Ozga (eds), *Policy-Making in Education: The Breakdown of Consensus*. Oxford: Pergamon Press.

Hargreaves, A. (2009) 'Labouring to lead', in C. Chapman and H. Gunter (eds), *Radical Reforms: Perspectives on an Era of Educational Change*. London: Routledge.

Haslegrave, H. L. (1969) *Report of the Committee on Technician Courses and Examinations*. London: HMSO.

Haydn, T. (2004) 'The strange death of the comprehensive school in England and Wales, 1965–2002', *Research Papers in Education*, 19 (4): 415–32.

Hennessy, P. (2006) *Having It So Good: Britain in the Fifties*. London: Penguin Books.

Higham, J. and Yeomans, D. (2011) 'Thirty years of 14–19 education and training in England: reflections on policy, curriculum and organisation', *London Review of Education*, 9 (2): 217–30.

Hirst, P. H. and Peters, R. S. (1970) *The Logic of Education*. London: Routledge & Kegan Paul.

Hodgson, A. and Spours, K. (2008) *Education and Training 14–19: Curriculum, Qualifications and Organisation*. London: Sage.

Hoggart, R. (1996) *The Way We Live Now*. London: Pimlico.

Hughes, B. (1979) 'In defence of Ellen Wilkinson', *History Workshop*, 9 (7): 157–60.

Hughes, C. (1993) 'Education: what every parent should ask', *The Independent*, 1 April.

Jackson, B. (1964) *Streaming: An Education System in Miniature*. London: Routledge & Kegan Paul.

James Committee (1972) *Teacher Education and Training. Report of the Committee on Teacher Training*. London: HMSO.

Jenkins, S. (2010) 'Gove's claim to be "freeing" schools is a cloak for more control from the centre', *Guardian*, 28 February.

Jensen, A. R. (1973) *Educational Differences*. London: Routledge.

Jones, K. (1989) *Right Turn: The Conservative Revolution in Education*. London: Hutchinson Radius.

Jones, K. (2003) *Education in Britain: 1944 to the Present*. Cambridge: Polity Press.

Joseph, K. (1975) *Reversing the Trend*. London: Centre for Policy Studies.

Joseph, K. and Sumption, J. (1979) *Equality*. London: Murray.

Kavanagh, D. (1987) *Thatcherism and British Politics: The End of Consensus*. Oxford: Oxford University Press.

Kenneth Richmond, W. (1978) *Education in Britain since 1944*. London: Methuen.

Kerckhoff, A., Fogelman, K., Crook, D. and Reeder, D. (1996) *Going Comprehensive in England and Wales: A Study of Uneven Change*. London: Woburn Press.

Kogan, M. (1971) *The Politics of Education: Edward Boyle and Anthony Crosland in Conversation with Maurice Kogan*. Harmondsworth: Penguin Education Specials.

Kogan, M. (1978) *The Politics of Educational Change*. Manchester: Manchester University Press.

Kogan, M. (1987) 'The Plowden Report twenty years on', *Oxford Review of Education*, 13 (1): 13–21.

Kogan, M. (1991) 'At the Education Ministry: an official's view', in A. Gold (ed.), *Edward Boyle: His Life by His Friends*. London: Macmillan.

Kogan, M. (2006) 'Anthony Crosland: intellectual and politician', *Oxford Review of Education*, 32 (1): 71–86.

Kogan, M., Van der Eyken, W., Cook, D., Pratt, C. and Taylor, G. (1973) *County Hall: The Role of the Chief Education Office*. Harmondsworth: Penguin Education Specials.

Kynaston, D. (2007) *Austerity Britain 1945–51*. London: Bloomsbury.

Kynaston, D. (2009) *Family Britain 1951–57*. London: Bloomsbury.

Labour Party (1961) *Signposts for the Sixties*. London: Labour Party.

Labour Party (1997) *New Labour. Because Britain Deserves Better* (election manifesto). London: Labour Party.

Labour Party (2001) *Ambitions for Britain* (election manifesto). London: Labour Party.

Labour Party (2005) *Britain Forward Not Back* (Labour Party manifesto). London: Labour Party.

Laming, H. (2003) *The Victoria Climbié Inquiry*. London: Stationery Office.

Lawrence, I. (1992) *Power and Privilege at the DES*. London: Cassell.

Lawson, J. and Silver, H. (1973) *A Social History of Education in England*. London: Methuen.

Lawson, J. and Silver, H. (1985) 'Education and social policy', in I. McNay and J. Ozga (eds), *Policy-Making in Education: The Breakdown of Consensus*. Oxford: Pergamon Press.

Lawton, D. (1968) *Social Class, Language and Education*. London: Routledge & Kegan Paul.

Lawton, D. (1994) *The Tory Mind on Education 1979–94*. London: Falmer Press.

Levacic, R. (2008) 'Financing schools: evolving patterns of autonomy and control', *Educational Management, Administration and Leadership*, 36 (2): 221–34.

Levacic, R. and Jenkins, A. (2006) 'Evaluating the effectiveness of specialist schools in England', *School Effectiveness and School Improvement*, 17 (3): 229–54.

Limond, D. (2007) 'Miss Joyce Lang, Kidbrooke and the Great Comprehensive Debate: 1965–2005', *History of Education*, 36 (3): 339–52.

Lowe, R. (1988) *Education in the Post-War Years: A Social History*. London: Routledge.

Lowe, R. (1997) *Schooling and Social Change 1964–1990*. London: Routledge.

Lumby, J. (2001) *Managing Further Education. Learning Enterprise*. London: Paul Chapman.

McCulloch, G. (1998) 'Education and economic performance', *History of Education*, 27 (3): 203–6.

McCulloch, G. (2002) 'Secondary education', in R. Aldrich (ed.), *A Century of Education*. London: RoutledgeFalmer.

McKenzie, J. (2001) *Changing Education: A Sociology of Education Since 1944*. Harlow: Pearson Education.

McNay, I. and Ozga. J. (eds) (1985) *Policy-Making in Education: The Breakdown of Consensus*. Oxford: Pergamon Press.

McSmith, A. (1994) *Kenneth Clarke. A Political Biography*. London: Verso.

Maguire, S. and Thompson, J. (2006) *Paying Young People to Stay on at School – Does It Work? Evidence from the Evaluation of the Piloting of the Education Maintenance Allowance (EMA)*, SKOPE Research Paper No. 69. Oxford University.

Major, J. (1999) *The Autobiography*. London: HarperCollins.

Manning, A. and Pischke, J. S. (2006) *Comprehensive Versus Selective Schooling in England and Wales: What Do We Know?* Available online at: http://cee.lse.ac.uk/ceedps/ceedp66.pdf (accessed 14 February 2012).

Mansell, W. (2005) 'Playing politics with our exams', *Times Educational Supplement*, 25 February.

Mansell, W. (2007) *Education by Numbers: The Tyranny of Testing*. London: Methuen.

Manzer, R. A. (1970) *Teachers and Politics: The Role of the National Union of Teachers in the Making of National Educational Policy in England and Wales since 1944*. Manchester: Manchester University Press.

Marsden, D. (1973) 'Politicians, equality and comprehensives', in R. Bell, G. Fowler and K. Little (eds), *Education in Great Britain and Ireland*. London: Routledge & Kegan Paul.

Ministry of Education (1945) *The Nation's Schools: Their Plans and Purposes*, Ministry of Education Pamphlet No. 1. London: HMSO.

Ministry of Education (1959) *Fifteen to Eighteen*, Report of the Central Advisory Council for Education (England) (The Crowther Report). London: HMSO.

Ministry of Education (1960) *The Youth Service in England and Wales* (The Albermarle Report). London: HMSO.

Ministry of Education (1963a) *Half Our Future*, Report of the Central Advisory Council for Education (England), Cmnd 2165 (The Newsom Report). London: HMSO.

Ministry of Education (1963b) *Higher Education* (The Robbins Report). London: HMSO.

Mongon, D. and Chapman, C. (2009) 'New provisions of schooling', in C. Chapman and H. Gunter (eds), *Radical Reforms: Perspectives on an Era of Educational Change*. London: Routledge.

Morris, E. (2002) 'Why comprehensives must change', *The Observer*, 23 June.

Morris, M. and Griggs, C. (eds) (1988) *Education – The Wasted Years? 1973–1986*. London: Falmer Press.

Neary, M. (2002) *Curriculum Studies in Post-compulsory and Adult Education: A Teacher's and Student's Study Guide*. Cheltenham: Nelson Thornes.

Ofsted (2003) *Excellence in Cities and Education Action Zones: Management and Impact*. London: Ofsted.

Ozga, J. (1989) *Open University Unit 7 Parent School Relationships*. Milton Keynes: Open University.

Powell, J. Enoch (2004) 'Law, Richard Kidston, first Baron Coleraine (1901–1980)', rev. *Oxford Dictionary of National Biography*, Oxford University Press, 2004; online edn, January 2011, http://www.oxforddnb.com/view/article/31338 (accessed 24 April 2012).

Powell, M. (2000) 'New Labour and the third way in the British welfare state: a new and distinctive approach', *Critical Social Policy*, 20 (1): 39–60.

QCA (1998) *Education for Citizenship and the Teaching of Democracy in Schools: Final Report of the Advisory Group on Citizenship*. London: QCA.

QCA (1999) *Qualifications 16–19: A Guide to the Changes Resulting from the Qualifying for Success Consultation*. London: QCA.

QCA (2007) *The National Curriculum: Statutory Requirements for Key Stages 3 and 4*. London: QCA.

QCA/DfEE (1999) *A Review of the National Curriculum in England and Wales: The Consultation Materials*. London: QCA.

Ranson, S. (1985) 'Changing relations between centre and locality in education', in I. McNay and J. Ozga (eds), *Policy Making in Education – The Breakdown of Consensus*. Oxford: Pergamon Press.

Reay, D. (1998) 'Micro politics in the 1990s: staff relationships in the secondary school', *Journal of Educational Policy*, 13: 179–95.

Reynolds, D. and Farrell, S. (1996) *Worlds Apart: A Review of International Surveys of Educational Achievement Involving England*. London: Ofsted.

Ribbins, P. and Sherratt, B. (1997) *Radical Educational Policies and Conservative Secretaries of State*. London: Cassell.

Richards, C. (2010) 'The English primary curriculum and its assessment: a critique of three recent reports', *Education 3–13*, 38 (4): 389–94.

Roberts, K. (2001) *Class in Modern Britain*. London: Palgrave.

Rubenstein, D. (1979) 'Ellen Wilkinson re-considered', *History Workshop*, 7, Spring: 161–9.

Ryder, J. and Silver, H. (1970) *Modern English Society*. London: Methuen.

Sallis, J. (1987) 'Parents and the Education Act, 1986', *Management in Education*, 7 (4): 39–45.

Salter, B. and Tapper, T. (1981) *Education, Politics and the State: The Theory and Practice of Educational Change*. London: Grant McIntyre.

Sanderson, M. (1987) *Educational Opportunity and Social Change in England*. London: Faber & Faber.

Sharp, P. (2002) 'Central and local government', in R. Aldrich (ed.), *A Century of Education*. London: RoutledgeFalmer.

Shephard, G. (2000) *Shephard's Watch. Illusions of Power in British Politics*. London: Politico's.

Simon, B. (1991) *Education and the Social Order, 1940–1990*. London: Lawrence & Wishart.

Smith, G., Smith, T. and Smith, T. (2007) 'Whatever happened to EPAs? Part 2: Educational Priority Areas 40 years on', *FORUM*, 49 (1&2): 141–56.

Smithers, R. (2005) 'Last stand', *Education Guardian*, 26 April.

Sumner, C. (2010) '1945–65: the long road to Circular 10/65', *Reflecting Education*, 6 (1): 90–102.

Swann Report (1985) *Education for All*. London: HMSO.

Sylva, K. and Pugh, G. (2005) 'Transforming the early years in England', *Oxford Review of Education*, 51 (1): 11–27.

Taylor, W. (2008) 'The James Report revisited', *Oxford Review of Education*, 34 (3): 291–311.

Thatcher, M. (1993) *The Downing Street Years*. London: HarperCollins.

Thrupp, M. and Wilmott, R. (2003) *Education Management in Managerialist Times: Beyond Textual Apologists*. Buckingham: Open University Press.

Timmins, N. (1996) *The Five Giants*. London: Fontana.

Tomlinson, S. (2005) *Education in a Post-Welfare Society* (2nd edn). Buckingham: Open University Press.

Torkington, K. (1986) 'Involving parents in the primary curriculum', in M. Hughes (ed.), *Involving Parents in the Primary Curriculum* (Perspectives 24), School of Education, University of Exeter.

Vernon, B. (1982) *Ellen Wilkinson 1891–1947*. London: Croom Helm.

Watts, R. (2002) 'Pupils and students', in R. Aldrich (ed.), *A Century of Education*. London: RoutledgeFalmer.

Whitty, G. (2002) *Making Sense of Education Policy*. London: Paul Chapman.

Whitty, G. (2008) 'Twenty years of progress: English education policy 1988 to the present', *Journal of Education Management Administration and Leadership*, 36: 165–84.

Williams, S. (2009) *Climbing the Bookshelves*. London: Virago Press.

Williams, S. (2010) Interview [see Chapter 3].

Woods, R. G. (1972) 'Philosophy of education', in R. G. Woods (ed.), *Education and Its Disciplines*. London: London University Press.

Woods, R. (1981) 'Margaret Thatcher and secondary reorganisation, 1970–1974', *Journal of Educational Administration and History*, 13 (2): 51–61.

Yates, A. and Pidgeon, D. (1959) 'The effects of streaming', *Educational Research*, 2 (1): 65–9.

INDEX